The Golden Sea
Man's Underwater Adventures

The Golden Sea Photographers

Daniel Audrerie	Stan Keiser	Steve Shane
Bernie Campoli	Steve McCarroll	Joseph W. Shaw
Ron Church	Jack McKenny	Bradley Smith
Natalka Czartoryska	Robert Marx	Peter Stackpole
David Doubilet	Naval Undersea Center	Akira Tateishi
Steve Fochios	Perry Oceanographics, Inc.	Ron Taylor
Frank J. Frost	Coles Phinizy	Valerie Taylor
Al Giddings	Carl Roessler	Paul Tzimoulis
Peter Gimbel	Flip Schulke	Robert K. Vincent Jr.

The Golden

Sea

Man's Underwater Adventures

BY JOSEPH E. BROWN— Edited by Bradley Smith

PUBLISHED BY PLAYBOY PRESS  A Gemini-Smith Inc. Book

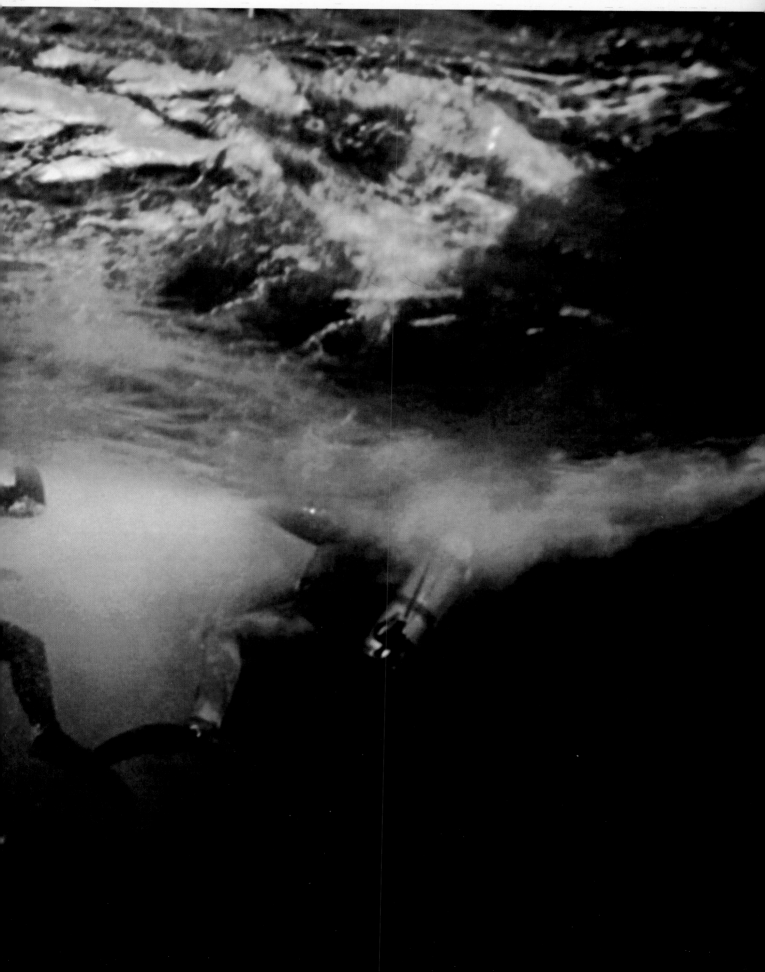

(Above) Treasure hunters cut through the hull of the multi-million dollar liner Andrea Doria. *(Overleaf) Demonstrating a sport of the future, aquanauts, using powered sleds compete in a unique Grand Prix.*

World rights reserved by Gemini-Smith, Inc.
Published by Playboy Press,
747 Third Avenue, New York, N.Y. 10017
A Gemini Smith Book
Copyright 1974 Gemini Smith Inc.
and Bradley Smith
Library of Congress catalog No. 74-80348
ISBN No. 87223-412-6
Simon and Schuster No. 16830
Printed in the United States of America

CONTENTS

Weighing up to 3500 pounds and equipped with powerful, batlike wings, the graceful manta ray is a docile creature and has rarely harmed a human diver.

ix

Introduction

One sunny morning 23 years ago on the north coast of the island of Jamaica, I discovered the sea. Until that moment I had sailed the surface of the Caribbean in small craft, crossed and recrossed the Atlantic on huge ocean liners, splashed in the surf of the Pacific Ocean and off the quiet coasts of the Caribbean. But the sea had remained an impersonal, undulating, solid sheet of water with an ever changing hue. To me it was primarily an enormous highway upon which I, along with countless others, had traveled since the beginning of civilization.

I did not feel much like an explorer as I stood on the powdery white sand and looked out to where a tall, muscular black man sat in a small flat-bottomed boat. "Come out and see the sea," he called. "Take a look under the reef and watch the life go by." I motioned to him and he came close enough for me to wade the few steps to the boat. We struck a bargain, the best I've ever made, for in return for a few dollars he allowed me to discover the wonder and mystery of the sea.

I knelt on the bottom of the boat, shading my eyes as we moved through tangled beds of rockweed and kelp into a brilliant green world of sea lettuce where tall fronds of sea fans waved gracefully and perpetually. As we neared the reef, bright flashes of Silversides fish moved by in formation and swiftly changed course as though from a silent signal. Then we reached the coral reef, abode of hundreds of kinds of sea life. The reef was eye-dazzling with long spines of antler coral (named because of their close resemblance to deer antlers) reaching up almost to the boat bottom; round, convoluted brain coral, ranging in size from that of a clenched fist to a giant head, decorated the tropical seascape.

Every conceivable style of architecture was represented in the multi-colored coral formations. There were coral spires, reminiscent of cathedrals, surrounded by coral trees and coral shrubs. Coral polyps were building their complex and endless houses. At the same time, mollusks bored into them and the ocean waves battered the structures. In dark doorways and in irregular window openings, by concentrating intently, I could discern an octopus stretching its tentacles, a pencil-thin school of barracuda moving around the edge of the candelabra-like coral. Occasionally, a huge, ugly gray grouper or a graceful yellowtail glided between the surrealistic edifices.

There are real cities as well as coral ones to be explored in the pages of this book, settlements that have disappeared beneath the waves between two and ten thousand years ago. Today these cities are being rediscovered. Walls of ancient settlements and fortresses have been found in the Mediterranean, the Red Sea and even off the Bahama Islands. As each region is discovered, another page of man's knowledge of his history is written.

My guide brought me out of my reverie. "Look, mon, if you really dig this, you ought to get into it." He threw out a small anchor and brought out two face masks. "I can fit the mask but you'll have to do without flippers because you can see that mine are too big. You just lie down on the water and look around—and remember, don't put your feet down because that coral can slice into your flesh and leave a painful wound." He proceeded to give me a snorkeling lesson while still sitting in the boat. I put the mask on (he had rubbed the glass plate with a piece of potato to keep it from clouding up). Then I pushed the long, black breathing tube up through the side of the mask so it stuck out directly above my head and I clamped the mouthpiece between my lips and teeth. Breathing was not as difficult as I expected. My instructor helped me over the side before sliding over himself.

An instant and absolute sense of quiet, of peace, of mental relaxation absorbed me and I felt relatively secure cradled by the sea. Below and surrounding me was infinite space—or so it seemed at first. But after only a few moments my perceptions sharpened, especially my visual sense. Along the sandy bottom and clinging to the sides of the coral were shapes that not even the most exotic artist ever painted. Below the fluted edges of the kelp, sea grape and rockweed, were purple starfish, redbeard sponge, flat sand dollars with their semicircular five-pointed design, the serrated small domes of the sea urchins (when this peculiar growth sheds its shell and its tiny spines are exposed, one must be careful not to step on it for its sharp, mildly poisonous spines can go through a rubber flipper). Blue crabs, green crabs and brown rock crabs moved sideways concealing themselves first under one, than another, rock or sunken object. Remnants of metal and wood had become encrusted and alive with barnacles, sponges and limpets. The life within the reef continued even under the surface of the sand where fiddler crabs burrowed, flounders hid themselves and sea worms dug tiny tunnels in the soft sand.

I didn't recognize all of these strange and colorful forms of life on that first memorable snorkeling expedition. But as I continued to snorkel day after day with my new found friend and teacher he never tired of identifying the marvels of the reef. The surprising, the unexpected, never failed to appear as we glided effortlessly through the water. But what of the dangers? That they exist is not to be questioned. Yet it is a welcome danger—a danger almost sought after—the kind of danger that all explorers are prepared to face when they don't know what they will discover on the other side of the reef or of the mountain.

Joseph Brown (who I first met when he was the editor of OCEANS Magazine) has illuminated the life within the depths in-

timately and vividly. He has described the protective devices of both the mammals and the fish that inhabit the warm and the cold waters of the world. Yet, after acknowledging the dangers, they seem to be far less threatening than those faced daily on land. The underwater traffic is not a hazard; fish, even the big ones, usually avoid humans. There are no thieves or murderers, no danger of falling and no contagious diseases; indeed, the sea seems to me a comparatively safe environment.

Perhaps my greatest thrill after learning to snorkel and dive was finding a Spanish coin off the north coast of Haiti not far from the very spot where Columbus' flagship, the *Santa Maria*, sank on Christmas Eve in 1492. I was snorkeling along, gazing intently downward (one is always intent when snorkeling; there seems to be an implied command to look, and certainly one sees more and concentrates more on seeing in the sea than on land). There was a little round dot and I thought it might be a bottle cap. But it turned out to be a coin, not from the earliest Spanish expeditions, but one dating back to the 17th century, well worn, but with enough left to identify it. It is now in the small museum in Port-au-Prince, Haiti. I did not continue seeking treasures and have always regretted it. Now, after reading Joe Brown's provocative narrative describing the riches to be found in the golden sea, it seems increasingly important that I take up the quest again.

So I discovered the sea, and, even though I have snorkeled and dived, I have never lost the feeling of peace and excitement that comes each time I move below the surface of the sea. Yet I know the sea and its depths are not for everyone. So I have fashioned a theory, perhaps not too scientifically accurate, but completely satisfying to me. It goes like this; As humans evolved in different parts of our world at different times, they carried with them something similar to what the psychologist Carl Jung called race memories. I call them evolutionary memories. Somewhere deep within the subconscious many humans retain their connections with the sea

that go back to the beginning of sensation. And these people are at home in the sea—in it, on it, near it. They feel little sense of danger and quickly become familiar with their surroundings in the depths. There is another group, and I have come to know many of them, who seem to carry in their subconscious a later evolutionary phase. I call them bird people. They love to fly and are completely at home in the air, in small planes, gliders, even parachutes. Then, of course, there is a great majority of us that have largely lost both of these "memories." We are the land people and it takes us time and effort to bring back, to re-alert and rebuild, our lost faculties. But it is worth it.

My discovery of the sea is miniscule compared to the new discoveries being made almost daily which involve man's dependence upon the sea and its importance to his survival. It is probable that the sea will, as this book suggests, be farmed as effectively as the land; that the resources of the sea will be controlled; that man will adapt to living harmoniously with the sea and its inhabitants.

In the never-ending search for areas in which our increasing population will live, that the sea will afford artificial islands and underwater cities is no longer a fantastic prophecy. With the opening of Japan's International Ocean Exposition, the underwater city becomes a reality.

It is as though man has discovered a new world, another space, far more important to his immediate future than outer space. For the sea can provide a new source of nutrition for millions. On a less scientific level, the sea offers an increasing variety of experiences for the adventurous. Great fortunes lie waiting to be discovered beneath the restless waters; adventures to awaken the most primitive instincts of man await the snorkeler and the scuba diver. Man has looked across the seas and up into the skies. Now he must look *down* into the underwater world of natural beauty and incredible natural resources, for therein lies his new world.

—Bradley Smith
La Jolla, California

The Dark Sea

Below, it is peaceful. Graceful sea plants sway in a mute, slow-motion ballet, their leaves bathed in shafts of sunlight percolating down from the surface. Fish swim past, some inquisitive, some indifferent, some cautious—a few, perhaps, even hostile. Around, above and below, a panorama of intense beauty unfolds. It is a strange, mystifying world of dazzling colors, diverse creatures and awesome topography. The details vary with the locale: the turquoise of the Mediterranean, the soft monotones of the Arctic, the emerald lushness of the California kelp forest. But the excitement is constant, the impact unending.

To the neophyte aquanaut, changes in the sensory system are startling. The gravity and acceleration stimuli are greatly altered, for instance. Once in the sea, buoyed by water and unshackled from the bonds of gravity, the diver revels in a giddy new freedom. A flip of his hand sends him spinning in any direction. Weightless, he drifts up, down, sideways. He may stand on a single finger, upside down, propel himself long distances with an effortless flick of a rubber-finned foot. Even in his weightless state, however, he is aware that the liquid presses him ever tightly with each inch of descent. Other senses demand readjustment. His hearing tricks him. Sound travels faster in water than in air; the diver finds, however, that it takes longer to determine the source or direction of sound. Vision is distorted; even in clear water, it takes the human eye 50 percent longer to adjust to visual details. Objects, magnified and distorted by the water and face mask, appear larger and closer than they really are. Beckoned by their beauty, the diver is astonished to find that they elude his reach. Yet he also soon learns to temper this curiosity with caution, for some of the sea's most exquisite creatures are also its most painful, even its most lethal.

Man's natural apprehension in the sea is well founded, for the liquid environment is as charged with dangers as it is alive with beauty. Though his own dim, primeval origins can be traced to the oceans, he is only a temporary trespasser here, an intruder who is merely tolerated. And for the privilege of visiting and beholding, the sea demands utmost respect and understanding.

Unlike the fish that glide past, the human diver must inhale air constantly to remain alive. During the past six millennia, man has fashioned increasingly remarkable devices to extend this ability, so that he may venture deeper and remain longer. Once, cocooned in a ponderous, pressurized steel cylinder, two men touched the floor of the deepest part of any ocean, seven miles down in the Pacific. Although that dive offered only a fleeting and as yet unrepeated glimpse of the pitch-black world of the abyss, it confirmed for the first time that life—uniquely adapted, primitive life—does exist there, and therefore it exists in every region of the seas.

Today, technology is pushing the safe depth limit of the free diver—the diver unencumbered by surface apparatus or confined to bells or submarines—past the 200-foot mark, a barrier that has existed for decades. Modern submersibles regularly plumb much greater depths with only an occasional accident. And for periods of up to several weeks, diver-scientists have lived and worked in self-sustained chambers anchored to the sea floor, forerunners, perhaps, of entire underwater communities to which future generations of aquanauts may someday come to flee the din and congestion of their terrestrial cities.

Despite this progress, man often finds himself frustratingly inadequate when he visits the alien undersea world. Its immensity dazzles even the most jaded mind. No terrestrial training or experience adequately prepares him emotionally for his first (or one hundredth) descent; an astronaut readying himself for a voyage to Outer Space is perhaps better conditioned than the aquanaut traveling in aquaspace. Each dive is a totally new experience, for the liquid world is a place of constant change, constant challenge, and constant danger.

In his terrestrial environment, man has been evolving for several million years. Even with the advanced intelligence and physical adaptation thus developed, he is at the genesis of a totally new evolution in the sea. To an otherwise superior mortal, this realization is a bit humbling. With modern weapons, tools and other technology, he may easily dominate the fishes and other animals that live in the sea, yet he is helpless to precisely emulate them. Perhaps he experiences his greatest frustration when he encounters marine mammals—the sea lions, whales and dolphins to which, of all the sea's creatures, he feels the closest affinity. Once land-bound themselves, these mammals long ago preceded man in returning to the sea, yet they are still capable of sustaining themselves equally well in the great depths or breathing the same air that humans breathe. And they survive against predators whose very presence may unnerve even the boldest human diver.

About three decades ago, just after World War II, millions of landlocked humans discovered the exciting playground beneath the sea for the first time. Off the Riviera resort of Cannes, skindivers began soaring over jeweled coral beds of reds, violets, purples and yellows. Others prowled the spectacular grottos of Australia's 1,250-mile-long Great Barrier Reef. Still others, armed with sling spears or simple underwater cameras, hunted elusive barracuda and groupers on the sandy floor of the Gulf of Mexico.

Later, this Wet Revolution grew still more purposeful. Oceanographers whose previous research had been limited to dangling instruments into the depths from decks of ships, donned wetsuits and scuba gear and went down to see for themselves. As divers gained increasingly deeper diving capability, long-lost ships carrying valuable treasures loomed suddenly—and tantalizingly—within reach. And with finite resources dwindling on land, the rich bounty of oceanic minerals, food and water took on a new meaning.

Man has literally only tapped the surface of the wet frontier. Beneath that surface, virtually unexplored, are immense challenges. The possibilities are almost unlimited for research and development of natural resources, for locating artifacts of lost civilizations and treasures of lost ships, both for profit and in order that science can fill in missing gaps on how ancient civilizations lived, worked and played.

This can only be accomplished, however, with a thorough knowledge of the undersea world, and by pursuing that knowledge with respect and caution.

The Element

An astronaut peering down at his home planet from space might well wonder why it is named Earth. More appropriately, it might be called "Water," because 70.8 percent of its surface is covered by the oceans. There are four of them altogether—the Pacific, Atlantic, Arctic and Indian—plus numerous smaller seas. Together, they hold 350,000,000 cubic miles of salt water, accounting for more than 97 percent of all the earth's water. Because of the oceans, Earth is the only planet on which a repetitive cycle of erosion and sedimentation is constantly altering the surface. The ocean is the source of rainfall; evaporated from the sea, rain gradually washes away the terrestrial mountains, and the debris is carried by rivers and streams onto the lowlands and into the ocean once again.

Earth was the logical name, however, for it was not until recently in the span of history that man began to comprehend the size of the oceans, or their dominance of earth. Less than four centuries ago, for instance, maps of the famous geographer Mercator showed land and water portions of the earth divided about equally. Interestingly, that was even after the voyages of Columbus that opened a new hemisphere to exploration, after John Cabot reached Canada, after Vasco da Gama found an all-sea route linking India and western Europe, after Balboa discovered the Pacific and Magellan sailed across it. In Mercator's time and before, no one could be faulted for such geographically lopsided thinking, for in their world, water meant the Mediterranean Sea or the Black Sea, surrounded by dry land. The Atlantic was there, too, but was it not merely a river extending around the rim of a terrestrial world?

Had it been possible to somehow scoop the water out of the ocean basins and set it aside temporarily, the sight of what lay below would have amply satisfied anyone whose notion of the earth was one of plains, mountains and abyssal canyons. In the sea are mountains higher than Everest, canyons that would humble the Grand Canyon, barren deserts rivaling the Sahara. Off the coast of Peru, for instance, a mountain whose base is anchored on the sea floor rises 25,000 feet to the surface, then another 23,000 feet as an extension of the Andes chain. If placed next to Everest, the peak of this mountain would peer down three miles to the neighboring pinnacle. The ocean's most spectacular geologic rise, however, is not a single peak, but its system of ridges. Mid-oceanic ridges stretch fully 35,000 miles, touching all oceans; they rise from 6,000 to 12,000 feet above the bottom.

At the opposite end of the geographic scale are the deep trenches, the abysses that have existed in a perpetual midnight blackness in the millions of years since the oceans were born. In the abysses there is less movement than at the surface, since their floors lie far below the tug of ocean currents, tides and storms. In the oozy sediments of the abysses—in some places 12,000 feet thick—is written the history of the earth itself.

For years, scientists assumed that in the great depths, where no sunlight penetrated and where pressures are so enormous, no life existed. In January, 1960, that belief was finally shattered. During a 37,800-foot descent to the floor of the Challenger Deep near Guam—the deepest known point on Earth—U.S. Navy Lieutenant Don Walsh and Jacques Piccard, the adventurous son of famous Swiss scientist-inventor Auguste Piccard, were startled by an incident that occurred moments after their vehicle, the Navy bathyscaphe *Trieste*, settled through a cloud of silt on the bottom. Noting that the pressure at that depth was nearly nine tons per square inch, Walsh later excitedly wrote of the event:

As we sank through the clear water near the bottom we had a tremendous piece of luck. Peering through the tiny porthole, Jacques spotted a fish. It appeared to be browsing, searching for food along the ocean floor. It looked like a sole or flounder, flat with eyes on the side of its head. It was about a foot long. Our sudden appearance in his domain, with our great light casting illumination such as he had never seen before, did not seem to bother him at all.

Even as diving technology continues to race ahead with lightning-like speed, few divers living today may ever experience the kind of thrill of discovery that Walsh later described, in a masterpiece of understatement, as ". . . an exciting event." Yet it would require several lifetimes to explore even the fringe of the world's coastlines and continental shelves where marine life is most abundant. By both accepted custom and international law, the continental shelf is defined as that outward slope of the continents to a water depth of 600 feet, or 100 fathoms. That depth happens to coincide with the deepest point that, in most parts of the world, sunlight penetrates the sea. The edge of the shelf, therefore, becomes a sort of dividing line between two major ocean zones one pitch black, the other illuminated. Nine-tenths of all life in the oceans thrives on the continental shelves. One reason, of course, is food. Continental shelves are formed by vast deposits of silt that wash down from rivers and canyons on the continents; this same run-off brings to the sea great quantities of minerals, which diatoms, among the smallest forms of marine life, require to build their microscopic shells. Diatoms are at the very bottom of the marine food chain, the life-giving pyramid which dictates that tiny organisms shall provide food for increasingly larger organisms.

Continental shelves vary in width. Off the West Coast of the United States the shelf is relatively narrow, extending outward only about 20 miles. The East Coast shelf is much broader, extending an average of 150 miles. And in the Arctic it is broader still—up to 750 miles wide at one point. Another factor that determines the range of marine life on these shelves is temperature. Except for mammals and birds, the forms of animal life found on Earth are unable to maintain stable body temperature.

The oceans themselves and their shorelines, however, are a constantly changing region of earth, and a diver revisiting any coastline after an absence of several years may find the underwater landscape markedly altered. Wind and tide gnaw hourly at the coasts. The surf carves once-level beaches; over years of time, boulders are polished to fine-sand consistency on one beach, while the original sand of another may be carried away to expose older boulders underneath.

Deep within the sea, below the floor, fissures of the still-cooling earth are continually active. Normally, the periodic convulsions of this volcanic activity occur too deeply to be heard or felt by humans. Occasionally, however, the outbursts spew upward to the surface to write spectacular new pages in Earth's history. Early on the morning of November 14, 1963, for instance, the captain of a fishing boat cruising off the coast of Iceland heard a deep rumbling in the sea and saw a column of dense smoke rising from its surface. Three hours later, alerted by the fisherman's radio report, journalists and scientists began swarming to the site; by the 19th day, awed by repeated explosions that tossed ash and debris 1,200 feet into the air, they had witnessed the birth of a new island. Later it was named Surtsey, the first island created by a volcanic upheaval in the Atlantic in more than a thousand years.

Eighty years earlier, in 1883, another oceanic volcanic eruption occurred in a narrow strait between Java and Sumatra, half a world away from Iceland in the tropical Pacific. But this time the explosion, containing the force of one million atomic bombs and probably the most violent explosion in recorded history, signaled not the birth of an island, but the near-death of one. The island was Krakatoa. When the dust of the explosion settled weeks later, 37,000 humans had perished.

Although water represents the genesis of his own existence, man is quite tardy in his return to this ever-changing water environment that engulfs his planet. Only for an eye-blink in the millennia of earth time has he existed at all; the period in which he has developed the means of voyaging across the ocean's surface and probing its depths shrinks to a fraction almost too infinitesimal to measure.

Although estimates vary, most geologists agree that the earth was born sometime between 3 and 4.6 billion years ago. Although that expanse of time is difficult to grasp, there is a more manageable, if only imaginary, yardstick. For the moment, think of the earth's history as compressed into a single, 24-hour day. As the clock of this day ticks its first tick, the earth is born in a cataclysmic convulsion of the sun. Four hours later, at 4 A.M., this molten mass begins to cool, and a crust forms. Two more hours, and the oceans begin to appear. They are not the oceans we know today, however, but massive, globe-ranging seas that will continue to ebb and flow across the lifeless, void land masses for millions of years.

Now it is 6 A.M. It is appropriate that the hour of the appearance of the primeval ocean coincides with the first traces of dawn in our day, for without the oceans the dawn of life would not have occurred. Even so, the clock ticks on through the morning and afternoon and into the evening before the first dim forms of life finally do appear. It is about 9 P.M.—600 to 700 million years ago in real time—before the first microscopic, bacteria-like, soft-bodied forms begin to show up in the ocean.

Forms of life that left fossils date to the Cambrian period—500 to 600 million years ago, or after 9 P.M. of our imaginary day. In the next half-billion years—less than one-quarter of the earth's history—life evolved slowly at first in the sea, then began a migration to the dry land of the continents. During the Ordovician period (440–500 million years ago), while half of North America remained a land mass still drowned under salt water, the earliest known vertebrates appeared. Sometime during the Silurian period that followed, a primitive, scorpion-like animal half swam and half crawled ashore from the sea for the first time. That creature, half-aquatic and half-terrestrial, was an arthropod, the earliest member of the phylum of the animal kingdom that even today dominates both the land and sea in terms of numbers. On land, we know them as insects. In the sea, they have evolved into crabs, lobsters and their hard-shelled, multi-legged cousins, so well known to divers and tide-pool hunters.

In Silurian seas, fish began to evolve, followed by amphibians and primitive reptiles. Evolving plant life helped tame the terrestrial world and make it habitable for creatures struggling out of the sea, by establishing soil from crumbling rocks, by preventing the soil thus established from being washed back into the sea, and by providing food.

Between 9 and 11 P.M., the pace of developing life quickened. Both in the sea and on the land, some forms rose to dominance and then disappeared. For a while, huge, terrifying reptiles roamed the earth before disappearing into oblivion. Possibly for self-protection, birds learned to swim against an ocean of air as their ancestors had learned to swim against the liquid currents. Many of the large land animals—huge, serpentine, grotesque monsters—returned to the sea about 170 million years ago, during the Triassic period. They, too, eventually vanished, though they are preserved in literature and art as sea serpents, sea monsters and other such terrors of the deep.

Finally, in the Tertiary period, which dates back 70 million years or so, came the mammals. They were primitive creatures at first, developing later as the forebears of the higher forms we know today. Perhaps 50 million years ago, many of these mammals also abandoned life on the land and re-entered the sea. Their descendants are the air-breathing whales, dolphins, seals and sea lions.

Man himself did not show up until the clock of our imaginary, time-telescoping day was ticking out its final minutes. At about ten minutes before midnight—more than one million years ago—he began to evolve from a race of terrestrial mammals whose hands had developed the ability to manipulate and examine objects and who, in the final years, developed a brain of remarkable power, one that could reason and plan and thus compensate for the small physical stature of the body that housed it. Even as midnight approached, however, man did not begin his own return to the mother ocean until an infinitesimal fraction of the final second.

The Descent

Because he left no written record of the feat, the first human to dive into the sea will forever enjoy a ghostly anonymity. That dive, simple and short as it must have been, occurred at least 4½ millennia before the birth of Christ, since archaeologists digging the ruins of a Mesopotamian site dating from 4,500 B.C. have found shells that could only have been brought up from the sea by divers. No doubt dives were made even earlier for utilitarian purposes: to hunt fish that ranged near the surface, to snare lobsters, clams or other seafood, or to recover valuable objects accidentally dropped from boats or the shore.

The early descents, as those of today, were limited in both depth and in time spent at that depth. Though divers no longer are limited in undersea exploration by having to hold their breath, new breath-diving depth and duration records in modern times have become a challenge akin to flagpole-sitting, marathon dancing or barrel-jumping. The world's official depth record for breath-diving is held by an American naval petty officer, Robert Croft. In 1968, Croft reached a depth of 240 feet off Florida by descending along a Manila line lowered into the sea, holding an assemblage of heavy weights. Paralleling such efforts have been those of duration.

Early man, however, was not in search of mere records.

He entered the sea first for food, later to bring up objects that had commercial value, such as sponges, and shells that had value both as money and in the food they contained.

Humans who performed well in the sea were held in high esteem by early societies. In the period between 2500–1400 B.C., one performed so well he became the first god worshipped by divers. He was Glaucus, who began life as a mortal fisherman in the Cretan village of Anthedon, and who was elevated to divine status when he reported the discovery of a plant that possessed miraculous powers; apparently the plant, eaten, helped Glaucus to greatly extend his lung power and thus to recover exceptional quantities of sponges, which were a valuable commodity in the early Greek world.

No one knows how the early free divers rated as depth- or duration-record setters, though a consideration of what they brought up gives us a clue. Besides sponges, which the Greeks used for a variety of purposes from armor padding to canteens, pearls and their shells and corals used for dyes were other highly prized items. The Chinese particularly valued red coral, used for jewelry and ornaments; in fact, this coral was a valued commodity in trade between Eastern and Western civilizations. Red coral, however, is seldom found in water shallower than 100 feet; to harvest it, divers probably had to remain down at least two or three minutes. Considering the pressure at that depth and the fact that divers had to expend energy to chip the coral loose, the feat looms even more remarkable, an indication of superb strength and physical conditioning.

Even today, such skills have not been outmoded by technology in many parts of the world. In Japan, for instance, pearls are still harvested by women divers called *amas*, who wear face-clinging masks but who carry no air storage devices of any kind. Few, in fact, wear even swim fins. And on the island of Tuamotu in the Marquesas Archipelago, among other areas of the Pacific, skindivers work at depths of 100 feet or more to harvest not the pearl itself, but the valuable mother-of-pearl shell.

The neophyte diver today usually embarks on his underwater career just as did ancient man, the *amas* and the Tuamotu divers. Today, however, he has at his disposal three additional, and quite helpful, implements: rubber fins for faster propulsion, a face mask for improved vision and a snorkel to assist breathing while floating on the surface.

There are literally dozens of variations of these devices on the market; for instance, the glass of face masks now can be fitted with prescription glass for wearers of glasses.

The snorkel is merely a refinement of one of the earliest devices used by diving man. Aristotle mentioned submerged divers drawing air from the surface through a reed or hollowed-out stem; quite possibly, the original designer drew his inspiration from the trunk of an elephant he saw half-submerged in a jungle pond. The use of reeds for military purposes—by soldiers who advanced unnoticed against an enemy by breathing through the hollow stems as they walked across a river underwater—appears in many legends.

Today's snorkel is usually made of plastic, with a mouthpiece of rubber. Most divers thrust the tube through the strap of their face mask to prevent it from flopping about. Some snorkels are equipped with a ball attachment at the top, which shuts out the water when the diver submerges; others, considered much safer, have no ball, the user merely holds his breath when submerging and blows out the water that half fills the tube when he surfaces again.

The snorkel is truly a window to the sea. Wearing it, the diver may float at the surface literally for hours, face-down, raising his head only if he cares to do so. Many marine animals are startled by the motion of a large object, such as a diver, on the surface, especially if there is repeated splashing from raising and lowering the head for air. The diver using a snorkel, however, disturbs underwater life very slightly and thus stands a better chance of seeing the panorama of life there.

For prolonged periods underwater, and for deep-water exploration, scientific research, underwater photography, marine archaeology or treasure salvage, some form of breathing apparatus is a must, but millions of underwater enthusiasts receive their initiation without it. Many diving clubs, as a matter of fact, require time spent as a breath diver as a condition of membership, and many clubs as well as some nations prohibit the spearing of fish while wearing scuba—self-contained underwater breathing apparatus.

Ultimately, however, the free-swimming diver, once "hooked" on the thrill of his new sport, graduates to more sophisticated equipment. Historically, that important second stage in the evolution of diving has involved various devices by which the diver could be fed air from the surface. Among the earliest of these devices—forerunners of the modern snorkel—were tubelike inventions through which the diver sucked in air from the surface while he was submerged.

One of the earliest was designed by Leonardo da Vinci at the request of the Venetians, who needed something to assist divers during Venice's war against the Turks in the 16th century. Leonardo, already an accomplished inventor, came up with a rather elaborate solution. It was a leather helmet, complete with windows, which fitted over the diver's head; extending upward from this was a tube that was attached to a float on the surface. The Venetian Senate was pleased with the gadget, until a flaw was discovered that sent Leonardo back to his drawing board. The enemy, the Senate reasoned, might spot the floating tube, and the element of surprise would be lost. Leonardo did indeed eliminate this possibility in his second design—a complete underwater suit, the forerunner of later suits—but it was never put to use. Leonardo explained later that his reluctance to see the device built was not an indication of his lacking confidence in its workability but, rather, was one of morality. "The use of such a suit," he wrote, "would lead to murder at the bottom of the sea."

Inventors following in Leonardo's footsteps continued to experiment with similar innovations; for a while, diving bells were the rage, though they enjoyed only minor success until two Greeks designed and built one in 1538 that was demonstrated before Spanish Emperor Charles V. Large enough to hold both inventors, its design relied on the basic principle of physics that air will not escape from an open-ended container held level with the water itself. To prove that the bell was functional, the inventors entered it holding a lighted candle; when they later returned to the surface, they proudly pointed to the still-lighted flame.

Diving bells remained in use until the mid-20th century. In 1934, two Americans, William Beebe and Otis Barton, descended to a record depth of 3,028 feet off the Bahamas in an enclosed bell they called a bathysphere. Unlike earlier descents in which duration was limited by the amount of air naturally trapped in the bell, the completely closed sphere included a cylinder of compressed air, which greatly extended their diving time. The 1934 descent was a major milestone in diving history, but short-lived; successors continued to shatter the 3,028 foot mark until the ultimate was achieved—the 37,800 foot plunge of the bathyscaphe *Trieste* in the Pacific 26 years later.

Neither bells nor bathyscaphes, however, allowed the diver much freedom once on the ocean floor. He still needed some means of receiving air from the surface without being confined to a surrounding chamber. The breakthrough in this technology is credited to a German engineer, Augustus Siebe, whose invention in 1819 of a diving suit and helmet became the forerunner of "hard hat" gear still used in some salvage work today. Siebe's device consisted of a brass helmet into which air was pumped from surface compressors, and a leather-and-canvas suit. The diver, therefore, was completely enclosed as he had been in a bell, but was also relatively free to walk about on the sea floor.

"Hard hat" or "pot gear" equipment revolutionized salvage work almost overnight. It is, in fact, a basic method used by the American Navy, since it can be used in water much deeper, and for longer periods, than can scuba. The Navy began using diving suits in the 1870s. It established a series of diving schools, and although regulations at first limited divers to descents not exceeding 60 feet, the experience thus gained helped establish pioneer diving and decompression tables that today are accepted as standard all over the world. It was not, however, until 1898—more than a quarter-century after the Navy entered the diving business—that bluejacket salvors had an opportunity to demonstrate their prowess in wartime. When the battleship *Maine* was blown up in Havana harbor that year, a detachment of Navy hard hats was immediately dispatched from the East Coast. Working in shifts around the clock, the divers successfully retrieved many valuable instruments and cargo from the sunken man o' war, plus its cipher code, thus preventing it from falling into enemy hands.

Meanwhile, during the developmental years of diving technology, much was being learned about the hazards of pressures and other physiological facts of life. At the surface, the average human can fill his lungs with about seven quarts of air. During a dive, however, water pressure gradually compresses the air in the lungs; this increasing pressure is a basic physiological hazard in diving. At sea level there is also pressure—14.7 pounds per square inch (known as one "atmosphere")—but because it is exerted equally from all directions and the human body has adjusted to it, it poses no problem in everyday living. When man descends into the sea, however, adjustment problems increase dramatically. Salt water weighs about 64 pounds per cubic foot. At a depth of 33 feet, therefore, the pressure exerted by this weight is equal to a second 14.7 pounds per square inch (p.s.i.). Added to the normal 14.7 pounds p.s.i. at the surface, this means that at 33 feet the diver is subjected to 29.4 pounds p.s.i., or two atmospheres. The effect of this pressure on the diver was summarized long ago in Boyle's Law, the first rule memorized by every diver. It dictates that "the volume of a given mass of gas at a constant temperature varies inversely with the pressure exerted upon it." Thus, when the diver has reached a depth of 100 feet, the original seven quarts of air in his lungs has been compressed to about two quarts.

Remarkably, however, the human diver is able to adjust to pressures at depths of 1,000 feet or more, as long as air supplied under pressure to him equals the pressure from without. It must, however, be applied equally to all internal air spaces, not just his lung cavity. If for any reason the increased pressure is not applied equally to all body surfaces, severe pain may result. The principle explains why Leonardo's early snorkel, though laudable in intent, could not possibly have worked.

Even at a depth of three or four feet, a diver wearing the suit could not possibly have taken in air from the surface, because increasing pressure on his body from the water would have made chest expansion impossible.

Even with a method that supplies the diver with compressed air at a pressure equal to that of the outside water pressure, only the major physiology problem has been solved. The human body contains several natural air spaces, principally the sinuses and middle ear spaces. If any of these are blocked—by congestion caused by a cold or hay fever, for example—air pressure inside the body cannot reach these vital spaces, and the membranes can easily be ruptured. This is why one of the first rules of diving dictates that no one should dive if he has a cold or similar illness.

Although Boyle's Law was well known previously, its importance skyrocketed when the aqualung, designed by French oceanographer Jacques-Yves Cousteau and engineer Emile Gagnan, revolutionized the sport of diving in the 1940s. The principle of the Cousteau-Gagnan device was not entirely new. As far back as 1900, Louis Boutan, a French professor of biology and pioneer underwater photographer, designed a simpler rig that allowed him to work underwater without attachments to the surface. In 1925, another Frenchman, a naval officer named Yves Le Prieur, improved on Boutan's design, and necessities created by World War II spurred American research that led to the bubble-less underwater breathing devices used by Navy frogmen during that conflict.

The Cousteau-Gagnan lung, however, has one major innovation. It has a demand valve, a control that permits the user to receive air under pressure only when he wants it, instead of it being pumped in continuously with resulting waste, as in previous models. When a diver using an aqualung breathes out, the exhaled gases open an outlet allowing them to escape. The air supply controlled by the diaphragm demand valve is switched off. When the diver starts to breathe in, the outside sea pressure closes the outlet valve and opens the intake valve.

Because the world was then at war, the impact of the aqualung's advent in 1942 caused few if any ripples outside the small and somewhat elite group of adventurers who had been diving professionally up to then. When the war clouds cleared, however, the impact was astonishing; in the decade following, skindiving became a major worldwide sport, afflicting the affluent and average alike.

Meanwhile, other limits to diving, about which relatively little had been known previously, spurred new study and research. One was the phenomenon of nitrogen narcosis—"rapture of the deep"—which occurs between 150 and 300 feet, when the nitrogen in the air behaves more and more like an anesthetic, and produces symptoms very much like an alcohol intoxication. This euphoric condition can become fatal. Also, at depths as shallow as 33 feet, divers breathing pure oxygen were found to develop seizures like an epileptic fit. This occurred with any gas mixture when the partial pressure of oxygen exceeded two atmospheres.

Since the advent of scuba, underwater research has zeroed in on various gas mixtures and more sophisticated equipment that will enable divers to penetrate the 200-foot depth barrier with regularity and in safety. Such undersea pioneers as Dr. Edwin Link, Dr. George F. Bond and Cousteau have publicly predicted that within the lifetime of all of us, that barrier will be pushed down to 3,000 feet or more.

What is it like, wearing only scuba gear, to descend, alone, below the level of sunlight, into the cold pitch-blackness of Inner Space? Until the 1960s when technology began pushing the depth barrier down with regularity, 1,000 feet was considered a mark to be attained by only a few hardy men, and an exceedingly dangerous undertaking. Despite the risk, many accepted the challenge. Hannes Keller of Switzerland and Kenneth MacLeish of the United States in 1961 attained a depth record of 728 feet in Italy's Lake Maggiore, in a "free" dive. Because that was below the safe limit for the use of compressed air, they breathed a mixture of oxygen and helium, plus an additive. Lake Maggiore, of course, is not the open ocean; for years the title of champion diver in the sea itself belonged to Lieutenant Commander George A. M. Wookey of the British Royal Navy. His dive—600 feet—occurred in Norway's Oslo Fjord on October 13, 1956.

Eight years later, almost totally unnoticed, Wookey's record was broken. On a damp, cloudy fall morning in 1964, a young Californian named Mark Rogers bettered Wookey's mark by an even 100 feet in the submarine La Jolla canyon off San Diego, California. Like Wookey, Rogers had developed a breathing mixture of oxygen and helium, but he added a third gas—hydrogen. Mixtures of oxygen and helium were first used in 1939 when Navy divers raised the sunken submarine *Squalus* from 243 feet of water in the North Atlantic. Mixtures of gases other than compressed air vary according to the depth to be achieved, the physiology of the diver and many other factors. A gas that proves satisfactory in diving experiments at one depth may prove toxic at another, too cold for the human system at still another.

Preparing for his dive, Rogers faced two related obstacles. Mixing the three gases might prove dangerous at the surface because of the hydrogen, so he had to carry them in separate tanks and mix them underwater by turning valves that fed into a common cylinder. And this with fingers numbed by the deep-water cold. A miscalculation could have proved instantly fatal: too much oxygen, and Rogers would suffer from gas poisoning; an error in the mix, and an explosion could result. The second problem was the sheer weight and size of the equipment. Deep diving requires proportionately more breathing mix at progressively lower levels, since greater amounts of gas must be breathed in to offset the pressure outside the body.

Rogers had been diving for about ten years. During the year prior to his record attempt, he had experimented with various gas mixtures in simulated dives, using a decompression chamber in Los Angeles. From the Library of Congress he obtained a bibliography of almost every book ever written on diving physiology, borrowed the books, and pored through them. Nothing, however, could prepare him mentally for the descent, because there was no precedent for it. No one, wearing only scuba gear, had ever dived below 600 feet.

Anticipating that there would be skeptics, Rogers assembled a group of San Diegans to monitor the dive. He arranged to photograph plastic markers tied at 100-foot intervals along a length of Manila line down which he would descend, hand over hand. A local television cameraman provided the roll of film, marking it for identification just before Rogers submerged, planning to receive it upon his surfacing.

A few minutes before 9 A.M. on October 24, 1964, Rogers began the descent. Beyond 200 feet, because of the overcast sky above, daylight began fading. Somewhere between 300 and 400 feet, the pressure proved too much for the flashlight he carried; its lens exploded with a loud pop. Now, the only light was the faint glow of Rogers' wristwatch and air tank dials. It grew increasingly colder. At the 500-foot marker, he was almost overcome with dizziness; correctly determining the cause, he readjusted the mixture and the giddy feeling vanished.

"Below 500 feet," Rogers recalled later, "the cold was incredible. My fingers had no feeling, as if frozen to the Manila line, I lost all sense of direction; I kept telling myself, *don't let go of the line or you're lost*! At each new marker, the only way to determine where to point my camera was to pop off one flashbulb, look around in that split second of light, then take a second photo. I felt suspended in time; it was like drifting around in a vast barrel of oil."

At 600 feet, Rogers thought momentarily about British diver Wookey. With each succeeding hand-over-hand tug down the line, he would be further obscuring the Britisher's long-standing depth mark.

Finally, Rogers' numbed fingers gripped the last plastic marker: 700 feet. The temperature was 49 degrees, the pressure on his body a punishing 21 atmospheres—more than 300 pounds per square inch. Under the pressure, Rogers' wet suit was squeezed to tissue paper thinness. Denied its warmth, Rogers felt his body convulse with the chill. Only 30 seconds did he linger at that depth; slowly, he began his ascent to the more familiar world of fresh air and sunlight and human voices.

Gradually, the light from above began trickling down around him. Rogers remembers it now as "a very special sunrise." At 100 feet, he could dimly make out the form of Dick Whidden, a diver friend who had prearranged to help Rogers switch from his own air supply to that in safety tanks at the 100-foot level. Rogers gulped the air; as he did so, Whidden felt Rogers' pulse and was startled to find it so weak. The two remained below the surface until Rogers' decompression was completed. Finally, after 90 minutes in the cold dark world below, Rogers struggled aboard the waiting boat, shivering with chill and utterly exhausted.

Since 1964, scientists have made great strides in the development of efficient, safe gas mixtures and more reliable equipment. The Navy has conducted a series of experiments in the technology of saturation diving, which may enable humans to remain days, even weeks, at great depths.

Ultimately, perhaps, man may reach the pinnacle of diving physiology—being surgically fitted with fish-like gills that will enable him to "breathe" water and be set free as a fish for years beneath the sea. Eyebrows arched with disbelief when Jacques Cousteau predicted that possibility two decades ago in his now-famous projection of *Homo aquaticus*. In 1973, an event occurred that gave the possibility some credence. At Drexel University in Philadelphia, two physicians announced the development of a machine that enables mammals to breathe liquids as easily as air. The machine has been successfully tested with dogs, and though its major application would be in certain types of lung surgery, its possible use in aquaspace travel did not go unnoticed.

Meanwhile, man will undoubtedly continue to use more conventional equipment to enjoy the wonders of the liquid world to which he is returning after thousands of millennia.

The Dangerous Sea

Shortly before dusk on September 9, 1973, 37-year-old Albert Schneppershoff was pleasure diving with his 10-year-old son, Al, and two friends near Guadalupe Island, off the Baja California peninsula of Mexico. An experienced diver and a member of the Long Beach Neptune Diving Club of California, he had won a number of trophies only weeks earlier in the National Spear Fishing Championships held in Los Angeles; friends described him as "a skilled, capable diver, and as cautious as they come." That night, however, Schneppershoff was to make his final dive.

While his son waited in the boat with the two friends, Schneppershoff swam away alone about 100 yards, periodically submerging and surfacing as he looked for more fish to add to the fat string of albacore, black sea bass and tuna speared earlier in the day.

Suddenly, those aboard the boat heard an anguished scream out of the gathering gloom. Hastily, they pulled up the anchor and sped to the direction of the sound. When they found Schneppershoff a few minutes later, the reason for the scream was instantly apparent: the calf of his right leg was hideously ripped open, and dark red blood splotched the water where he drifted, unconscious. Despite frantic efforts to revive him, Schneppershoff never regained consciousness. He died less than an hour later.

The witnesses correctly surmised that a shark attack had occurred. Later, after examining photographs of the leg wound and inspecting two teeth fragments extracted from it, James Stewart, chief diving officer of the Scripps Institution of Oceanography confirmed the suspicion, and determined that the killer could only have been the species most feared of all: the great white shark.

"There was no conclusive proof," Stewart said later, "but the attack had every earmark of a great white. From the teeth marks left on the victim, we reconstructed a pattern of the shark's mouth. It fitted a great white. But, more convincing, was the method of attack. It was not a repeated ripping that characterizes most sharks, but one, massive, stunning bite."

Possibly because it had occurred in a remote area rather than near a populated resort, Schneppershoff's death received only brief mention in the press. Stewart's later investigation, made on behalf of the Shark Research Panel, wasn't reported at all. Yet it underscored once again the savage fury, and unending danger, of this most feared and fearsome creature of the sea—the shark.

In the water jungle of the ocean where predators of every description wage a never-ending battle of survival, nature has equipped many with the means of inflicting pain or even death upon man. Statistically, these species may seem an insignificant nuisance, yet the diver who is well aware of their presence and knows how to avoid them will enjoy the wonders of the underwater world with considerably more self-assurance and peace of mind. Fully 300 species of fish are considered either poisonous or dangerous, for example, and throughout the various environmental niches of the sea there exists a bewildering array of other animals that can bite, sting, squeeze, paralyze, pierce or otherwise make life somewhat uncomfortable for the unwary human visitor. But it is to the shark, a splendidly adapted relic of the past, that man assigns his utmost respect and awe.

With the exception of larger members of their own kind, possibly the killer whale, and, of course, man, sharks have no major natural enemies in the sea. It was once believed that sharks feared porpoises and that porpoises fatally rammed sharks at will with their tough, blunt noses. Recent experiments with the two animals in captivity at the Mote Marine Laboratory in Sarasota, Florida, suggest otherwise. "In self-defense, perhaps, porpoises will indeed ram sharks," explains Dr. Perry Gilbert, a ranking expert on both sharks and porpoises and director of the laboratory. "But, in captivity at least, we've learned that porpoises try to *avoid* sharks; in fact, we've had to teach them to attack."

Given so few enemies, then, sharks managed to survive the era of prehistory that the German geologist Johannes Walther described as "the time of the great dying," the Cretaceous period of some 63 million years ago, when the dinosaurs became extinct on the land and the last "sea monsters" disappeared from the ocean. The sharks survived, and they haven't changed much since. The lack of change, perhaps, explains why there are so few species of sharks compared to other fishes. Out of more than 30,000 fishes (by far the largest group of back-boned vertebrates either on land or in the sea), only about 300 are sharks. In the human mind's eye, the number seems to shrink even smaller; most of us tend to think of only a single shark—very large, very heavy, and very menacing. Some sharks are just that, of course, as the record of shark deaths around the world amply verifies, yet the world of sharks—like many domains of Nature—is filled with curious contradictions.

Some of the most savage, even fatal, attacks against man have been made by very small sharks; even the nurse shark, normally unobstrusive, has been known to turn on a human tormentor. Yet the whale shark, at 50 to 70 feet long easily the largest fish in the sea, is, by comparison, a docile kitten. Both the whale shark and its close cousin, the basking shark, *look* menacing, because of their habit of swimming with huge jaws agape to scoop up the thousands of plankton and bait fish their systems require daily just to replenish the energy required to move their huge bodies about. Yet neither has ever been known to harm a human.

Riding whale sharks, in fact, has become a popular sport among divers. Never has there been a reported incident of one of them turning on the rider; whale sharks apparently worry no more about humans clutched to their fins than they do about the remoras and pilot fish that likewise ride along. Before his death in a European cave-diving accident in the early 1960s, diver-scientist Conrad Limbaugh of Scripps Institution of Oceanography made a detailed study of these huge creatures, and frequently rode their backs as a means of gathering data on their habits. Once, in the Pacific 200 miles west of Baja California, Limbaugh encountered a whale shark he estimated to be between 35 and 42 feet long, and decided to hitch a ride. When Limbaugh approached, hundreds of black-and-silver-banded pilot fish scurried away, but the shark paid him no heed whatsoever.

"The mouth opened and closed with mechanical regularity," Limbaugh reported. "By swimming fast, our group of four swimmers, equipped with swim fins, could keep up with the shark. We clambered over it, examining it closely, even looking in its mouth. It showed no concern, except that when we examined its head, it slowly dived out of sight. But it soon returned to the surface and allowed us to climb aboard again."

Sharks vary widely in size, habits and disposition. The ground shark, perhaps the most common, is found in all warm seas. Considered relatively harmless to man, it inhabits inshore regions such as bays or harbors, and is a popular gamefish.

Tiger sharks grow larger—up to 30 feet; the tiger-like stripes that give them their name identify only the younger fish and gradually disappear with age. They roam farther at sea than the ground sharks, usually in warm waters, and are feared in many parts of the world, although the only authenticated attacks on man have occurred when the fish has been provoked.

No so the blue shark, a seagoing species that ranges up to 12 feet in length. Though blues have never made a verifiable attack on humans that caused injury, numerous divers have reported having to drive them off with spears or other instruments. The blue is one of the most abundant of the sharks, and during the summer months when the water is temperate, huge packs have been sighted off the coast of New England.

Two of the strangest looking sharks are the hammerhead and the thresher. A glance establishes how the former got its name; the head is broad like a hammer, with eyes placed on the two flat projections on either side. Because the head functions as a sort of rudder, hammerheads, which grow to about 15 feet, can turn more swiftly than most other sharks. The thresher's peculiar adornment is its tail, an elongated member shaped like a huge, upswept scythe. Like most sharks, threshers are found in warm, temperate seas.

The mako shark is the most streamlined and the fastest swimming of all sharks—and a real trouble-maker where divers are concerned. Known as the porbeagle in some parts of the world, the mako has been known to attack man, particularly in small boats. Makos are popular as gamefish, and in turn they terrorize other gamefishes, such as the swordfish, which they have been observed pursuing at high speeds. Ernest Hemingway relished fishing for the mako; one he caught, weighing 786 pounds, stood for years as the Atlantic record. Another mako fishing enthusiast was Western novelist Zane Grey. No stranger to purple prose, Grey in 1934 described the last moments of a mako he had hooked with tackle off Florida. Despite its abundance of adjectives, the passage succinctly describes the fighting fury and aggressiveness of this species:

At last he showed broadside, limned against the blood-stained water . . . his terrible jaws spread, his wide, weary tail churning the water. He was overcome but not beaten. He had the diabolical eye of a creature that would kill as he was being killed. And as Reuban [a companion] *lassooed that waving tail, the mako lurched with snapping jaws, half way up to the gunwale, to sink his teeth in the side of the boat. That was his last gesture.*

The title of grand champion in the ferociousness department, however, indisputedly belongs to a single, terrifying species: the great white shark. The word "great" is not used here as an adjective. It is part of the shark's common name, although it also describes both the shark's tremendous size (up to 40 feet) and the respectful distance that most knowing observers place between themselves and this fish.

The great white shark has been the subject of several books and a popular movie, *Blue Water, White Death*. In the final moments of the latter a shark, captured at the end of a near-fruitless search for a photogenic specimen, left no doubt about the savage, unrelenting fury of its species; not until the moment of death did the shark cease its bloodthirsty charges against jittery photographers protected in an iron-barred cage.

White sharks have spawned countless legends. No doubt they have caused many a tall sea story to be stretched even taller. Some Biblical scholars have suggested that the whale in the story of Jonah might actually have been a great white shark.

The great white shark is clearly not only a man-killer, but a man-eater as well; in many cases, the hunger of attack is not surfeited until the last morsel of a victim is consumed. V. M. Coppleson of Australia, a leading authority on shark attack, believes it possible that once sharks such as the great white have tasted human flesh, they may acquire an appetite for it, roaming the seas in search of more. More than one treasure hunter has undoubtedly wondered about this possibility. And at least one has wondered in print whether the thirst for human blood might not be passed along from one generation of great whites to another. Reporting on his lifetime search for a fleet of Spanish ships sunk near Florida's Cape Canaveral in 1715, with a great loss of life to both storm and sharks, treasure salvor Kip Wagner noted that sharks gathered "by the dozens" nearby as his crews worked the wreckage underwater. "Only at this spot," he continued, "have any of us seen sharks along the coast in such numbers. Could it be this particular school retains a 'tribal memory' of the Great Feast of 1715?"

Unlike the skeletons of most fishes, that of a shark consists of cartilage instead of bone; this may explain why sharks have left so few fossil records. The few fossils found, however, indicate that the sharks of millions of years ago weren't much different from those that anglers hook—or divers encounter—today. An indication of their hardy ability to survive lies in their reproduction habits. Some fish lay literally millions of eggs, though only a few of the young survive. Most sharks, however, bear their young live—only about 50 or 60 at a time—and most of the young survive.

Sharks have tiny brains; seldom does that of even large sharks exceed three inches in diameter. They have no air bladders like other fish, thus they must swim constantly to maintain position in the water. Most are endowed with downward-protruding snouts, forcing them to exert considerable energy in swimming to avoid sinking. There is considerable debate about the state of development of shark senses. They seem insensitive to pain; during feeding frenzies they have been observed slashing at boat propellers until they have hacked themselves to pieces. Yet other senses—the olfactory and acoustical systems, for example—seem remarkably well developed. Sharks can pick up the scent of dead or decaying fish hundreds of yards away (though for some reason they avoid approaching decaying flesh of their own kind). Although some scientists say sharks have poor eyesight, others insist, just as vehemently, that their vision is excellent.

Good or poor, a shark's vision is obviously limited in turbid water or in poor lighting conditions; witnesses to Albert Schneppershoff's death suggested that since seals and sea lions had been sighted in the area, the attacking shark perhaps mistook the diver for one of these animals in the gathering dusk.

There is no argument, however, about the shark's teeth, or the shark's ability to use them. Hans Haas, the underwater photographer, calls them "revolver teeth," because, like the rapid reloading of bullets into a revolver, the shark has the ability to quickly regenerate new teeth for any he has lost. In 1966, a study of the young of one species disclosed a phenomenal turnover ability; in the upper jaw, teeth were replaced every 7.2 days; in the lower, every 8.2 days. Shark teeth are arranged in several rows, one behind the next, so that when one row becomes worn, another is available to take its place.

How the shark puts his teeth to work, during a feeding frenzy, is one of the most fascinating sights in the sea. It is also a good time for the diver to put considerable distance between himself and the feeders, for even the most harmless sharks seem to lose all sense of courtesy when competing for food.

Dr. Perry Gilbert, who has been studying shark behavior for more than two decades, once induced a feeding frenzy with captive sharks at Bimini, and captured the results on movie film. Gilbert found that when a large dead fish such as a 400-pound marlin was offered, lemon sharks in the tank first circled warily at a distance of about six feet. Then, the sharks began to swim faster, the circle tightening until one shark darted in for the first bite.

Perry's observations and others have punctured the

long-standing notion that sharks roll to one side before attacking. Braking their forward motion with their pectoral fins, they point upward so that their mouths can make contact with the bait. The jaws open wide, the lower one dropping downward and the upper one jutting out from behind the thin upper lip. With the great white shark as a single exception, sharks usually jab forward several times to get an adequate bite, ripping and tearing their prey repeatedly. They shake their heads violently from side to side to tear meat loose. Then, with perhaps 10 or 15 pounds of food in their mouth, they swim away.

But not for long. As blood and other body juices spew out from the wound, a sort of primitive and instinctive electricity shocks the rest of the pack into action. The feeding frenzy begins. "The behavior of the animals at this point seems to be determined entirely by the visual sense," Gilbert reported on the Bimini experiment. "An observer can substitute tin cans and wooden boxes for the bait, and the sharks will indiscriminately attack and consume them. It is clear that any effective shark repellent will have to take effect long before the animals go into a feeding frenzy."

Most sharks are carnivorous; given a choice, they prefer meat. But if meat isn't available, or if they are competing in the kind of feeding frenzy Gilbert observed, they rate as perhaps the all-time-champion scavengers of the sea. All manner of debris has been found in the stomachs of captured sharks. One, caught in the Adriatic, yielded three overcoats, a nylon raincoat and three automobile license plates. From another, caught off the Florida Keys, came an assortment of tin cans, a dozen cow vertebrae and the cow's head...minus the horns. In still another account, the entire body of a human, except for the head, was removed from a 22-foot shark captured by fishermen in the Mediterranean in the 9th century. What made this so unusual was that the body was completely encased in battle armor!

But the strangest find, perhaps, was that taken from the belly of a shark caught in 1799 off Jamaica. In the stomach were documents that proved that the United States brig *Nancy*, captured by the British during the Revolutionary War, had been giving aid to the enemy and was therefore a legitimate prize of war. The papers, along with an affidavit of a naval officer who recovered them, are displayed in a museum case at the Institute of Jamaica in Kingston.

The danger to divers from sharks varies from species to species, and after years of research scientists know that even within a single species, behavior is not always consistent. They urge the diver approaching, or being approached by, a shark to proceed with utmost caution. "In our experience," says Hans Haas, "the sharks are the most dangerous marine creatures.

Even though their aggressiveness has been greatly exaggerated, they certainly have been responsible for a sufficient number of grave injuries and deaths. Their teeth are among the most terrifying murder instruments in the animal kingdom. A 12-foot shark can cleanly bite off an arm or leg; a 22-foot shark can bite a human body in two."

As the result of numerous encounters with sharks, Jacques Cousteau agrees. But he adds that while their presence in the sea is something divers should regard with caution, it is also something they can do little about. Of sharks, he once wrote, "I and my diving companions fear them, laugh at them, admire them, but are forced to resign ourselves to sharing the waters with them."

It was during World War II, when thousands of airmen and seamen were forced to ditch in shark-infested waters, that shark research received its greatest impetus. In the beginning, with little experience to go on, there was a tendency to minimize shark danger. Two entries in the Navy's *Shark Sense*, the basic manual used by naval airmen in learning how to survive at sea, are an excellent illustration of a change in attitude. The first entry, dated 1944, reads:

The natural conclusion is that the shark offers no unusual hazard to a swimming or drifting man.

In the 1959 edition of the same book, the passage had undergone a rather remarkable change of direction:

All you have to do is look at the record. Never count on a shark not attacking you. He may do it.

The record has been growing for more than 30 years. Internationally, several panels of researchers are devoted to compiling data on shark attacks, and convening conferences to discuss what can be done about them. In the United States, the Smithsonian Institution in Washington is the major storehouse of shark attack knowledge; there, the Shark Research Panel, operating under the auspices of the American Institute of Biological Sciences, has compiled a massive bibliography of shark lore dating back almost two centuries. When the vast number of swimmers, bathers and divers around the world is considered, the shark hazard dwindles considerably. But the ratio is hardly consoling to the occasional diver or swimmer who encounters a shark, especially if the shark is large, and more especially if it has drawn a blank that day in its search for food.

During one five-year period selected by the Shark Research Panel for specific study—1962 to 1966—researchers came up with these statistics: worldwide and without apparent provocation, sharks attacked 30 small boats and 161 inshore swimmers, waders, surfers and water-skiers. Twenty-six other people who had provoked the sharks (for instance, prodding them with sticks or spears) were likewise attacked. Offshore, as the result of air crashes and ship sinkings, another 476 were attacked. None of the small-boat or provoked attacks proved fatal. In the offshore attacks, 350—the majority—were fatal, though the panel pointed out that there is no way to tell how many of the victims succumbed to other injuries.

The attacks knew no geographic limitation. They ranged from Australia to South Africa, from the United States to the Philippines, from Fiji to Greece. At one time, swimmers in British or European waters had seemed exempt, since no attacks had been recorded there. But in July and August of 1960, two unprovoked attacks off the coasts of Scotland and England shattered that illusion of immunity.

Statistically, divers below the surface are generally less prone to shark attack than are persons wading or bathing in the surf. Nearly half of the 1,406 attacks that occurred between the middle of the 19th century and the present, selected for study by Leonard P. Schultz of the Smithsonian Institution, involved victims either swimming at the surface, or wading, or standing in knee-deep to chin-deep water. It must be remembered, however, that waders and bathers offer a larger target numerically; especially at popular beach resorts, they far outnumber divers. In other respects, Schultz's study proved one thing: The only predictable thing about sharks is their unpredictability.

Schultz found that hungry sharks care little about weather; attacks have occurred both on sunny days and on stormy ones. They attack in murky water and clear water. They attack in daylight and darkness. They attack in any region of the oceans, from the open sea to shallow, narrow rivers feeding into the seas from the continents. And water temperatures seem of equally slight concern; shark encounters have been recorded in a range of temperatures upward from 53° F.

Schultz's study was based on records of the Shark Research Panel, which collects data only on shark attacks that are first reported in the press (the panel then follows through with interviews of witnesses, if any). Of attacks that have gone unreported, or close brushes by divers with sharks, there is no adequate record. But to the diver experiencing such an attack, no matter how bold he may be, the encounter is hardly forgotten. Dr. Donald R. Nelson, now a professor of biology at California State University in Long Beach, had such an encounter in 1960 that chills his memory to this day. Even in 1960, Dr. Nelson was no stranger to sharks, nor they to him. Long interested in the relationship of sharks and sound, he had spent many hours diving on Florida reefs during his graduate study at the University of Miami; later, he conducted extensive shark research for the Navy, and produced an award-winning film on sharks.

On New Year's Day of 1960, Dr. Nelson and Marty Roessler, a graduate student, spent the morning spearfishing near Florida's Grassy Key, then moved their boat to deeper water. Roessler remained in the boat while Nelson, armed with a pneumatic spear gun, swam seaward, hoping to find more fish on deeper reefs. About 150 yards from the boat, in water 40 feet deep, Nelson suddenly became aware of a dark form near the surface, slowly swimming in circles but 30 feet away.

It was a great white shark. "To me," Nelson recalled later, "the shark seemed enormous. It was nearly 12 feet long and especially heavy-bodied, weighing about 1,000 pounds. When the shark turned and began swimming directly at me, my mind abruptly shifted from identification to self-defense."

Nelson reflected momentarily on his prudence in bringing the spear gun along, "but I decided against firing my one spear except as a last resort. The shark came so close that I had to withdraw the gun for fear of touching its snout and possibly exciting it." Instead, he shouted and brandished the gun at the shark. The shark turned, but only slightly, and made four more passes—possibly withholding an actual attack only because of Nelson's presence of mind in repeatedly shouting and waving the gun. Meanwhile, Nelson managed to work himself closer to the boat into which, after the fourth pass, he scrambled with an alacrity befitting a man who fears for his very life.

Hans Haas, whose pioneering underwater photography won him an Oscar in 1951, recalls a shark encounter perhaps even more blood-curdling. One morning in the early 1950s, Haas descended alone on a reef in the Red Sea, where he had been told hammerhead sharks had been sighted; although his camera had captured many other shark species, he had never filmed a hammerhead. As he sat on a ledge of coral about 45 feet below the surface, a black-tipped shark about 10 feet long swam into view and began making slow, lazy circles. Denied a hammerhead, Haas decided to film the black-tip anyway, especially since its circling suggested an ideal film sequence.

So engrossed in filming did Haas become that he failed to notice the approach of a second shark, which had worked itself into a position behind his back, barely five feet away. Instinct warned Haas of imminent danger. Turning his head he confirmed the danger: six feet of menacing great white shark. Haas reflected momentarily on the foolishness of diving alone; he had violated a cardinal rule of all divers. Worse, he had put the spear gun he carried aside while filming the first shark. The great white was now between him and the only means of defense except for his bare hands.

Haas shouted—a means of defense against sharks that he insists even today is the best weapon a diver has—waited until the shark's head and mouth passed by him, then slammed one hand against the shark's gills. Momentarily startled, the predator turned away, but Haas barely had time to retrieve his spear before the shark returned once more. Then the incredible occurred. The first shark now joined the attack; Haas suggests the psychology involved was perhaps like that of an otherwise meek dog attacking another from envy, when the second one finds a bone. Fortunately, Haas had not strayed too far from shallow water and, keeping the two sharks at bay with the spear, he pulled himself, nearly exhausted, on the reef. For awhile, the two frenzied sharks swam about just beyond the reef. Finally, giving up the fight, they moved away.

From such experiences, shark researchers have suggested a number of rules by which divers may lessen the chance of shark attack. The first rule, obviously, is to stay out of water where sharks have been recently sighted. Under no circumstances should a shark be provoked. Since blood attracts and excites sharks, divers who have suffered a bleeding wound should stay out of the water. They should also avoid water that is turbid or murky, and should avoid diving at night. Above all, they should not panic. Divers are safer from sharks while submerged than on the surface.

"Divers," says Dr. Eugenie Clark, noted ichthyologist and former director of the Cape Haze Marine Laboratory in Florida, where she conducted shark behavioral experiments, "are in relatively little danger when completely submerged in clear water. Even a hungry shark generally takes time in investigating a possible meal; almost always the diver has time to leave the water if he is not far from a boat or shore. But no swimmer can outrun a shark, so he shouldn't do anything to excite it."

Sharks, however, represent only the most familiar hazard facing swimmers and divers in the sea. Far more numerous—but seldom as serious—are the injuries inflicted by 300 species of poisonous or dangerous fish the diver is more apt to encounter, or stinging animals such as jellyfish or the Portuguese man-of-war, or even the painful annoyance of several species of sea urchins. Like sharks, many of these creatures are quite unpredictable. Barracuda, for instance, are considered dangerous fish and many attacks on humans have been verified. Yet this apparently occurs only with Atlantic species of barracudas; those in the Pacific generally ignore the diver or swimmer. "Live and let live" is a good axiom for the diver to keep in mind, for most marine animals will avoid man unless provoked. The teeth of the moray eel, for example, can inflict a painful bite. Most morays, however, prefer to remain hidden in crevices and caves along the sea bottom, and there is no verified case of one pursuing and attacking man without provocation. Recently, an award-winning film was produced in which one sequence depicted a bikinied woman diver feeding tiny fish scraps to a moray that she had practically made a pet of during several visits to his underwater lair.

The octopus, another overrated "monster of the deep," likewise usually avoids the human's approach, often fleeing in a camouflage of inky substance. Yet there are dangerous species. One of them, only four inches long, carries enough toxin to kill 10 men; fortunately, its population and range are quite limited, and it bites only when one extends an unwary hand into a crevice where it lives.

Two animals deserve final mention, for with certain marine lizards they share the common heritage of the reptilian age when sea dragons swam the oceans as dinosaurs roamed the continents. They have never lost their savage instinct for survival. They are the sea snake and the salt-water crocodile.

There are about 50 species of sea snakes altogether; the venom of all is deadly. Growing to a maximum length of only about five feet, they are found mostly in the tropics, hunting food at night and capturing their prey by swift jabs of their tiny mouths. The venom kills within a few minutes. According to Ben Cropp of Australia, an underwater naturalist and photographer who has helped capture these snakes alive for scientific research, they are almost 15 times more venomous than cobras, and there is no known antidote. Sea snakes, entirely marine, feed mostly on small fish, especially the wrasses. Fortunately for the human diver, the snakes' mouths are so small that they are unable to grip a broad surface—such as a diver's arm or leg—and many divers have survived attacks without fatal results. But because that possibility exists, the government of Australia not long ago launched an extensive program to seek an antidote to the sea snake's venom, which would provide divers with added peace of mind when visiting their habitats.

The salt-water crocodile is doubly feared, because it can attack and maim or kill its prey on land as well as in the water. Growing to 20 feet in length, salt-water crocodiles normally live in marshy areas of the tropics, particularly near New Guinea and nearby islands, but mariners have sighted them swimming, alone or in twos or threes, hundreds of miles at sea. Because game hunters prized them, the Pacific population of these animals was kept to a minimum until World War II when, because no one was hunting them, they began to multiply.

Before the war, a few of the animals had managed somehow to migrate to the Palau Islands, an archipelago in southwest Micronesia a few hundred miles from New Guinea. Not many years later, this population had proliferated to the point where it became dangerous to man. Periodic reports of crocodile-caused injuries and fatalities among Palauan islanders began trickling out of the area, which was administered by the U.S. as a trusteeship of the United Nations. Finally, in the late 1960s, the frequency of attacks triggered demands upon local authorities to do something about the problem. The solution: an invitation to an Australian hunting team to come to Palau. Within a few weeks of hunting, the crocodile population was thinned down once again to a relatively safe level.

Robert Owen, an entymologist in Palau and conservation officer for the United States-administered Trust Territory of the Pacific Islands, has made a lifetime study of this crocodile species. "I have witnessed nothing on earth that will attack—anything—with such blind, unprovoked fury," Owen says. "A dog that wanders within 10 feet of a salt-water crocodile has a life expectancy of one jump. In captivity, salt-water crocs of unequal size cannot be placed in the same cage; the larger will invariably eat the smaller. A parent will kill its young. Once, I cracked open an egg to study the embryo inside. Immediately, it began snapping its tiny jaws at my finger."

Measures to control the populations of crocodiles, sharks and other dangerous animals of the sea have been attempted, in varying degrees and with varying success, in many parts of the world. Obviously, man cannot hope to eliminate them entirely—nor should he. The sea's marvelously adapted stinging, biting, piercing creatures are as vital to the ecology of the marine world as are wasps, poisonous snakes or predator cats to the land. The diver should be wary of them, of course, and should inquire locally about their known presence before venturing into an environment in which he is, despite his modern devices, a relative stranger. Yet, at the same time, by watching the intricately balanced drama of undersea life that unfolds before him, including the battles of predator and prey, his own existence may perhaps become more meaningful. Without the shark, the stonefish, the barracuda and the deadly sea snake, the ocean might be a safer place for the diver. But a great measure of its mystery—and value—would also be lost forever.

Danger!

Few sights are more terrifying to the diver than the swiftly approaching form of a shark. The fear is well founded, for despite twenty centuries of accumulated written and visual data on these terrors of the depths, they are probably the least understood and most unpredictable of the 20,000 species of fish in the oceans. Of all large creatures in the sea, only the shark is a major menace to man. Saltwater crocodiles, for instance, have killed humans, but both their number and their range is extremely limited compared to those of the shark which is found in all oceans of the world.

Even the killer whale, once feared perhaps even more than the shark, has proved to be friendly to man, at least in captivity. Sharks are primitive creatures, seeming to embody all that is evil, and when man seeks a symbol to denote wickedness or viciousness, the shark is one of the most easily identifiable. The French, for instance, chose the word *requin* as the name for the shark itself. It is drawn from *Requiem*, the word describing the mass for the dead, and there is an entire group of sharks—harmful ones—described as the Requiem group.

Scientists believe that sharks date to the Cretaceous period, meaning that the first ones probably appeared in the seas about 300 million years ago. They have no true bones, however, and thus left few fossil records, though dim traces of one ancient shark, dating perhaps even earlier than 300 million years, were found near Cleveland, Ohio, in the 1800s. Undoubtedly the most feared of the sharks is the great white or whitetip (shown on the opposite page) although many smaller species have caused harm to divers, and are a constant danger. In Australia, where the shark menace is particularly acute, mesh nets rigged by concerned local officials have snared more than 9,000 sharks—more than half rated as man-killers—since the control program began in 1937. Along with other dangerous creatures of the sea, sharks add a fascinating element to underwater exploration. Until scientists learn far more about their unpredictable habits, however, divers would be prudent to temper their curiosity with caution.

Despite one near fatal attack, Australian diver-adventurer Rodney Fox continued to hunt great white sharks like this menacing 12 foot man-eater.

32

Underwater cages are usually used by cameramen when filming sharks. This one, however, risks a face-to-face encounter to obtain a dramatic close-up.

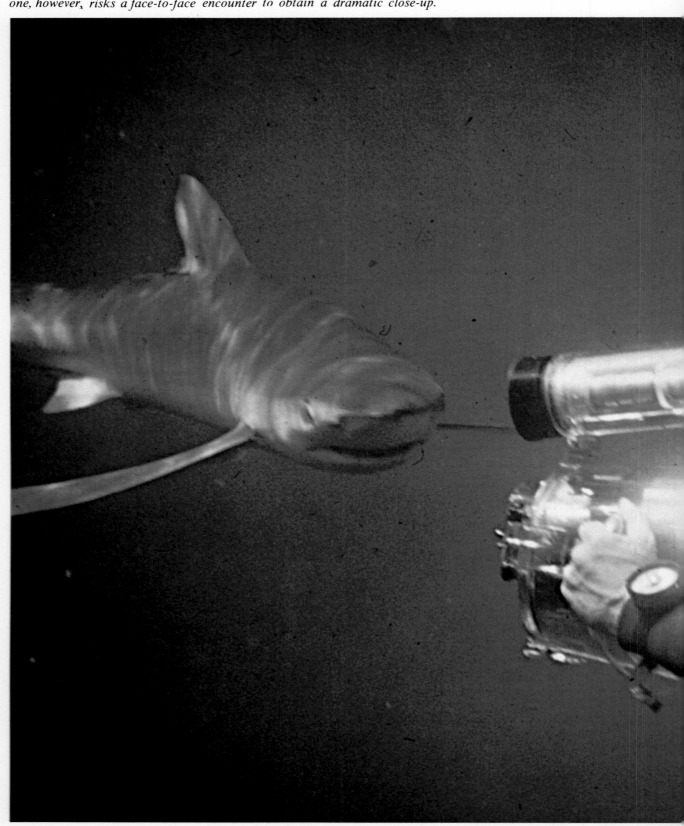

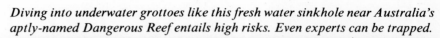

Diving into underwater grottoes like this fresh water sinkhole near Australia's aptly-named Dangerous Reef entails high risks. Even experts can be trapped.

Moray eels generally avoid divers, but they attack with a vicious, painful bite when provoked. Contact after spearing requires the diver's utmost caution.

The rubber suit worn by this daring diver offers only slight protection from the bite of a deadly sea snake, whose venom can produce death in a few minutes.

Members of the cat shark family number about 60 species and are noted for their very decorative spots, stripes or bars. Most are found in shallow water.

Even a small shark can be dangerous. This one is hiding on a reef near Cozumel Island in the Caribbean. Below, a killer whale displays the rows of menacing teeth that can destroy an animal much larger than himself in the open sea, but which have proved quite harmless in his performance as an oceanarium star.

Barracuda are unpredictable fish; this school ignores a diver as it swims leisurely by, but others, especially in the Atlantic, sometimes have attacked man.

Cameras Underwater

With so few predators to worry them, marine animals in the Galapagos Islands, like this seal, exhibit no fear at the approach of the photographer.

The underwater world is a region of earth that should be seen to be fully appreciated. While not everyone can enjoy the boundless undersea adventure firsthand, the modern underwater camera can provide a vivid record of exploration with its results available to millions. The camera often proves to be a valuable extension of man's own vision, a visual aid in an element where turbulence sometimes limits the range of human eyesight to only a few feet. Underwater photography need not be complicated for underwater cameras are much like land cameras. It has become a logical science, a creative form that can be mastered with only a basic knowledge of photography itself and relatively simple and inexpensive equipment. A knowledge of diving must come first. But once acquired, using the camera underwater is a natural second step. As man moves deeper into the sea, the camera becomes an increasingly important tool, both to produce a record for scientific study and for purely aesthetic pleasure. In even shallow waters may be found some of the sea's most breathtaking panoramas—waiting for the explorer with a camera to preserve its beauty.

A snorkeling photographer warily inspects a dangerous moray eel as she explores the 1,250 mile Great Barrier Reef off the eastern coast of Australia.

The manatee, an amiable, cowlike sea mammal, is fast becoming extinct. Here, Joyce Church, famous diver, is taken for a ride in a river of Florida.

Equipment developed to assist the underwater photographer ranges from the basic, simple breathing device used by this lensman recording a Nassau grouper to more sophisticated, powered sea sleds, below, which are produced for more advanced work. Such power greatly extends the diver's range.

Flash bulbs, floodlamps or electronic strobe are not only necessary when photographing in deeper water, but often help attract subjects toward the camera.

As he prowls a crevice in a local underwater promontory of the salty Red Sea known locally as Moses Rock, a diver finds an abundance of film subjects.

47

The Unseen Sea

One day in 1893, an enterprising and inquisitive French zoologist named Louis Boutan donned a diving suit and helmet, struggled with a huge boxlike contraption that weighed several hundred pounds, and slipped into the warm waters of the Mediterranean Sea. The box, sealed tightly with heavy bolts and boat caulking, contained a camera. When Boutan surfaced later, he brought up something of immense historical significance: the first known underwater photograph.

By today's standards, Boutan's picture, which depicted a Mediterranean spider crab, was of poor quality: grainy, of extreme contrast, and somewhat out of focus. But from that humble beginning have evolved thousands of photographs and generations of improved cameras and related equipment, which have added an exciting new dimension to man's exploration of Inner Space.

Boutan's years-long struggle to develop a way of preserving what he saw beneath the sea was born of a scientist's frustration. In underwater investigations, unlike research on the land, he noted in 1900 in his book *Underwater Photography and Progress in Photography*, there was no way to retain a visual record of what had been studied. "If one can photograph a landscape in open air," he asked himself in the book, "why should it not be possible to make a photograph on the bottom of the sea?"

After his initial experiment, Boutan worked constantly to improve both equipment and technique. To overcome the problem of the great bulk and weight of his housings, he began suspending them from empty wine barrels that floated on the surface. Later, he added a huge arc light that, because it greatly illuminated the undersea scene, allowed him to snap his shutter much faster than the 1/50th of a second that had led to blurring in earlier photographs. Meanwhile, Boutan's contemporaries and successors improved even further on his designs, and by 1914 an Englishman, J.E. Williamson, had filmed the first underwater motion picture. By the time the aqualung revolutionized diving in the early 1950s, underwater photography had emerged as an art form in its own right. Within another decade, American cinema audiences had become as addicted to Cousteau's classic *The Silent World* and to re-runs of *Flipper* and *Sea Hunt* on television as they had been earlier to Westerns and whodunits.

Today, most divers rank their underwater cameras equal in importance to their swim fins and snorkels. Underwater photography is more difficult than surface photography, because of the physical limitations of diving and the fact that shooting through water adds visual problems that do not occur in air. Water acts as a filter, absorbing both natural light and artificial light as a sponge soaks up water. In addition, the distortion of objects underwater (the same that the diver encounters in viewing them through his face plate) must be reckoned with. Yet today's camera technology has advanced so far that even the most inexperienced amateur can bring home a creditable and permanent visual record of his descent.

Most underwater photographers begin with very simple equipment. Dr. Walter A. Starck II, a marine biologist who has conducted one of the most intensive studies of coral-reef life, began his photographic career with nothing more than a simple box camera housed in a rubber bag. Many of Starck's contemporaries, whose photography later earned both awards and acclaim, experimented with housings equally as simple—in some cases, plastic bags—before graduating to sophisticated equipment. With these devices, they learned from experience some of the basic rudiments of the art.

The first lesson to be learned is that taking submarine pictures is something like shooting in a fog; plankton and other particles suspended in the water may not unduly hamper human vision, but they show up embarrassingly on film. In shooting in clear air on the surface, distance between camera and subject is not critical—but underwater, distance often spells the difference between success and failure. Artificial light, from either flash bulbs or electronic strobe, only compounds the problem, because the light bounces off the suspended particles. Depending upon the type of equipment and the clarity of the water, therefore, a good rule of thumb is to shoot no more than six feet from the subject. Using this distance as a maximum, it is then a good idea to preset the focus, shutter speed and aperture (the lens opening, determined either by an underwater light meter or from prior experience). The undersea world is a world of constant motion, and seldom is there time to change these settings when a subject suddenly comes into view.

It is not the purpose of this chapter to present detailed information on either the involved technology of underwater photography or equipment. However, since photography has become such an integral element of diving and marine exploration, some basic guidelines and suggestions are presented here, followed by capsulized descriptions of the enormous variety of underwater shooting backgrounds that are available to the diver in different parts of the world.

Almost any camera suitable for surface photography can be adapted for underwater use, as can accessories such as light meters, artificial light sources and other gadgets. Because this equipment must be operated quickly and against restrictions of the fluid medium, however, each piece should be of a type that assures simplicity and ease in handling. Numbers on dials and levers should be large enough to be read easily in poor light. Because of the buoyancy of water, all accessories should be attached either to the diver or to the camera and housing, so they won't float away or sink.

Obviously, everything must be absolutely watertight. To achieve this, a number of specialized, ready-made housings for various types of cameras are on the market. A number of make-it-yourself kits are also available, though mass production has lowered the cost of most ready-made housings to within reach of the average diver.

A guiding principle in the selection of a housing should be the maximum depth at which it will be used. The increasing pressures that confront the diver are also at work on housings and cameras underwater; although simple housings are sufficient for very shallow photography, they are subject to implosion at greater depths. The cost of such housings, therefore, usually increases with the maximum depth at which they are guaranteed to withstand crushing.

There is a camera that combines many of the requirements of submarine photography but requires no housing at all. The Nikonos, based on a design of Jacques Cousteau, is a 35mm. camera that is simple to operate and has achieved widespread use. The body of the Nikonos, sealed against moisture, is itself the housing. The camera can be used either in the sea (to depths of 180 feet) or for surface photography. It is absolutely essential when using a Nikonos that it be dried off thoroughly before being opened to remove the film; even the tiniest drop of salt water can wreak havoc on delicate inner parts. (Incidentally, should *any* camera be accidentally dropped in salt water, manufacturers recommend that immediately after retrieval it be totally immersed in *fresh* water, sealed in a container, and shipped to the maker for repair.)

Photographers debate constantly on the relative merits of 35mm. cameras and those designed to accept 2¼ × 2¼ film. Larger negatives generally assure better quality enlargements than do smaller ones, but because 35mm. film is manufactured in 20- and 36-exposure rolls, the diver using it is required to surface less often to change film than with 2¼ × 2¼ film, which comes only in rolls of 12 exposures.

Whatever the camera size selected, the lens used should be a wide-angle lens—and the wider the better. Water distorts objects seen by the camera lens as it does those viewed by the human eye; a photograph taken at six feet will appear as if shot at four. A normal (50 or 55mm.) lens, used underwater, functions as a telephoto lens would on the surface, narrowing the field of view. Wide-angle lenses increase the peripheral range that the camera "sees," and in so doing, help capture objects that move into view on the fringes of the scene.

Lighting problems are also magnified underwater. Shooting good pictures in clear water, particularly in shallow depths, is not so difficult, but the problems increase proportionately with both depth and the condition of the light filtering down from the surface. Light varies even from one geographical location to another. One very experienced underwater photographer, an award-winning professional, once confessed absolute frustration when the quality of his work began deteriorating. He studied the problem and finally determined what had gone wrong: most of the better photographs had been taken in warm, clearly lighted tropic seas; when he began shooting in colder northern waters, he had not adequately compensated for the substantial difference in both lighting conditions and background colors. The change was undetected by his eye, but the camera noted it quickly. Because of the critical importance of good lighting in submarine photography, a wide range of artificial light sources—from flash bulbs to electronic strobe—has been developed by the photographic industry, in addition to a variety of filters to compensate for color imbalances caused by water.

Where and what is there to photograph? The answer to that question is as broad as the seas themselves. The patient beginner who stations himself with a simple camera at a single shallow-water site near his home will produce enough images to enliven many an evening of viewing. But like diving itself, underwater photography inevitably stimulates a desire to see more, to film more. And the ocean, in its enormous and infinite variety, literally opens a new world of possibilities.

The Living Reef

Diving on a coral reef is an exploration of life. Not only does the reef teem with perhaps the widest and most diverse assortment of creatures found in any zone of the sea, including one fifth of the 20,000 known species of salt-water fish. It is also a living form itself. Because corals die if exposed to air, the entire reef community is hidden from surface view; through the environmental niches, bizarre, colorful and uniquely adapted animals compete for food and protect their territories with a fierce intensity. Reefs themselves consist of living organisms piled atop dead organisms. Soft, tiny animals called *polyps* fasten themselves to the skeletons of their dead predecessors until they, in turn, die.

Coral reefs are among the sea's most fragile environments, which explains why they are found only in limited zones of the ocean. Four conditions are required for reef growth; denied any one of these, the reef will perish. The first is a constant current, from which the polyps extract their food by extending tiny tentacles that catch minute zooplankton. Second and third are requirements for high salinity and an ambient water temperature of at least 68° F. Finally, the water must be clean, or silt will plug the feeding filters of the polyps, literally starving them to death. The first three conditions are generally constant in the sea and are seldom affected by man. Human activities, however, have polluted the oceans in some sections of the world, causing once-magnificent reefs to deteriorate.

In the process of reef-building, polyps secrete skeletons of calcium carbonate, or limestone, in a breathtaking range of colors, shapes and sizes. A reef's existence also depends upon a type of algae called *zooxanthelle*, tiny cells that live within the polyps. These cells apparently aid the polyps by increasing the oxygen supply and removing waste. Since these algae require sunlight, coral reefs are usually found at levels no deeper than 150 feet. All, therefore, are within reach of the scuba-equipped photographer. (There are corals in deeper and colder seas, but they are solitary animals that do not build reefs.)

Photographically, coral reefs beg to be preserved on color film. They are vivid rivals of the rainbow, and much of their visual impact is lost when they are photographed in black and white. Their beauty, however, can easily deceive the diver; some of the most colorful specimens of coral, as well as other organisms, can bring pain to those who unwittingly touch them. There are species of the cone shell, for instance, that can cause paralysis or even death if stepped on or touched. A small fish variously called the lionfish or zebrafish, gorgeously colored, is likewise dangerous. But the rewards of coral reef diving far outweigh the hazards, and with caution the chances of being bitten or stung are extremely remote.

At first glance the reef community may seem disorganized, but the opposite is true. Perhaps nowhere in the sea has evolution proceeded with such a high degree of purpose and specialization. Generally, reef organisms divide themselves into two types: fixed (sessile) and swimming. The corals, alcyonarians (soft corals), algae, sponges and a few of the mollusks (such as the giant clam, *tridacna*) are included in the first group. The swimmers include the fishes, other mollusks, echinoderms (generally symmetrical animals such as starfish and sea urchins) and crustaceans.

Coral forms and fishes vary dramatically from one zone of the tropics and subtropics to another, and they number so many altogether that there are species of both that have not yet been classified by scientists. The fish range in size from the tiniest, brilliantly colored tropical fishes, including the angelfish and parrotfishes—to the larger predator gamefishes, such as the barracuda and shark—to members of the tuna family, which roam the fringes of the reef in search of food.

Patience is the byword of the reef diver and photographer. Douglas Faulkner, one of the world's leading photographers of marine life, suggests that the human visitor is much better off in selecting one spot on a reef and waiting there for the drama of life to unfold before him, than in swimming aimlessly in search of it. Unlike most photography on the surface, that on the coral reef is never the same. Film shot underwater by two photographers visiting the same site a half hour or even minutes apart will be quite different.

And drama it is, indeed. There are constant battles of predator and prey. Watching, the diver becomes transfixed by the fierce territorial behavior exhibited by even some of the tiniest fishes, at the risk of their lives. The phenomenon of symbiosis—the tolerance of two organisms for each other for mutual benefit—is another noted feature of the reef. For instance, many species of sea anemones—beautiful, flower-like animals of the sea—kill their prey with stinging tentacles, yet they allow symbiotic fishes to swim among the tentacles without harm. Other fish serve as "cleaners," gaining protection in return for picking off parasites or removing injured tissue from the bodies of larger fishes.

At night, the reef drama intensifies. Diving after dark is not for the novice, however. The altering of some senses occurs even in the lighted sea, and the diver is denied orientation further by the absence of light. The only way a scuba diver can tell whether he is ascending or descending at night is by casting artifical light on his air bubbles. His mind plays tricks on his emotions, and often he imagines objects that do not exist. But given adequate experience in daytime diving, and by rigidly adhering to the basic diving rule of never venturing into the sea alone, he witnesses activity in the night sea that he wouldn't see in years of daylight diving.

Many marine animals that hibernate during the day come out to feed when sunlight vanishes. Corals cast eerie shadows and shapes in artificial light. Already magnified by the natural prism of water, some animals appear frighteningly large, and the distance between them and the diver seems to narrow considerably, if only in the mind's eye.

What reefs are best for diving photography? Obviously, those less frequently visited by man, those that have not felt his full impact, are less disturbed and are more closely preserved in their natural state. In the Florida Keys, for instance, the southern reefs, farther from Miami, enjoy the greatest immunity. But many reefs around the world still offer a tremendous opportunity for marine photography, and no two are the same.

Easily the longest, Australia's 1,250-mile Great Barrier Reef flanks almost one entire coast of the Down Under continent, and stretches north into the teeming Coral Sea. The reefs of the Red Sea had seldom been visited until skin divers discovered them en masse in the mid-1960s. These reefs still provide spectacular diving, but access is subject to the recurring political turmoil of the Middle East. For fish-watching, a convergence of currents in the Galápagos Islands, where Charles Darwin first pondered the origin of coral reefs in 1837, stimulates an unusually great number of species. Other noted reef areas are in Belize (formerly British Honduras), site of the world's second longest barrier reef, and at Andros, Grand Cayman and Cozumel islands in the Caribbean.

Finally, there are the reefs of Palau. On a map of the Pacific, the scattered islands of the Palau chain form the western half of the Carolines Archipelago, cupped by the giant geographic arc of the Philippines, Indonesia and New Guinea. Administered by the United States as a United Nations trusteeship since 1947, Palau was virtually undiscovered as a diving mecca until Micronesia opened the doors to tourism in the early 1960s. Today, a single diving spot—a coral wall near the island of Esengel, south of Korror, the Palau district capital— has become perhaps the most desired destination of divers in the world. There, a diver can wade across a shallow reef in water only ankle deep, then descend along a sheer 800-foot coral wall as deep as his equipment will take him.

Paul Tzimoulis, a noted photographer, magazine editor and diver, describes Palau's wall as "the best single diving spot in the world." Photographer Douglas Faulkner has written and photographed an entire book about these islands. Other divers agree that Nature has smiled with special benevolence on Palau. Unlike the jellyfish found in most parts of the world, for instance, those of Palau are stingless. The spines of the local sea urchin, elsewhere a prickly nemesis of bather and diver alike, bend harmlessly at the touch. More important, while most ocean zones are touched by one or two nutrient-delivering ocean currents, Palau has four—the Kurisho Current, the North and South Equatorial Currents, and the Equatorial Countercurrent—each stimulating the marine life that makes Palau one of the world's most spectacular living reefs.

Forests of the Sea

Hardy survivors of the Ice Age, the brown kelps of the marine algae family represent true forests in the sea: lofty, dense, thickly populated underwater jungles that support an intense variety of life, from microscopic to mammalian. There are about a thousand species of kelps altogether. Many are very small, clinging to walls of tidepools along seashores of the world. Without doubt the grand champions in terms of sheer size—the sequoias and redwoods of the sea forest—are two species found primarily off the West Coast of North America—*Macrocystis* ("giant" kelp) and *Nereocystis* ("bull" kelp). Both of these kelps stretch as much as 100 feet from the rootlike *holdfasts*, which anchor them to rocks on the sea floor, to the tough, leafy canopies that spread across the sea's surface.

Kelp forests provide a rich bounty for the diver armed with either spear or camera. They provide not only shelter for a great number of marine animals, but oxygen and food as well. One of the greatest delicacies of the sea, the abalone, thrives here, and hunting it has made the West Coast kelp beds a popular diving Mecca. A succulent, one-shelled mollusk, the abalone protects itself from predators by clamping onto rocks with a thick muscle, feeding on plankton that drifts past. Abalones are free-swimming animals, but seldom will the diver find one anywhere but clamped tightly on a rock. The primary tool of the abalone hunter is the pry-bar; it is inserted under the shell and then pried quickly and forcefully to loosen the shellfish.

Often, especially at low tide, the leaves—*fronds*—of the kelp forest form an almost impenetrable mat at the surface, supported by large, balloon-like air sacs. The sight of this heavy mat often discourages the fledgling diver, though quite unnecessarily, because immediately below it there is plenty of room to swim among the less-dense trunks or *stipes* of the plants. The trick is to remain submerged as much as possible; skin divers often spend hours floating just below the surface with only the tips of their snorkels visible on top.

Underwater Parks

At several locations around the world, governments have wisely set aside underwater acreages as parks or preserves, so that divers may enjoy the sea floor in its natural entirety. Universally, regulations prohibit spearfishing, the taking of artifacts or the removal or destruction of any natural features; scientific collecting requires a special permit.

As a result of this "look but don't touch" policy, the untrammeled marine life in these parks is a treasure trove for the marine photographer. Fish of all kinds, their instincts seeming to tell them no hunters are allowed, proliferate and often become as tame as deer or squirrels in a land sanctuary.

Buck Island Reef, two miles from St. Croix in the Virgin Islands, is a spectacular shallow-water park; along a two-mile underwater trail, the diver is guided by small signs that identify prominent coral species and other marine life. No scuba gear is necessary; the entire park is within snorkeling reach of even the most inexperienced visitor. Trunk Bay at St. John, also one of the Virgin Islands, is another snorkeler's paradise; the area abounds with parrotfish, brain coral, three species of angelfish, small turtles and schools of rainbow-hued tropical reef fish. Fifty miles south of Nassau, in the Bahamas, 176-square-mile Exuma Cays Land and Sea Park is perhaps the largest of all underwater playgrounds, and because of its remote location it is also one of the least visited.

Two marine parks are located in California. In the 5,000-acre La Jolla Underwater Park near San Diego, divers may swim through forests of kelp, and the even more adventurous may explore the upper reaches of the cavernous La Jolla Canyon nearby. To get a preview of what they may expect to find in the canyon, divers may first watch a television screen in the Scripps Institution of Oceanography Aquarium, on which a live image is relayed from a television camera dangled into the depths from the end of the Scripps research pier. To the north, Julia Pfeiffer Burns State Park, located on the edge of California's hauntingly beautiful Big Sur, is the nation's newest underwater preserve. The 2½-square-mile park touches both terrestrial and marine environments and thus is an ideal place for the diver-photographer to explore the active interface of sea and shore. Protected by law, the park is a rich storehouse of marine life, including kelp beds, various species of Northern California fish, sea otters, abalone, anemones and corals.

Perhaps the most popular underwater park of all, Florida's 75-square-mile John Pennekamp Coral Reef State Park, contains some of the world's most beautiful living reefs, a number of shipwrecks and a spectacular assortment of marine life. The park, named for the Miami newspaperman who championed its creation, has been credited with stimulating interest in similar parks elsewhere.

Pennekamp regulations are rigidly enforced by both the Florida Department of Natural Resources and the Marine Patrol, and the hands-off policy covers the shipwrecks as well as coral and marine life. The park lies athwart Key Largo, largest of the Upper Keys, and is only a 90-minute drive from Miami.

Altogether, 40 of the 52 corals found in the Atlantic Reef System can be seen at Pennekamp, and the varied appearance indicates how some of them acquired their common names: staghorn, moosehead, leaf, hat, finger, star, brain, flower, and cactus. The submarine coral growths are a spawning ground for brightly colored tropical fish, sharks, barracudas, eels, turtles, shellfish and other marine life.

An estimated 15 shipwrecks are scattered on the floor of this park. Most are completely broken up, but the remains of the 285-foot freighter *Benwood*, sunk after torpedoing in World War II by a German submarine, offers some of the most dramatic wreck-prowling in the entire Florida Keys. The *Benwood* sank in 1942 and was further demolished after the war when her hull, considered a hazard to navigation, was used for bombing practice. When the Pennekamp park was established by the Florida Legislature in 1960, however, the hulk received the same protection accorded marine life.

Fire in the Sea

Though it is hardly an everyday occurrence, the outpouring of volcanic lava into the sea can provide the diver fortunate enough to be on the scene with spectacular motion-picture footage or still shots. Near one undersea volcano, about 60 miles off the northeast coast of New Zealand, divers regularly explore hot water springs that bubble out from the side of a prominent fissure. The ocean floor there is an eerie sight, with odd marine growth affected by irregular lava flows, and hundreds of still-unidentified species of fish.

In the islands of Hawaii, which owe their very existence to volcanoes, there are unusual opportunities to explore underwater lava bores. Normally, only the solidified remains of past flows are available for inspection by the visiting diver; because of the rate of flow, the temperature of the lava and the cooling effect of the sea, some of the solidified goo has curled, forming tunnels large enough for a diver to crawl inside.

In March of 1971, however, a team of diving scientist-photographers had a unique opportunity to watch an actual lava flow underwater, and captured the results on film. Heading the team was Dr. Richard W. Grigg, assistant marine biologist at the University of Hawaii's Institute of Marine Biology, a former surfing champion and specialist in the study of deep-sea precious corals. Grigg's special interest was the effect of lava flows on coral communities.

Observers on the island of Hawaii had noted restless activity of the Mauna Ulu vent of Kilauea volcano as early as February of 1971; a month after the flow began, ten miles inland, the molten river finally reached the sea. In mid-April, the spectacle was still occurring, and Grigg flew from Oahu to join an observation team that had already been formed. At the point where the lava entered the sea, Grigg noted much less steam than he had expected to result from the meeting of substances having such diverse temperatures. Later, he postulated that tongues of lava, flowing into the sea, caused immediate volatilization of the water, producing a thin layer of steam that surrounded the lava and thus insulated it from the water itself. Meanwhile, during the month of activity, the flow had added 0.2 square miles of new land to the island of Hawaii.

Grigg and others on the team wanted to observe the flow as closely as possible for photographic purposes, but far enough away so they could escape if the lava suddenly bubbled too near their location. Finally, they found a spot between two lava streams where the flow had been consistent for several days. There, they entered the water and descended to a depth of 110 feet before gradually beginning to work their way back up the underwater slope. Grigg recorded his impressions later:

Suddenly I was aware of a strange mixture of noises: hissing, rumbling, grinding, roaring, intermittent concussions. The visibility now was about 10 feet; we still couldn't see any activity. Later, just ahead of us at a depth of 35 feet, the front of a nearly cylindrical tube cracked and burst open. Incandescent lava poured forward about a foot. For about five seconds it sizzled and hissed, vibrating at a blurred speed as the surface cooled to a crust. Seconds later it revived and the process was repeated twice. Upslope, red cracks appeared along several other twisted tubes where small buds were forming. All of us were shooting film like crazy, in spite of ourselves.

Returning to Oahu, Grigg found that his camera had recorded some of the most extraordinary activity of Nature anywhere on Earth. More important, however, was the scientific evidence the incident produced. A clear gap occurs, Grigg determined, between surface and submarine lava flows; if similar gaps found in older flows elsewhere can be dated, the information may be of extraordinary value in reconstructing the history of vertical changes in sea level or land masses, thus unlocking one more long-kept secret of the sea.

In the Wake of War

On the morning of February 16, 1944, the United States Navy launched a carrier attack against a fleet of Japanese warships and cargo vessels at anchor in 40-mile-wide Truk Lagoon, in the mid-Pacific. To the defending Japanese, who had prepared for an amphibious invasion and who had turned Truk into what they considered an impregnable bastion, the attack was a stunning and costly surprise. For 36 continuous hours, in more than 30 waves, naval aviators of Carrier Task Force 90 pounded the lagoon—with ordnance estimated to be 15 times greater than that used by the Japanese at Pearl Harbor 2½ years earlier.

The defenders were caught with some 60 warships, fuel tankers and cargo vessels still at anchor, and few of the ships had been idle. Most were in the process of being fueled, loaded, unloaded, or repaired, and thus were not ready for quick escape to sea. When the din of battle finally died, the Japanese surveyed a catastrophic loss: 15 naval vessels, 6 tankers and 17 cargo ships lay at the bottom. In addition, the wreckage of 250 defending aircraft—as well as 25 of the attackers—had plummeted either into the lagoon or onto the scattered small islands around its rim.

Because the assault had come so late in the war, no attempt was made by the Japanese to salvage the ships. And although postwar American administrators allowed salvage of wrecked ships elsewhere in Micronesia, of which Truk is a part, the strewn hulks slumbered untouched in their salt-water graves until as recently as the late 1960s.

Today the Truk ships, possibly the greatest number of vessels ever sunk at one time in modern history, represent one of the world's great underwater museums, a coral-encrusted tomb preserved almost intact for more than a quarter-century. Even now, the diver's first glimpse of the ghost ships, many of them in very shallow water or protruding partly above the surface, is as if the bombing attack had happened only the day before. Cargo that was in the process of being loaded remains on rusting decks. On one ship there is a Japanese Zero fighter aircraft, still bolted to its deck mountings. Considering the passage of time and the ravages of salt water, the state of preservation is indeed remarkable. Masts, rigging and superstructures are still solidly in place. Hatches and doors swing freely on their hinges. Portholes open and close. Some of the vessels were completely or partly overturned in sinking, while others, most of them in shallower water, settled upright.

For years, until a worried local government finally mustered up sufficient funds to remove them as a safety measure, tons of unexploded ammunition, including depth charges containing highly toxic picric acid, were also scattered about the lagoon floor. Today, that danger has been removed, but all else remains virtually untouched, as the ships have been declared a national monument by the tourist-conscious Trukese. By decree of the local legislature, it is illegal—punishable by a $1,000 fine—to remove any item from these ships. Even those who wish only to dive and photograph them must obtain a permit.

Of the total number of ships lost, about 16 lie only a half-hour boat ride away from the community of Moen, headquarters village of the Truk area. The largest, a 20,000-ton auxiliary cruiser, lies in very deep water off adjoining Dublon Island, which the Japanese used as naval headquarters for their mid-Pacific war operations. It can be reached only by scuba-equipped divers, but many others are within snorkel's reach. The other wrecks involve a wide variety of craft—destroyers, submarine chasers, tugboats, a seaplane tender and a submarine; as late as 1973, all had not been located or identified.

Sea Grottos

Exploring sea caves involves some of the world's most dangerous diving. But it also offers an opportunity to see an enormous density and diversity of marine life, unusual color patterns and, occasionally, some clues to the relatively recent geological history of the earth.

Sea caves are found on coasts of all continents, from Greenland to Australia, but they occur in the greatest number on coasts formed of limestone or other soft minerals. The island of Capri in the Bay of Naples, for instance, is dotted with 31 large caves, which have a total area of more than 750,000 square feet. The average sea cave ranges in size between a small room and a large house, but they also come in mammoth sizes. The largest one known, the Grotta del Blue Marina ("Grotto of the Sea Bull") on the east coast of Sardinia, can be followed at sea level for 13,275 feet, or more than two miles.

True sea caves are dominated by marine influences; in other words, they are connected to the sea by at least one opening. Many other caves, however, were created by the sea but are now on dry land; hollowed out by pounding ocean surf, they were left high and dry when the oceans receded or land was uplifted. These caves provide dramatic testimony to the changing relationship of land and sea during earth's history. On an island off the coast of Norway, for example, there is a tunnel nearly 400 feet above the sea, from which the pounding surf of an interglacial era carved out nearly 5 million cubic feet of granite rock. Scientists say its present elevation has been caused in part by the elastic, upward rebound of the earth's crust after the melting of glacial ice. Because many of these caves were created after man's appearance on earth, some of them, scientists believe, contain relics of early human habitation buried in the debris of their floors.

Whether exploring for ancient relics or merely studying and photographing present marine life in sea caves, the diver must meticulously obey certain safety rules. The first involves the obvious absence of any easy vertical escape route; while some sea caves contain air pockets between the surface of the water and their roofs, others are totally filled with water. Air supplies therefore must be carefully planned, with extra attention given to providing emergency supplies in case of equipment failure. As in night diving in the open sea, cave exploration requires artificial light of some kind, and the "spelunking" diver who finds himself suddenly in darkness is likely to panic easily in his search for direction.

From long experience (and a number of tragedies) divers have developed a basic set of safety rules that, coupled with rapidly improving diving equipment, may further open this fascinating region of the sea to exploration.

For example, sea cave dives should be attempted only by divers working in teams of no less than three members. Extra air supplies are left along the entire route, and divers hand-follow a safety line that is fastened securely at one end to an object near the cave entrance. Equipment such as compasses, spare lights, decompression computers and buoyancy compensators—not always necessary in shallow open-sea diving—are safety absolutes in cave diving. Every aspect and unknown hazard of the cave to be explored must be considered. For instance, divers who have plotted a course through a fully explored cave have sometimes run into trouble because they forgot to take into consideration the downward slope of their progress: in caves, just as in the open sea, air consumption increases with depth.

Sea caves are particularly ideal places to study filter-feeding animals, those that extract nutrients from passing currents and must rely on an abundant supply of passing water. Quieter than the open sea, caves are less affected by influences that disturb these currents. And because plants that depend on sunlight disappear within a short distance from the entrances of sea caves, filter feeders have no food competition from plants. They are therefore left to vie only among themselves for living space in a perpetually darkened world.

The Upside-Down World

In the sea, where up and down seem much the same, Nature sometimes has a way of performing curious flip-flops. One day in 1959, three diving scientists of Scripps Institution of Oceanography, Dr. Wheeler J. North, James R. Stewart and Conrad Limbaugh, swam into a sea canyon near Cabo San Lucas in Baja California to seek shelter from a storm. Suddenly, at a depth of 30 feet, they noticed a trickle of sand tumbling down a nearby slope. Following the downward flow they descended to 130 feet, where the trickle had become a veritable torrent, a "landfall" in the ocean as spectacular as any waterfall they had seen on land.

Fortunately, the divers were equipped with cameras, and they preserved the sight on film. Later investigation at the scene by another scientist, Dr. Robert Dill, disclosed that landfalls occur quite regularly, and that they often tumble to much greater depths than that the Scripps divers had reached; when Dill reached a depth of 250 feet, he could still see sand catapulting at least another 100 feet below. Nearly everywhere that divers have plumbed the continental slope they have found deep canyons and gouges etched into its face, closely resembling weather-eroded cliff faces in the surface world. What causes these landfalls is still speculation; however, many scientists believe they are triggered by powerful undersea earthquakes or strong turbidity currents. (The latter are rivers of silt-laden water that flow down the continental slopes; some roll along for hundreds of miles, laying down new layers of sediments as they go.)

Few divers have been fortunate enough to capture a repeat of the Cabo San Lucas phenomenon, since Nature does not always announce her shaking, rattling and rolling in advance. But the incident served to illustrate the value of having a camera always ready when exploring the underwater world.

Under Arctic Ice

Of all marine regions on earth, that of the Arctic is the least explored. Cold, forbidding, little understood, it remains a region of great mystery despite the fact that man has now traversed the North Pole both over the ice and beneath it. Yet the Arctic Ocean, most of it shielded from view by a year-around ice pack, continues to grow in importance because of its storehouse of minerals, its influence on global weather, its strategic geography, its abundance of marine life, and its potential as a natural laboratory for studying fragile ecosystems and the effect of pollution on them.

Because of the massive ice cap, we tend to regard the

Arctic as a land mass, even though it is not. Although it is the smallest of the four oceans, the Arctic Ocean is nonetheless an impressive feature of our watery planet: 3,662,000 square miles in area, or nearly four times the size of the Caribbean Sea. Perhaps most surprising is the fact that it has such a rich marine biota, the home of many of the great whales, thousands of species of fish that have adapted to an extremely harsh environment, and some astonishing giants of other phyla. The lion's mare jellyfish, for instance, with an 8-foot body and 100-foot tentacles, largest planktonic animal in the oceans, lives nowhere else.

Until recently, because of the overriding danger of extreme cold, man's exploration of the Arctic Ocean was confined to over-ice vehicles and under-ice submarines. But now, the day of the rubber-suited human diver has dawned, and full scale under-ice exploration by aquanauts is not far away.

In the late 1960s, the first significant attempt was made to determine how human divers must adapt to this environment. Headed by Dr. Joseph B. MacInnis, a Canadian physician long interested in diving physiology and a leader of his nation's man-in-the-sea program, a team of scientists and photographers spent several weeks exploring beneath the ice in the Canadian Arctic. They wore specially developed, heated diving suits and breathing equipment that had been tested under the most rugged conditions in laboratory experiments. As a safety measure, they stationed a microhabitat, the *Sublimnos Sea Shell*, at a shallow depth near where they planned to dive, so they could crawl inside for food and warmth, and if an emergency occurred.

There was little precedent to refer to when planning the Sublimnos project; until the late 1960s, no published literature existed on manned diving performance under Arctic open-sea conditions. In fact, few men had ever dived beneath Arctic or Antarctic ice at all, and those who had were divers who had gone down for very brief periods, usually for such utilitarian reasons as repairing ship or submarine hulls.

Altogether, MacInnis' group collected more than 200 hours of under-ice experience, thus ranking them as true pioneers of this new frontier of the sea. Based on the experiment, MacInnis concluded that diving technology has advanced to the point where under-ice diving can be conducted on a broader scale—but only with utmost caution and planning. Obviously, Arctic diving is not the same as diving at Bimini. For extended exposure in near-freezing temperatures, specially designed "thermal suits" are required to overcome the bitter cold and to permit the diver to function properly. Absolute teamwork and emergency planning is necessary. Diver-to-diver communication is imperative. But MacInnis feels that rigidly adhering to well-established safety rules will allow the door to be opened for under-ice Arctic exploration by human divers. And beyond exploration of purely utilitarian or scientific purpose—aiding in offshore oil recovery, for example, or making pollution or ecosystem studies—the new frontier offers adventure and esthetic stimulation of the highest order.

Every danger of the sea, every unsolved mystery, every human fear of probing an unknown and alien element, seems magnified under the ice. "It is impossible to know how Arctic marine animals will respond to a free-swimming man," MacInnis wrote in *Oceans* magazine at an early stage in the Sublimnos project. "Who knows what a massive seal or walrus might do if a diver wandered into his icy den . . . or the outcome of a sharing of an underwater pathway with an angry polar bear . . . or the results of being the first to meet the huge Greenland shark. . . ."

Yet in later dives, MacInnis found that the compelling beauty of the under-ice Arctic diminished his fears and lessened his anxiety. In a realm of bitter cold that would seem to retard all life, he found abundant, foot-thick tufts of algae and forests of kelp; in furrows gouged from the sea floor by ponderous, monolithic icebergs were thousands of sea urchins and brittle stars; small sculpins—well adapted to Arctic seas—were so forgiving of his intrusion that they showed absolutely no alarm when he picked them up with a gloved hand. And in such an atmosphere, MacInnis' group realized that they had become bound together by purpose as never before. The remoteness of the site, the primeval stillness, the awesome intertwining of shadows and colors served to cement, in MacInnis' later words, ". . . that precious blend of dependence and independence that is shared by men in an alien environment."

Today, several years later, nations are viewing the Arctic Ocean with increased interest. Following in MacInnis' wake, a group of scientists serving with the Royal Canadian Navy has launched cold-water diving experiments. The United States Navy, with a strategic responsibility at stake, has worked feverishly to develop new and better equipment, and new gas breathing mixtures for use at great depths in extremely cold water. And, stimulated by discoveries of petroleum deposits and other minerals in the frozen North, private industry has begun investing huge sums in research.

With the Arctic door thus cracked ajar by economic necessity, scientific curiosity and political indispensability, the day of diving under Arctic ice as a creative adventure cannot be far behind. And when that day dawns, man certainly will have taken one of the greatest strides yet in his return to the sea.

The Golden Sea

One sultry afternoon in 1955, an ashen-haired, middle-aged homebuilder named Kip Wagner idly poked his way along a low, sandy seaside bluff near Vero Beach, on Florida's Atlantic coast. Despite the heat, it was a grand day for beachcombing, a hobby Wagner had pursued almost daily since moving to Florida from his native Ohio just after World War II. A hurricane had raged through the area two days earlier. Kicking at stray tufts of seaweed as he strolled, Wagner was fascinated to see how the storm had completely realigned the shoreline, and he marveled at the toughness of the small marine grasses that had so staunchly resisted wind's fury and surf's deluge.

Suddenly, the glint of a bright, silvery object in the sand caught his eye. Assuming it was a seashell, and being a collector of them, Wagner scooped it up. Instead, its precise polygonal shape told him it had probably been made not by Nature, but by man; scraping through the thin layer of solidified residue, he could clearly make out a tiny cross and a date embossed on the surface underneath. It was a doubloon, a Spanish coin.

Like most romantics, Wagner, who often had heard old-timers in the area spin tales of "lost pirate treasures," was instantly whisked back in time to the spell of Stevenson's *Treasure Island*. In his daydream, he could hear the screech of Long John Silver's parrot: "Pieces of eight! Pieces of eight!" In his mind's eye, he could see a fleet of Spanish galleons, hull down in the sea under the weight of silver ingots, precious gems and chains of purest gold. And his imagination summoned up the winds of the fierce hurricane that was to send the ships and their cargoes foundering to the bottom, to be buried perhaps forever in the sands of time.

Unlike most romantics, however, Wagner could not shake himself from the dream. His chance discovery of a single Spanish coin that hot Florida afternoon was to set in motion a search that would result, after nearly a quarter of his lifetime, in the richest sunken treasure find of the 20th century. By 1970, despite a withering series of disappointments and almost daily dangers that surely would have discouraged men of lesser resolve, Wagner and later associates were to recover a record $6,500,000 in treasure—$1 million of it on a single day, the booty of an entire fleet of Spanish galleons that perished, with the loss of 1,000 lives, in a hurricane two-and-one-half centuries earlier.

Wagner's spectacular success was admittedly unusual. The motivation that drove him was not. "There is no way to escape from treasure," Joseph Conrad once wrote, "once it fastens itself upon your mind." Later generations of treasure seekers have verified Conrad's observations. Treasure fever is a malady with no cure, an affliction whose treatment—the finding of treasure—only worsens the suffering. The mere hint of sunken spoils can send otherwise rational men into restless daydreams; the diver who accidentally stumbles across a shipwreck, devoid of intrinsic value though it may be, becomes an addict for life.

Hunting for sunken treasure has always been considered a potluck adventure, a moonlighting, weekending avocation generated by armchair daydreaming or, in the case of a few men like Kip Wagner, by the chance findings of a single clue to a legitimate buried fortune. Although treasure hunting will doubtlessly continue to be a hobby for many, it has also, in the past few decades, become a full-time, serious and sophisticated big business for a few. The reason is technological. For one thing, remarkable improvements in diving equipment now allow humans to descend deeper and remain longer than was possible only a few years ago; thus, they are able to reach shipwrecks and to spend the underwater time necessary to salvage them. For another, a revolution has occurred in salvage equipment itself.

Certainly, there is no shortage of treasure. Someone has likened the floors of the oceans to a vast bank. Each time a ship sinks, each time an earthquake or volcano topples a seaside city into the depths, a deposit is made. And each time a successful salvor recovers some of the spillage, there is a withdrawal. Fortunately for the adventurous, the total deposits vastly outnumber the withdrawals. The contents of this vast marine vault have been increasing for hundreds of years, and only recently—not until the 20th century, in fact—has man been able to set about reducing them with any reasonable assurance of success.

The explosion of undersea exploration that was generated by military demand in World War II is turning up new shipwrecks every year. In the summer of 1973, for instance, Dr. George Bass, a marine archaeologist with the University of Pennsylvania, spent three fruitful months conducting a study of the seabed off the coast of Turkey. Using sonar equipment, underwater television and a midget submarine, Bass and his team of scientists found shipwreck after shipwreck that years of exploration by previous groups had somehow overlooked.

The Caribbean, its reefs littered with shipwrecks dating to Spain's three-century colonization of the New World, remains a skindiver's El Dorado. According to one reliable estimate, there are at least 300 unsalvaged wrecks containing valuable cargo off the Florida Keys alone. The Great Lakes hold thousands of other shipwrecks. And others abound in the Mediterranean, the Indian Ocean, Southeast Asia—anywhere that man has traveled in trading ships since the Phoenicians sailed the seas.

The Treasure Hunters

The adventurers who come to tap this underwater treasury are a diverse lot. Daniel Stack, whose firm Treasure Hunters, Incorporated, funded a successful five-year project to salvage a fleet of Spanish galleons at Vigo Bay, Spain, and who has watched treasure-hunters come and go over the years, divides them into four categories. First is the armchair adventurer. He gains his excitement vicariously from the treasure-hunting exploits of others. A mere hint of treasure whets his interest; although he dreams of buried riches and pirate booty, he is content to remain a silent partner in the quest, ". . . and he becomes positively ecstatic if the find actually turns out to be other than just another hoax."

The scientist occupies the second category. He is the marine archaeologist, the historian who gains pleasure in filling in missing pages of history. He cares little about the intrinsic value of a shipwreck; his satisfaction comes from classifying and cataloging, from proving and disproving.

The third group is composed of active adventurers, today's soldiers of fortune. They actually search for treasure, though, Stack adds, what they basically seek is adventure. "If it were the actual hard cash which they really sought, most of the searches would die aborning and never mature out of the cocoon of mental imagery into full-blown argosies, for these men do not take the trouble to do the research necessary to insure that the sought-for treasure ever really existed, or if it existed, what the real circumstances of the loss were."

Only a handful of men are found in the fourth and last group—the professional salvors. Yet, as Stack points out, they are usually the ones who consistently enhance their bank accounts, because "they bring to bear upon the glamorous world of treasure the vital resources of the mundane world of business." Their search is no hit-and-miss affair; with the huge sums of money required for professional treasure salvaging, it could not afford to be. Usually, these professionals incorporate into companies, sell stock, commit substantial capital, assemble the latest equipment, conduct meticulous research, and exercise utmost restraint in searching not by hunch but by proven scientific methods.

Though Stack's definition of the four groups is a good one, membership within groups seldom remains constant. Some who come to seek treasure are quickly discouraged, and just as quickly drop out. Others, whose original goal may have been mere vacation adventure, become so addicted that they quit prosperous jobs and give up equally prosperous businesses to become full-time (and sometimes poorer) treasure hunters. Still others, to whom intrinsic riches are the only goal at the outset, feel the tug of history as they prowl old shipwrecks and sunken cities; soon, they find themselves among the increasing ranks of amateur archaeologists.

Traditionally, marine archaeologists and treasure hunters have been adversaries, and with sufficient reason. In the past, many valuable historical wrecks around the world have been demolished by careless divers using dynamite or similarly destructive methods of salvage; as a result, many states and nations have now adopted strict laws protecting antiquities. Florida, for instance, requires licensing and bonding of treasure salvors, and the state collects 25 per cent of what is found. Texas permits no salvage whatsoever. Many Mediterranean nations permit salvage, but all artifacts retrieved must be turned over to the controlling nation.

In recent years, however, there has been a remarkable change of attitude. Though the two groups may still occasionally feud with each other in courtrooms and in the public print, in private each places high value on the skills and aspirations of the other, recognizing that science and profit can co-exist in the sea. As a result, few well-funded professional salvage teams these days are complete without at least one experienced marine archaeologist, and it is on the professional salvor—with his thirty thousand dollar proton magnetometer, his specially equipped fleet of boats, and his accumulation of valuable seismic-profile data—that the diving scientist relies heavily for logistical support.

Although the word *treasure* is usually associated with the recovery of shipwrecks and their cargoes, sunken ships are only a part of the much broader scientific discipline of marine or underwater archaeology. In the dictionary sense that treasure is, by first definition, "a store of valuable items," marine archaeology may then be divided further into four sub-classifications. The first includes refuse sites of past civilizations; in times past, just as today, coastal and inland waterways were used to dump garbage, trash and other debris no longer wanted. The dumped items were valueless at the time; today, however, they are of significance historically as clues to the way past civilizations lived. A good example is the *cenote* (from the Mayan word for a water-filled limestone sinkhole). On the Yucatan peninsula of Mexico, cenotes were used by the Mayans as dumping grounds for all sorts of castoff objects, including spears, ornaments and even human bones.

In a cenote at Dzibilchaltun, Mexico, one archaeological team in three months recovered some 6,000 artifacts, which proved the existence of a huge and previously unknown pre-Columbian city. Extrapolating from the number of human bones found in the well, archaeologists determined that the city was perhaps one of the largest in the New World, measuring about 20 square miles, and that it was inhabited continuously from about 2000 B.C. until after the Spanish conquest. From the artifacts, which included jars, flint and nearly 3,000 potsherds, they were able to trace, almost decade by decade, the evolution of that civilization over the centuries.

Material recovered from cenotes near Dzibilchaltun and Chichen Itza, also in Yucatan, has enabled archaeologists to reconstruct patterns of sacred and funeral ceremonies, including those of human sacrifice; such sites are a second major target of marine archaeologists. The third classification includes sites of former human habitation, both in the New World and the Old World, which were submerged in the sea as the result of either a sudden, violent occurrence such as an earthquake, or more slowly, as in one of the periods of melting during the Ice Ages. Some sunken habitation sites lie in very shallow water; others may have broken up, with the remains sliding into water too deep for present-day diving technology to reach.

The final category exclusively involves shipwrecks, and there are uncounted thousands of these scattered underneath the seas of the world. Like time capsules of the period of history they represent, and although the cargo they carried may have included no "treasure" in the usual sense of the word, they are of enormous significance to the diving archaeologist and historian. Unlike written records of history or artifacts found in buried cities, which may have been handed down from generation to generation, a shipwreck represents a single moment of time, a specific day during a specific era when a ship containing money, cargo, furniture, utensils or dishes, foundered and went to the bottom. Diving on a shipwreck, then, is more than a quest for riches: it is an expedition into history.

Ancient Shipwrecks

The origins of modern marine archaeology date to the year 1900 and an accidental discovery by a group of Greek sponge divers who were driven off course by a sudden storm en route home from North Africa. Seeking shelter from the tempest, the divers landed at the barren, sparsely populated islet of Andikíthira, northwest of the island of Crete. Demetrios Kondos, captain of the divers, thought they should take advantage of the enforced interlude and he suggested that for diversion, they dive for sponges near the island. He expressed doubt that any sponges would be found, but felt that by diving his men would feel less irritated over the delay in reaching home.

Kondos was correct; there were no sponges at Andikíthira, but what one diver found proved of tremendously greater value. At a depth of about 150 feet, Elias Stadiatis stared in astonishment through the blue Mediterranean water upon several huge columns of marble and bronze. Some had been sculpted into human forms, others were shaped as animals. When Stadiatis tugged at one of the bronze figures, an arm fell off in his grasp; startled, he yanked on the descent line to indicate he wished to surface. Once on board, he notified Captain Kondos who, correctly suspecting that the discovery was that of an ancient ship with a cargo of prized art objects, descended to the site himself and took tape measurements.

Returning home again to the island of Syme, Kondos described the discovery to an excited citizenry, and produced copious notes as proof of his claim. Word quickly reached Athens, and after a careful examination of the bronze arm—the only artifact recovered from Andikíthira—the first major marine archaeological expedition in modern history was organized. Kondos was retained by the Greek government to head the expedition.

The expedition held special meaning for Greece; for years, despite laws forbidding the removal of antiquities from the country, many valuable masterpieces had vanished without trace. To the Greeks, Andikíthira became a matter of national urgency and of national pride.

The hazards of the project were many. Divers had to work in depths of 160 to 170 feet, about the limit of human endurance in that pre-scuba period, and could remain down only for very short periods of time. One diver died of the bends and two others were crippled during the nine tedious months of excavation. Despite the losses, however, the Andikíthira project was to greatly elevate the role of the diver in the field investigation of science. Not only did divers bring up enough artifacts to fill an entire wing of the National Museum at Athens, rare and valuable works of art whose value could not even be estimated, but these and many other items helped rewrite entire chapters of early Greek history. One metal object of particular interest, for instance, appeared to be some kind of astronomical device, but years of corrosion had obliterated its details. Finally, in 1956, more than a half century after the Andikíthira expedition, the Greek government retained a noted British archaeologist, Dr. Derek de Solla Price, to reassemble the device and determine its function. After months of cleaning and study, Dr. Price announced a theory: the object was a remarkably complex early-day instrument, a form of astrolabe that apparently had been designed to calculate the movements of the planets in the heavens. Until then, historians had only been able to guess at the structure of such devices, based on writings of Arabs in 1000 A.D.; no first-hand evidence was available. The Andikíthira astrolabe, however, confirmed that scientists of the pre-Christian era had achieved a high level of technological achievement, a fact that had eluded archaeologists for more than 2,000 years.

Though the Andikíthira wreck was the first major archaeological triumph in modern history, the *oldest* shipwreck, dating to the Bronze Age, was one discovered by an underwater archaeological team from the University of Pennsylvania. It was also the first to which rigid methods of land archaeological "digs" were applied. Dated about 1200 B.C., the wreck located at Cape Gelidonya, Greece, had carried a cargo of copper and tin (from which bronze apparently was to be made), as well as an assortment of tools, weapons and other utensils, all of which were of great historical significance.

The Shipwreck Lanes

A few shipwrecks, like the ancient ship at Andikíthira, have been found by accident. In 1967, for instance, the rotting hulk of the brig *Leonora*, capsized and sunk in a hurricane in 1874, was inadvertently found near the island of Kusaie in the Pacific by the Scripps Institution of Oceanography research vessel *Horizon*. The research ship had been dragging sampling instruments along the ocean floor. Most wrecks, however, are found by applying logic and considerable research, and by acquiring a working knowledge of world maritime history.

Some ship sinkings have occurred in haphazard and unusual ways; scuttling by a mutinous crew, for instance, or an unexplained hull failure, or an intentional, clandestine deepwater sinking for insurance recovery by an impoverished shipowner. Ships sunk in naval engagements also fall into this category. By far the majority of shipwrecks, however, can be traced to patterns that have repeated themselves over and over through history, and their locations are found in clearly predictable areas. They are the wrecks caused by storms, strandings or collisions, and most have occurred along established shipping routes of their period. World maritime trade routes, therefore, suggest the richest hunting ground for the treasure salvor. Records, of course, grow increasingly dimmer and unreliable as the researcher works backward through time. In the 20th century there is a rather precise account of the location and exact circumstances of every major ship sinking, but tracing previous sinkings becomes far less exact than the more recent *Titanics, Andrea Dorias* and *Lusitanias*, whose precise locations are well known.

The earliest important trade routes were those in the Mediterranean, cradle of civilization, where some of the oldest ships in history lie buried. In later centuries, mariners began crossing the Atlantic after Columbus' discovery of the New World; Spain's three-century conquest of the Americas produced what is probably the greatest concentration of wrecks in one area in world history. Spain also established routes across the Pacific and southward from Panama to Peru, while Portugal found routes to the trading treasures of the Orient by sailing eastward.

No one knows the total intrinsic value of all the ships and their cargoes that have foundered along these routes, but it is massive, and most of it can be traced to the pre-1900s, before the steamship and radio made navigation comparatively safe, and before weather forecasting had become adequate. From records in the archives of Spain, however, a fairly accurate estimate can be made of the value of cargoes carried and lost during the period of Spain's colonization of the New World; projecting from these records, the probable total of valuable cargoes lost by all nations becomes staggering. In his authoritative *Treasure Divers Guide*, perhaps the most extensive and exhaustive summary of sunken treasure around the world ever published, John S. Potter, Jr. estimates that between 1500 and 1820, the Spanish fleets linking Spain and the New World hauled some twelve *billion* dollars worth of treasure, at present day exchange values. Of this amount, an estimated 5 percent was lost in storms or pirate attacks, and 2 percent—about $240 million—was never salvaged. The South Seas Armadas, carrying treasure from Peru to Panama for transshipment overland and reloading aboard the flotillas sailing to Spain, carried another $2 billion in silver and gold. Potter, who spent years researching archival records in Spain, estimates that at least $30 million of the $50 million lost was never recovered.

While these figures indeed seem impressive, it must be remembered that the treasure it represents is spread over literally millions of square miles of ocean; it is the skill of narrowing down the search to more manageable proportions that separates the successful salvor from the luckless amateur. Research, therefore, becomes a cardinal prerequisite to the salvage itself. To the professional, merely finding a wreck is not enough. He must positively identify it beyond any doubt, and at this point the task of research has only begun. To determine whether to commit the capital required for salvage, he must first know, for instance, whether the vessel was ever before salvaged, and if so, how much cargo was recovered. It is also helpful to know many other details: the last known port of embarkation, the character of the passenger manifest, any clues that nobility or high-ranking government officers might have been aboard (which would indicate that cargoes of equally high esteem were being carried along).

Treasure maps sold in waterfront bars, no matter how impressively printed on parchment they may be, usually return a profit to only one person: the seller. Professional salvors place far greater trust in such documents as insurance company records, ship manifests, logbooks (useful in determining the position of sinking), official reports, and letters and interviews with survivors. Naval archives of most countries contain millions of words of descriptions of naval battles, and records of courts martial or naval inquiries that customarily follow naval disasters also provide clues, not only to the location of sinkings, but of what was carried aboard and other sailing circumstances that frequently shed light on the value of the ship.

Since disasters at sea have been headline events for centuries, contemporary newspapers, magazines and pamphlets offer additional information, though they are best consulted only for general information, since these stories are generally written during the feverish excitement of the moment and not after a careful deliberation of the facts. Maritime and military museums and archives are yet another source. By far the most comprehensive archival records are those maintained by Spain. Those covering the three centuries of Spain's rule in the New World are housed in the Archivo General de Indias in Seville; researchers there have found literally millions of documents, bundled up, that have never been read since they were written. Rarely if ever has any nation documented its maritime activity as has Spain.

Research, therefore, is the key to successful salvage operations. True, a few very successful shipwreck recoveries have been made with only cursory research being conducted in advance, but these are very rare. Nowhere is the value of research more ably demonstrated than in the case of the *Girona*, a galleass of the Spanish Armada and one of 63 vessels that perished in the British Isles and along the west coast of Europe in a raging storm in 1588. Because it so well illustrates what can result from a well-planned salvage expedition, supported first by endless hours of research on dry land, this salvage project is worth describing in some detail here.

The Search for the *Girona*

The impetus for the long and arduous search that resulted in locating and salvaging the *Girona* originated with a single man with an insatiable curiosity and a restless spirit of adventure. He was a Belgian, Robert Stenuit, a diver, amateur archaelogist, writer, photographer and unquestionably one of the world's most patient men. Stenuit became fascinated with shipwrecks as a boy. Later, as a student at the University of Brussels, he began compiling a card-index file listing those wrecks which, from reading about them, he considered to be the greatest potential treasures in the world—from either the standpoint of their intrinsic value or their historical significance. At 19, yielding to the call of the sea, Stenuit gave up his studies, determined to somehow mate two parallel, intense personal interests: diving and historical research.

By 1967, after Stenuit had participated as a diver in his first major salvage expedition, at Vigo Bay in Spain, the *Girona* index card had moved steadily forward through his file to a place of special honor. He had first heard of the galleass (a large war galley propelled by both sails and manned oars) while working with archaeologist-writer John Potter at Vigo Bay. During lulls in the expedition, Potter was writing the first draft of a major encyclopedic work on shipwrecks around the world, and he invited Stenuit to comment and participate. Reading Potter's draft, Stenuit became fascinated with circumstances of the demise of the *Girona*. Set against a background of major sea battles during the period when Spain's King Philip II was attempting to defeat England with his Invincible Armada, and with additional background of storms and high drama, the manuscript described how a large portion of the cargoes of the other armada vessels had been transferred aboard the *Girona*, on the apparent assumption that her large size made her safer from the tempestuous sea. The *Girona* proved no more invincible than her sisters, however, and had gone aground off the coast of North Ireland in a disaster that only five crewmen survived.

The thought of the gold in the galleass' hold obsessed Stenuit, but her history obsessed him even more. "The prospect of the *Girona*'s cargo held less meaning for me than the weight of history in her," he later wrote, referring to the stricken armada. "But apart from replacing the word 'treasures' by 'historical wrecks,' I wouldn't change a word. I decided to devote myself completely, for just as long as it might take, to finding this vessel."

With so little specific information to start with, that would take some doing. While still in Spain, Stenuit began prowling through archival accounts of the Invincible Armada's assault on England, but while he found extensive references to the *Girona*, none were specific enough to warrant a costly, full-scale salvage attempt. When the first stage of Vigo Bay expedition ended, Stenuit returned to London. Exploratory oil drilling was just getting under way in the North Sea, and because Stenuit knew that body of water well from a lifetime of diving, he was retained as a consultant by Ocean Systems, Incorporated, an American industrial diving and underwater engineering company. On weekends, he continued to pursue his *Girona* research wherever he believed clues could be found: in the Bibliotheque Royal in Brussels, a storehouse of old Spanish publications; in the Archives Nationales in Paris, where microfilms of many of King Philip's correspondence were on file; and at the Amsterdam Naval Museum in Holland.

In London, Stenuit concentrated on British accounts of the armada. He set aside nine evening hours each week for the task, poring through records at the British Museum and the Public Record Office Reading Room. During the next 18 months, Stenuit amassed more than 600 hours of reading and note-taking; though it had produced a wealth of material on the entire Spanish Armada it had not, to Stenuit's increasing frustration, yielded much specific information on the elusive *Girona*. Through it all, Stenuit found himself asking one question. Records of the armada all agreed that more than than 2,000 cannon had been carried aboard the fleet of ships. If any of the armada's 26 galleons, 13 *urcas* (storeships), 20 *pataches* (tenders), and three galleys and galleasses had previously been salvaged, he asked himself, *why wasn't there even a single cannon somewhere in a museum*?

Stenuit decided to go out personally and look for the answer. In deciding where to start, he reviewed his research material once again, and from this he made some deductions. Several contemporary accounts of the *Girona*'s sinking indicated that the galleass had gone down on the northern coast of North

Ireland, and several other references narrowed down the probable site even more. From experience, Stenuit had learned not to rely too heavily on place names, because in some areas they change over the years. In *Girona* accounts, however, he found striking similarities; though spellings differed, for instance, there were frequent references to a "Giant's Causeway," "Dunluce" and "the rock of the Bunboyes." In June, 1967, Stenuit drove to the coast of North Ireland with a frequent diving companion and accomplished underwater photographer, Marc Jasinski, and the two men spent several days making local inquiries about the place names his research had provided. One notation particularly piqued his interest. It was a frequently repeated reference to the fact that the *Girona* had smashed ". . . against the rock of the Bunboyes . . . which is hard by Sorley Boy's House." Who was Sorley Boy? And where was his house?

One evening, the pieces all fell together. "Sorley Boy" had been the local nickname of a regional baron, Lord McDonnell, and his "house" was Dunluce Castle, perched commandingly on a high, windswept knoll overlooking a rocky coastline below. In studying 16th-century maps, Stenuit had found only two landmarks in the area he was searching: Dunluce and Boys River. By the 19th century, maps showed many additional names that suggested a Spanish influence: Spaniard Rock, Spaniard Cave, Port na Spaniagh, and Lacada Point. Could the *Girona*'s sinking have been responsible for the addition of the names? Stenuit felt confident it had and on June 27, he and Jasinski, deciding the seas had calmed enough, began their search. Although earlier weather had roiled the sea floor, reducing visibility to nearly zero, the water during the early dives was clear enough once they swam near rocks that were clustered throughout the diving area. Peering through the dimly lit water, Stenuit suddenly sighted an object sticking out of the sand not far away. It was about three feet long, triangular in shape, and Stenuit needed no further clue to tell him he had at last found the *Girona*. The object was a lead ingot. Stenuit had never seen one before, but his mind instantly flashed back to one evening months before when he had sat reading in the British Museum. During an 18th-century salvage of another armada vessel, near Donegal, a historian had recorded the finding of ". . . a piece of lead which [a salvor] had supposed to be ballast, a yard long, triangular, the sides being pointed toward the ends, getting thick in the middle." Stenuit's ingot fitted the description perfectly. He later wrote:

With some difficulty I managed to turn it over and found stamped on the upper face five Jerusalem crosses. I set off down a corridor, which led me straight to a bronze cannon, half-buried in the peb-

bles ... in a crevice further down I found a second cannon: a smaller breechloader, bearing the Spanish coat of arms.

With each subsequent dive, Stenuit and Jasinski retrieved one artifact after another. To Stenuit it almost seemed that the old galleass had waited the centuries out for his visit alone, as if rewarding him for the arduous hours of reading and note-taking that had prepared him for this moment. An anchor, coins, a link from a gold chain, more lead ingots ... the two divers could not withhold their elation as the sea continued to disgorge riches. With identity of the galleass established beyond all doubt, the two men now became concerned that others would hear of their victory, perhaps even attempt to steal some of the spoils; both to hide their artifacts and to protect them from deterioration that would have occurred in the open air, they piled the findings in a nearby sea cave.

Returning to London, Stenuit set about organizing a team for full-blown salvage of the *Girona*. Two noted French divers, Maurice Vidal and Louis Gorsse, were retained, as was Francis Dumont, a Belgian architectural student. The National Geographic Society arranged to assist in the financing of what loomed as a difficult and costly expedition. A company in Marseilles donated a truckload of diving equipment.

The long months of winter dragged on; for Stenuit, anxious to get on with the salvage, they seemed an eternity. Finally, in April of 1968, although the Irish north coast was being raked almost daily with gusts of sleet, he decided to wait no longer, and the team began its work. The *Girona* expedition, though lasting less than a year, turned out to be one of the most dangerous of its type ever undertaken. Because of the pounding surf, Stenuit was forced to abandon normal diving procedures. To survive, and to avoid being crushed to death on the rocky shoreline, his divers had to learn to become a part of the surf itself, timing their movements with its mighty surges, riding its force toward the sea, then diving quickly to cling to rocky pinnacles or tightly-fastened kelp stems as the surge returned to shore once again. Even in summer, the water was bitter cold, and despite several layers of wool underwear and sweaters, cramps, pain and numbness became accepted discomforts.

By September, however, Stenuit's group had devoted, collectively, more than 6,000 man hours to the salvage and by any standard the expedition could consider itself a success. In all, more than 12,000 artifacts belonging to the *Girona* were retrieved from the icy depths, including jewels, coins, utensils, remains of the ship itself, shot, instruments, and potsherds, all of which had been hidden underwater for nearly four centuries.

None of this would have been discovered, certainly, had Stenuit not devoted himself to the painstaking research years earlier. In retrospect he believes that the finding of a single clue—the description of the lead ingot—was worth all the time involved, as it alone told him that he had in fact found a Spanish vessel and not some worthless contemporary fishing smack or schooner on which he might otherwise have devoted weeks of useless and dangerous toil.

The *Girona*'s artifacts were literally worth a small fortune. Their intrinsic value, however, was of secondary concern to the Belgian. "My own wish," he later wrote, "was that rather than going under the hammer to the highest bidder and straight into the glass case of a few American or Swiss millionaires, the entire collection from the finest jewel down to the humblest cannon ball, should remain intact in a maritime or archaeological display museum." After years of negotiating with the British government, Stenuit's wish was granted. In June, 1972, a new "Girona Room" was dedicated at the Ulster Museum, North Ireland National Museum, where the collection was placed on permanent display.

Robert Stenuit's decision was not unusual, for the world of the treasure hunter, though landmarked by occasional riches, is first of all a world of high adventure, and rarely is success marked by dollar value alone. Perhaps it was Kip Wagner, after adventurous years of salvaging the buried wealth of the 1715 Plate Fleet, who put it best.

"When I look back on our struggles over the years," he once wrote, "the money value seems almost meaningless. The real treasure lies in our having touched hands with history. Every find comes as a gift from the sea, and our best reward will always be the unforgettable thrill of discovery."

The Drowned Cities

The answers to many intriguing questions about man's past lie buried beneath the sea, entombed in salt water, mud and sand. Only comparatively recently, especially since the advent of scuba and other modern underwater equipment, experts and enthusiastic amateurs have joined in a major effort to find these answers that have remained hidden for hundreds or thousands of years.

The seekers are the underwater archaeologists. Though they adhere to the time-tested regimen of the broad field of archaeology—locating, measuring, plotting, digging—they are in a way members of a very select family of science because of the alien element in which they must work, and because of the added hazards that often confront them.

Underwater salvage dates back many centuries. The first efforts were, however, made in order to find material riches that had inadvertently sunk to the ocean floor. Even in recent centuries, man has brought many valuable treasures to the surface without realizing their true worth. Bronze objects were melted in furnaces, and those of marble were burned for lime or pounded to bits as construction materials; little did their users realize

that many were actually priceless works of art.

With the chance discovery in 1900 of a collection of ancient, irreplaceable artifacts by a group of sponge divers near Crete, however, the modern era of underwater archaeology as a science and valuable adjunct of history was born. Since then, the list of accomplishment has grown considerably: statues, hulls of ancient shipwrecks, household utensils, coins, weapons . . . and remains of entire cities covered by the sea. The careful study of this accumulating wealth of artifacts has helped science provide new answers to questions of how older civilizations lived, worked, played and fought.

But the gain from exploring sunken cities is not limited to man's history alone. By assembling evidence from these artifacts, and by thus being able to more accurately pinpoint the time in which a city disappeared in the sea, geologists, for instance have been able to assemble more accurate information on where and when the sea level rose and fell.

For whatever reason, underwater archaeology has become a fascinating, important phase of man's major new effort to explore the world beneath the sea.

A diver uses a pole marked in meters to measure a column found in ruins of Sabratha, Libya, a Roman city located during an expedition in 1966.

...ords data on a 300-yard long wall which once formed part of the harbor of Amathus, Cyprus, built by the Phoenicians about 800 A.D.

Discovery of this structure near Bimini triggered rumors that "lost" Atlantis had been found at last; however, it proved to be Nature's handiwork instead.

This wall, however, was indeed man-made. Discovered on the Mani Peninsula of southern Greece, it was built by the Romans at the port city of Gythion.

84

(Above) These pottery fragments, dating from a wreck that occurred about 4 A.D., were retrieved from the sunken city of Plitharia. (Below) Portions of a large glass mosaic from a temple of the ancient Roman port of Kenchreai are visible both above and below water. When found, they were well preserved.

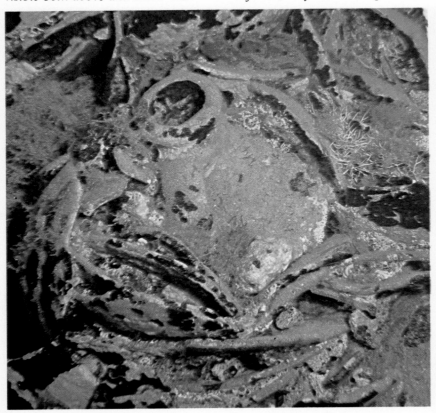

The type of tile and mortar wall construction used by the Romans has with-stood the centuries; this example was found in the sea near Asopos, Greece.

The ibis, a bird sacred to many early civilizations, is a figure frequently found by diving archaeologists. This mosaic was taken from a temple at Kenchreai.

The Sea of Submerged Civilizations

Whenever treasure hunters gather to boast of their achievements, bewail their defeats or merely to share their dreams, they inevitably get around to asking each other a question that goes something like this: Given unlimited time, equipment and money, what single unfound treasure in the world, of either intrinsic or historical value, would you most like to discover? Below the top-ranked treasure, just as inevitably, comes a variety of answers. An early Viking ship. The Treasure of the Incas. The Spanish galleon *San José*, sought futilely by a succession of Caribbean salvage expeditions. Any of the Manila Galleons, their holds bulging with gold, silver, silks, precious stones and art treasures, that perished from 1565 to 1815 along a trade route linking Acapulco and the Philippines. Or, of inestimable historical significance, the main hulk of Columbus' flagship, the *Santa Maria*, lost on Christmas Day, 1492 and only partly salvaged. Below the treasure ranked at the top, the answers literally wander around the world, the assignment of priorities evoking mild disagreement. But as to the most tantalizing prize of all, the Holy Grail of treasure hunters everywhere, the response is almost always unanimous.

It is Atlantis.

Until the legendary "lost continent" is finally found, or until the discrediting of its existence by physicists and geologists finally finds popular acceptance, Atlantis is likely to remain perhaps the greatest continuing mystery story on earth, and one of the great prizes of men who explore the sea. Certainly, Atlantis is one of the oldest and most hotly debated subjects in the history of mankind, a puzzle that has polarized philosophers, theologians, academicians, psychics, prophets and armchair adventurers since pre-Christian times. So deep is the chasm of opinion that divides the pro- and anti-Atlantis forces, it has occasionally triggered violence. A meeting at the Sorbonne shortly after World War I of the French Society for Atlantis Studies became so heated, for instance, that several members were routed by tear gas bombs tossed by other members who had argued, unsuccessfully, for a more scientific approach to solving the mystery. Atlantis has generated more than 5,000 books and pamphlets, most of them in recent years, as well as a proliferation of scientific and quasi-scientific organizations around the world. As another testimonial to the enormous appeal of Atlantis, its discovery was once chosen by a group of English newspapermen as the fourth most important news story they could imagine—several places ahead of the Second Coming of Christ.

Officially, Atlantis stands as a fable, a work of fiction that has endured the centuries. That's how Webster lists it: "A legendary island or continent supposed to have existed in the Atlantic west of Gibraltar and to have sunk in the ocean." But because of the difficulties of providing concrete proof that it did *not* exist, expeditions are periodically formed to seek new evidence that it did; and the fact that invariably they return empty-handed apparently is no discouragement for yet another search group. Throughout history, Atlantis has been reported "found" in almost all oceans and seas and even on dry land. Though not a single trace of physical evidence has withstood the test of the scientific laboratory, pro-Atlanteans have compiled a massive bibliography of material that has been offered in substantiation of their belief that Atlantis is fact, not legend, and that with diligence the "lost" continent may someday be found.

The legend has come down to modern times through Plato, the Greek philosopher. In the 4th Century B.C., he wrote in two of his dialogues, *Timaeus* and *Critias*, that the Athenian law-giver Solon had been told that Egyptian priests had written records of "an island continent beyond the Pillars of Hercules [the ancient name for Gibraltar] called Atlantis, the heart of a great and wonderful empire." Plato wrote that Atlanteans lived in golden-roofed cities, sailed mighty fleets and mustered large standing armies for invasion and conquest; an earthly paradise, Atlantis was "larger than Libya and Asia put together . . . a combination of mighty mountains, fertile plains, navigable rivers, rich mineral deposits and a large thriving population."

According to Plato's account, about 9,000 years before

his own time (or about 11,500 years ago) Atlantis disappeared beneath the sea in a single day and night. At that point, without even drawing any conclusions, Plato ended his account. Skeptics of the story were immediately joined by an esteemed spokesman. Aristotle, a former pupil who later founded a school of philosophy in competition with Plato, pointed to the story's abrupt ending as proof that it was merely a figment of Plato's imagination. "He who made it [Atlantis]," Aristotle wrote, "destroyed it." Although Aristotle was the first in a long line of distinguished critics, some believers have suggested that Plato was at least partially vindicated when Columbus discovered the New World in October, 1492. In Plato's time, after all, the continents of North and South America were also "lost," in the sense of being unknown to most of the rest of the world. Further, the existence of Pompeii and Herculaneum, destroyed by the eruption of Mt. Vesuvius in 79 A.D., was likewise widely doubted until ruins were eventually unearthed.

As described by Plato, Atlantis would have taken up most of the Atlantic Ocean, and its existence would probably have thus been known to peoples on both sides of the ocean. And a similarity of linguistics that is attributed to a "common memory" of the sunken continent is the evidence on which many pro-Atlanteans base their case. Several different groups of people living around the rim of the Atlantic have included the sounds A-T-L-N in designating a lost paradise, for instance. It was Atlantis to the Greeks, Antilla or Antilha to the Spanish and Portuguese, Avalon to the Welsh, and Atlas, Atalanta or Ataranta to the ancient North Africans. Residents of the Canary Islands used the name "Atalya" to designate themselves, whom they considered, because of their separation by water, to be the sole survivors of a "sunken continent."

One proposal holds that the moon approached the earth in some prehistoric period and exerted such a gigantic tidal force upon the sea that Atlantis was pushed beneath its surface. But this would have to have happened before Atlantis had any residents, because gigantic tides that could overwhelm an entire continent surely would have left their mark on the ocean floor, yet scientific examination of the sea floor of the eastern Atlantic indicates it has not been disturbed for millions of years. A variation on this theme suggests that instead of being pushed by the moon into the sea, Atlantis was *pulled* by it, and whisked away into Outer Space.

Meanwhile, on Earth, the relentless search for the missing continent continues, and each time any large, unexplained object is sighted anywhere in the sea, the great mystery story begins another chapter. In 1965, for instance, Dimitri Rebikoff, a French engineer and pioneer of underwater photography equipment, was flying over Grand Bahama Bank near the northern tip of Andros Island when a large rectangular structure about a quarter-mile long, just beneath the surface, caught his eye. Schooled in archaeology and an experienced explorer of underwater ruins in Europe, Rebikoff realized immediately that the symmetrical lines stamped the structure as being man-made. But what was it? It was too long to be the hull of a ship. Could it be the wall of a sunken city?

Weeks later, Rebikoff returned to the site in a boat, accompanied by Dr. Manson Valentine, an archaeologist with the Miami Science Museum, but they could not relocate the structure. Although Rebikoff reported seeing many other suspicious but smaller patterns near the site, the one he had spotted the first time had apparently been hidden once again by shifting Caribbean sands. The two men flew back to Miami and returned to other pursuits.

In the summer of 1968 a private pilot, Robert Brush, was flying between Nassau and Miami, and noted a square structure in shallow water in the general area searched by Rebikoff. He telephoned Rebikoff and Valentine, but before the two could assemble equipment to begin a search, the press also learned of the incident. As predictably as day follows night, Atlantis had been "discovered" all over again.

The Cayce Prediction

What particularly whetted adventurous appetites this time, however, was an incident that had occurred more than two decades earlier and had almost been forgotten until memories were jogged by the Andros object. In the mid-1940's Edgar Cayce, a noted psychic who held an amazingly accurate record of predicting future events, had joined the Atlantis controversy. Specifically, he predicted that in "1968 or 1969," the ruins of Atlantis would rise from the sea, in a location that coincided with that where Rebikoff and Brush had made their sightings. The press descended on Andros in droves. Not far behind the reporters and photographers were Robert Ferro and Michael Grumley, two avid followers of Cayce who had been excited enough by the earlier prediction that they formed yet another Atlantis society. The two were joined by Dr. Valentine, and a major search of the Andros area was organized.

The underwater structure this time was easily located; apparently the capricious Caribbean sands had shifted once again. Consisting of limestone block walls three feet thick, it measured 60 by 100 feet, and was obviously not a contemporary structure. But just how old was it? No one yet knows.

Although the incident generated a tremendous amount of interest and publicity, especially among devoted followers of

Cayce, later scientific investigation indicates the structures probably were not man-made at all. Although symmetry of design is usually an indicator of man's work, there are exceptions to the rule, and the Bimini "structure" may be just such a case.

Occasionally, because of certain geological situations, Nature shapes patterns along shorelines that are remarkably straight-lined, so symmetrical that it takes a trained eye, and scientific instruments, to detect the difference.

Core samples taken of the formations at Bimini by a scientific party sponsored by the National Geographic Society now indicates that it was indeed natural forces, not an ancient civilization, that was at work.

Even in the face of such scientific evidence, however, proponents of the Atlantis theory no doubt will insist that they somehow may relate to the long lost continent.

An even more recent and unusual Atlantis expedition, in the summer of 1973, involved 55 students and teachers who paid $2,800 each for the privilege of going along and was sponsored jointly by an organization called the Ancient Mediterranean Research Association (AMRA) and Pepperdine University of Los Angeles. AMRA furnished the logistical support, including a team of parapsychologists who had agreed to lend psychic talent to the search, while Pepperdine offered the participating students six academic credits. The undersea search took place along the southwest coast of Spain. Scuba divers reported finding a number of man-made columns in water 75 to 95 feet deep about 16 miles from the Spanish port of Cadiz, but the project was terminated by the Spanish government before detailed exploration began.

The columns could have been made by any number of civilizations that settled along the Atlantic coast of Spain. However, Dr. Edgerton Sykes, a British archaeologist, points out that because no settling of land is known to have occurred near Cadiz for at least 8,000 years, any structures must predate 6000 B.C., and therefore could not have been built by the Phoenicians, Romans or Greeks. Like its predecessors, the 1973 expedition returned no proof that would have either vindicated Plato, or established him as an early-day Clifford Irving.

Dr. Nicholas C. Flemming, a noted British geologist turned archaeologist, suggests that the fundamental difference in the oceans and continents makes Atlantis impossible, as well as another legendary "lost" continent, Lemuria, which supposedly sank in the Pacific. Continents are composed of light, sedimentary rocks resting on igneous rocks, containing large amounts of silicon and aluminum, Dr. Flemming explains, and these in turn rest on a layer of denser rocks containing silicon and magnesium. The continents are about thirty miles thick and float on the denser layer with a deep root like an iceberg.

By contrast, the dense layer on the ocean floor is much thinner, and comes to the surface. "While it is possible for changes of level at the edges of the continents to submerge cities and large tracts of land by ten feet or more in only a few thousand years," he continues, "it is not possible for continents to be transformed into ocean except over periods of many millions of years. Since man has inhabited the earth for only a little over one million years, and has approached civilization only in the last ten thousand years, it is clear that no advanced civilization can have occupied the middle of the Atlantic or Pacific."

Whether Atlantis is fact or fancy, its story certainly has an element of truth. In various parts of the world, sudden cataclysms such as earthquakes, or the gradual subsidence of land masses and the rising of sea level, *have* caused settlements and islands to be engulfed by the sea. The ruins of some settlements have been located and artifacts have been brought to the surface. Undoubtedly there are others yet to be discovered, which, though not as massive as Atlantis was supposed to have been, would nevertheless loom as major archaeological finds that would help fill in blank pages of world history.

In her classic *The Sea Around Us*, Rachel Carson described a "lost island," Dogger Bank, which lies in the North Sea. Dogger Bank first became dry land when ocean waters were frozen in glaciers during the Pleistocene, lowering the world's sea level. The island was inhabited by humans and lower animals, its soil tilled with a variety of crops, its forests hunted for game; then, as the glaciers melted and sea level rose, it was flooded over. Nearly as large as Denmark, Dogger Bank was accidentally discovered when North Sea fishing trawls began bringing up objects not normally associated with the sea: large masses of peat, for example, and unidentified bones that seemed to belong to terrestrial, not marine, animals. Suggesting that descendants of the drowned civilization must have retained pieces of the account in their memory, Miss Carson found a parallel with the Atlantis legend:

In the shadowy beginnings of human life on earth [*she wrote in* The Sea Around Us]*primitive man here and there must have had knowledge of the sinking of an island or a peninsula, perhaps not with the dramatic suddenness attributed to Atlantis, but well within the time one man could observe. The witnesses to such a happening would have described it to their neighbors and children, and so the legend of a sinking continent might have been born.*

Elsewhere in the world, where there are only vague stories about the locations of underwater cities, archaeological discoveries are yet to be made. Since early man sought shelter in caves, for instance, many archaeological treasures are thought to be buried in the sediments in sea caves. On the coast of Hawaii, a village known to have existed has vanished without a trace; scientists at the University of Hawaii suggest it may have been buried, or pushed into the sea, by lava flowing from one of the island's volcanoes. There are many flooded cities and causeways off Yucatan and Honduras; their dim forms can be seen by aircraft, yet they have never been explored from the sea. There are other such sites in the Mediterranean, off the Atlantic islands and, of course, at the still-unexplored ruins near Andros Island in the Bahamas. Certainly there must be more, especially since man from the dawn of history has chosen the shifting rims of the oceans as a favorite place of habitation.

How many sunken cities are there throughout the world? Dr. Flemming, who founded the University Diving Club at Cambridge, England, personally has investigated more than 100, and if all the smaller, submerged coastal settlements were added up, the total may well run into the thousands.

Although earthquakes, which with volcanoes are perhaps the most spectacular and violent phenomena on Earth, account for many cities having sunk, they are but one of the many causes. Most of the cities sunk in the Mediterranean resulted from earthquakes. Yet, asks Dr. Flemming in his book, *Cities In The Sea*, what would account for a number of caves found on Gibraltar, each containing evidence of human habitation, that lie fully forty five feet or more below the ocean surface?

The answer is that the level of the world's seas has changed many times throughout human history. Except for an infinitesimal amount lost to Outer Space, the total mass of moisture on earth is constant; an increase of moisture in one place must lead to a corresponding decrease someplace else. Most of the earth's moisture is contained in the sea, and in the icecaps and glaciers of the polar regions. If the global temperature drops and these locked-up blocks of ice expand as they absorb moisture, most of the moisture will come from the sea, and its level consequently will drop. On the other hand, if the global temperature warms up and the icebergs and glaciers melt, the sea level will rise.

The warming or cooling can be very slight, yet the result may be a rising or lowering of sea level by several feet. And since humans from the dawn of history have clustered on the shores of the continents, building their cities and harbors there, a difference of water level of only two or three feet would affect thousands of coastal cities around the globe.

Dr. Flemming notes that evidence from old glacial valleys and deposits which used to cover Canada and Scandinavia show that during the last million years there have been about six advances and retreats of the ice, while submerged beaches and caves show that each time the sea level dropped by 300 to 450 feet. At the beginning of the Ice Age—the term used to describe the entire sequence of events—the world sea level was probably 600 feet higher than it is now. One geologist has calculated that if the polar icecaps were melted entirely, the present sea level would rise by about 300 feet.

A second reason for the change in sea level is continental drift. Confirmed by the continuing Deep Sea Drilling Project, which has been retrieving core samples of the ocean floor around the world, the continental drift theory postulates that the earth's crust is not composed of a single, solid mantle, but of a series of plates that shift about, causing the continents to crumple and deform. Just as the water level in a bucket would rise if the side is dented in, the sea level is changed by the deformation of the continents as well as by changing temperature patterns.

The Mediterranean's sunken cities hold particular fascination for the archaeologist for two reasons. One is that there are so many of them, enabling scientists to piece together many interlocking clues to various periods of human history. The second is the manner in which most sank beneath the sea: violently and rapidly, whipsawed by the tremendous force of earthquakes. Unlike cities which became submerged more slowly as the sea level changed gradually, those destroyed by earthquakes are like frozen time capsules, demolished almost instantly with no opportunity for their inhabitants, noting a rise in the level of nearby waters, to remove their belongings to higher and drier ground.

Submerged Cities of the Ancient World

Occasionally a sunken city is found, only to be lost a second time. An example is Helice, a Greek community that toppled into the Gulf of Corinth during an earthquake in 4 A.D. Helice lies in 50 to 130 feet of water, less than a mile from the shoreline. Both Ovid and Pliny referred to the catastrophe that befell it in their writings and described how, in their time, its outline could be seen beneath the blue waters of the Mediterranean. In 1950, a team of French divers attempted to explore the ruins of Helice, without success. They did, however, find the rusting hulk of a World War II ship on the site. Because it was nearly buried under layers of silt, they speculated that centuries of shifting mud and sand must have covered the ruins of the city even deeper.

Not so elusive are the ruins of Caesara, chief port of Rome's eastern colonies, which lie off Israel's Mediterranean coast. Completed about 10 years before the birth of Christ, the city was captured from the Romans by the Arabs in 639; its ownership changed hands a second time about four centuries later when Caesara fell to the invading Crusaders. In 1300, it was the Arabs' turn once again; apparently still smarting from the earlier loss, they sacked the city. The destruction was total, and it included a dam-like aqueduct the Romans had built as protection from the Mediterranean. The town was soon covered by water.

Today, once-proud Caesara lies partly under the earth and partly under the sea. Protected by Israeli law, rows of marble columns and piles of debris containing amphorae and giant building blocks, used by the Romans to construct the sea-wall, remain intact. Divers, who may buy supplies from a nearby dive shop established especially for Caesara-exploring, have reported spending fascinating hours prowling the ruins. Caesara holds a special fascination for theologians; in this city Pontius Pilate resided, and St. Paul was imprisoned.

Another sunken city that divers may explore is Emborium, in the Aegean Sea just off the island of Melos. Although covered with water, many of Emborium's city walls still stand. And on the French Riviera near Marseilles, a team of diving French archaeologists from 1948 to 1952 excavated the sunken ruins of Fos-sur-Mer, a onetime Roman villa that later had become a summer playground for vacationing French families before it was abandoned and covered by the mud of the Rhone River. The name of the village means "ditch on the sea." In about 100 B.C. the Romans had literally dredged the site out of the Rhone, building a massive wall to protect it from further incursion. Fos-sur-Mer was a major seaport during the Roman period, but by the Middle Ages it had become just another fishing village. During their four-year excavation, the French archaeologists recovered—well preserved by layers of Rhone mud—many valuable artifacts, including a Roman house altar and household utensils, an ivory sculpture of the head of Aphrodite, an Italic vase, Campanian pottery and many amphorae. All are now displayed in a museum near the site.

While the ruins of Fos-sur-Mer had been well known and thus were easily located, those of another important Mediterranean city, Pheia, were found by accident. The existence of Pheia had been well documented in Greek records. In the *Iliad*, Homer mentioned that King Nestor had distinguished himself by fighting on the walls of the city, which had been a Greek stronghold; in the *Odyssey*, young Telemachus was reported to have sailed past. But the closest anyone was able to pinpoint the site was that it was somewhere on the Peleponnesus, an island-like peninsula on the eastern shore of the Ionian Sea. Because of the many references, scholars had tried for years to locate Pheia—or to establish, as an alternative, that the city really had never existed.

One day in 1956 two young Greek snorkelers spotted part of a large Ionic column in 25 feet of water, just off the Pelepponesian coast. They immediately notified Dr. Nicholas Gialouris, curator of the museum at nearby Olympia. Gialouris donned mask and snorkel; a few dives convinced him that the ruins were remnants of Pheia. Further research disclosed that a major earthquake in 6 A.D. had toppled Pheia into the bay, had caused the collapse of buildings at Olympia, 12 miles inland, and had also created lakes that flooded the city of Samikos.

Captivated by the discovery, Gialouris hastily organized a team of divers and underwater photographers. During the day, they searched the area in a grid pattern. At night, Gialouris pored through available records that might help in narrowing the area to be investigated. One night, he found a single notation that convinced him he was on the track of a major archaeological find. Prior to World War II, a British archaeological team had uncovered sherds of identifiable types of pottery from a hillside fronting the bay where Gialouris was now investigating. So Gialouris dug an exploratory trench on land and unearthed a number of bronze fragments. He theorized that the earthquake must have sent only a part of Pheia into the bay, that the rest was buried on land.

Day by day, Gialouris' group continued to find artifacts that substantiated the existence of a city: amphorae, columns, building stones of cut marble, part of a limestone wall. Later exploration retrieved two stone bathtubs, vase fragments, 7th-century Corinthian vases, and the head and neck of a bronze griffin. The most important find, however, was the remainder of a wall that had been erected around Pheia to protect it from attack. It was built of local limestone, was about 250 feet long and 2 feet thick, and its location helped to determine the boundaries of the rest of the ancient city.

Dr. Gialouris continued his work for nearly ten years, beginning in 1957. For part of this time he was assisted by Dr. John E. Hall, an American archaeologist who had led many underwater expeditions in Greece under the auspices of the Greek Ministry of Archaeology, and who later was to become an assistant professor of archaeology at the University of Miami. Even after leaving Greece for the United States in 1960, fascination for the Pheia project lingered in Hall's mind;

twice he returned, once with a team of archaeology students from Florida, to experience the thrill of discovery. In 1969, he summed up that feeling:

Exploring the ruins of an ancient sunken city can be an eerie experience. As you descend from the surface you go back more than 2,500 years. When you drift over the stone wall that once encircled the city, you wonder how many soldiers of invading armies have scaled that same wall. You pick up a broken wine jar and wonder who was the last person to drink from it. Was it a lovely woman? An elder statesman? A thirsty sailor just off the ship? What was life like on that fateful day about the year 550 A.D. when the world suddenly came to an end for the people of Pheia?

Exploring drowned cities thus can be a heady experience, but achieving scientific goals requires considerable patience and arduous work as well. An example is the city of Apollonia, on the northern coast of present-day Tunisia, which was twice investigated by Dr. Nicholas C. Flemming and a team of Cambridge University undergraduate students in 1958 and 1959.

Apollonia was the port city of Cyrene, the ancient capital of Cyrenaica, one of the greatest Greek colonies. Founded in the 7th Century B.C., Apollonia lies east of Benghazi and almost due south of the island of Crete. Cyrene itself is about ten miles inland, and is connected to Apollonia by a narrow roadway. Today, Cyrene is a tiny Arab town with one twisting street shaded by graceful eucalyptus trees. The ruins of once-magnificent temples, baths and palaces are sprinkled throughout the community, and goats and camels nibble at grass and bushes in the outskirts.

Arriving at Apollonia in 1958, Dr. Flemming found a city half submerged and half dry. Because of its tremendous size, he knew that plotting its original boundaries and determining where its major buildings were located would be a major undertaking. Because of Apollonia's role in both Greek and Roman empires, however, its study was considered an important contribution to modern archaeology.

In 91 B.C., following more than four centuries of Greek rule, Cyrenaica became part of the Roman Empire, and its rich grain-produce was exported to Rome via Apollonia and Ostia, the port of Rome. While in Italy, Dr. Flemming and his team visited Ostia to retrace the important grain route across the Mediterranean.

In 115 A.D., the Jews in North Africa rebelled against the Romans and the grain trade diminished. While this part of history was well documented, Dr. Flemming was unable to clear up the mystery of how Apollonia sank into the sea, and this riddle remains unsolved even today.

Below the surface of the harbor, Dr. Flemming sized up the effort that lay ahead. Later, he wrote:

At first we could only find disconnected walls, scattered rubble and broken amphorae. But we came across larger buildings after awhile and learned to recognize our position in relation to these. The sea was calming down; we could cruise effortlessly through the warm clear water, following the green weed-grown lines of walls, checking and rechecking corners and alignments, until each building was accurately drawn.

Diving near a reef to the west of the city, where the archaeologists could see the entrance to a tunnel, required particularly careful maneuvering. "The water was so full of bubbles that it was difficult to see much," Dr. Flemming recalls, "and the sharp rocks would suddenly loom up in front of us; it was like driving in a heavy London fog with the disadvantage that the road kept rushing backwards and forwards as well."

In almost every hollow, Dr. Flemming remembers, "we found explosive shells from a wrecked ammunition ship. When Dick Longbottom [one of the undergraduate students] carried one triumphantly out of the water to show us and we told him what it was, he dropped it with horror!"

Despite the obstacles, Dr. Flemming's group had familiarized themselves with the major features of Apollonia by the end of the third day, established a baseline, and prepared to begin the foot-by-foot survey. As they worked, the party drew an ever-increasing audience of curious Arab youngsters. To older villagers, however, the serious intent of the expedition was puzzling. "To people of a country which is struggling to make up for its lack of industrialization, it must be strange that we spend time and money on the problems of a dead civilization," he later wrote.

As the survey continued, the Cambridge team discovered a number of slipways and buildings, and old pots and jars, buried under a black mud, turned up everywhere. One of the students found the arm of a large statue, but a determined search for the rest of the object proved fruitless.

The first Apollonia expedition lasted four weeks. A year later, in 1959, Dr. Flemming returned for further work and in addition to enlarging upon the site survey and producing the first accurate map of the port city in more than twenty five centuries, he recovered many valuable artifacts which have helped to determine how its citizens lived.

One of the most treasured finds during the expedition was another statue, this one of marble and almost intact. It was located in the scattered ruins of a fish tank, a large, rectangular, brick-lined sink in which the ruling Romans once gathered fish from the sea.

By far the most significant excavation of a sunken city in the Western Hemisphere was that of Port Royal, Jamaica, the pirate "Hellhole of the Caribbean" that was destroyed by an earthquake in the late 17th century. The project involved the talents of a number of underwater adventurers and scientists, and is still continuing.

Despite its relatively brief half-century of existence, Port Royal attained an unparalleled reputation as a center of debauchery, riotous living and great wealth. A clue to the city's lifestyle is the fact that in its heyday Port Royal, which was founded by the English in 1655 after they had captured Jamaica from Spain, boasted of one tavern for every ten inhabitants. The city's geographic location near the center of several major trade routes made it a bustling crossroads of the Caribbean. Because its spacious harbor could accommodate 500 ships at one time, it was an ideal staging area from which English privateers could launch attacks against the heavily laden Spanish galleons that were then hauling wealth from the New World across the Atlantic to Spain. Free-booting pirates converged there for the same reason. Near the end of the 17th century, Port Royal was therefore one of the busiest port cities in the Caribbean, with a population of more than 8,000 and 2,000 buildings, many of them three and four stories in height.

The catastrophe that befell Port Royal began with a sharp rumbling shortly before noon on June 7, 1692; a second and then a third quake struck within minutes, followed by a tremendous tidal wave that first lashed through vessels anchored in the harbor and then engulfed the town itself. Port Royal's citizens, like other people everywhere, did not move their city because of earthquakes, although only four years earlier the town had been struck by one. Of lesser intensity, it demolished several buildings, damaged others, and shook ships with such violence that guns were knocked loose from their gunports.

Port Royal was a shambles within minutes of the 1692 quake; when the dust settled, more than 1,800 buildings were demolished, 2,000 lives had been lost, and most of the townsite had sunk beneath the harbor. (Of the thousand Port Royal survivors who moved across the harbor to found Kingston, many later died from epidemics resulting from the catastrophe.) All but about 10 acres of Port Royal was swallowed by the sea.

Although in more recent years the undersea ruins have

been a choice target of salvors, their quest has usually been for historic value and not treasure, because they believed that most of Port Royal's riches had been reclaimed in the exhaustive salvage efforts that began almost as the final tremor subsided. They were correct in this assumption, but since the records indicated that only a single valuable artifact had been found—a cluster of three leopard's teeth covered with gold—no one knew for certain whether any intrinsic treasure remained.

No part of Port Royal lies deeper than 50 feet, and by the end of the 17th century, salvage operations at such depths had become quite proficient. However, because of Port Royal's prominence in history, a reconstruction of its final days seemed significant. As an indication of just how important, one historian suggested as an imaginary counterpart the sinking of San Francisco into the sea during its riotous period of prosperity following the discovery of gold in California. Even if restoration of Port Royal was to be purely a historical venture, the Jamaican government thought well enough of the idea to assign it a high priority, and to allocate the necessary funds.

The first attempt to piece together the city's past was begun in 1956 by Edwin Link, the Hoosier-born aviator-turned-aquanaut whose famed Link Trainer had helped more than 2 million pilots learn how to fly. Link had discovered the sea in the late 1940s, when he decided to try to win a Florida-to-Cuba yacht race aboard his 43-foot yawl, the *Blue Heron*, not by using traditional marine navigation techniques but by applying new theories of celestial navigation he had developed. Link won the race handily, but only after a massive search for his ship (his navigation was so superb that he quickly outdistanced the opposition, and it was reported that *Blue Heron* had disappeared at sea). Fascinated by archaeology, Link had long thought about Port Royal. Although in his first brief expedition there he did establish the general outlines of the sunken city, he was frustrated to find that the equipment he had brought along was inadequate to penetrate the eight feet of debris under which the city lay. He came back to the United States determined to develop special equipment for the kind of work that Port Royal demanded.

In 1959, Link returned to Jamaica aboard the specially constructed *Sea Diver II*, and spent 10 rewarding months bringing up valuable artifacts and mapping the site. This time, his expedition was sponsored jointly by the National Geographic Society, the Smithsonian Institution and the Institute of Jamaica. But Port Royal was too enormous a challenge for a single expedition, or even two, and the task of continuing the work Link had started was passed on to other hands.

The second major expedition was headed by Robert

Marx, a former Marine who had achieved notable success in salvaging important shipwrecks throughout the Caribbean, and who later had developed a strong interest in historical aspects of marine archaeology. In 1963 Marx was appointed as a marine archaeologist by the Institute of Jamaica, and he began organizing a team that was to spend the next three years at Port Royal. In all, Marx's expedition produced more than 10,000 artifacts, although even this number, he maintains today, may be only 10 percent of that still awaiting recovery by future archaeologists. Among the artifacts salvaged were thousands of clay pipes, more than 500 bottles, a complete copper mill, pewter plates and tankards, brassware, a human jawbone and hundreds of coins. In terms of scale and duration, it was probably the most extensive marine archaeological excavation ever undertaken in the world.

Like Link, Marx had decided at the outset that equipment should be developed especially for the project. To avoid the burden of heavy and bulky air tanks on divers backs, Marx used hookah gear instead—air pumped to the divers through hoses from a compressor floating on the surface. With this constant air supply, the divers could also work below all day without surfacing. Assuming that many of the artifacts might be very fragile, Marx decided that all digging should be done by hand, and to avoid breaking artifacts that were flushed out of the mud, he chose an airlift with a tube much smaller than is normally used in underwater digs.

In addition to the artifacts, the salvage produced two shipwrecks. During the early months, Marx stumbled upon the mouldering wreckage of a 74-foot ship that proved to be the *HMS Swan*, a British warship sunk during the 1692 earthquake. Later Marx found the second wreck, a French warship that had sunk during a hurricane in 1722. Her hold yielded thousands of 150-pound mortar balls.

Exploration of the buildings buried in Port Royal's mud—a tavern and a cookhouse, for instance—brought more historical treasures. Marx considers the most exciting to be a beautiful 14-inch-high statue in Chinese porcelain of a woman holding a child in her lap. His research disclosed that it was the goddess of fertility and childbirth, dating from the Kuan-Yin Dynasty and made in Tu-Hun, China. Another treasure was an elaborate gold watch whose markings indicated it had come from a London jeweler; it had been well preserved by nearly three centuries of coral encrustation.

The project was not without dangers. Sharks, for instance, were a common nuisance in the harbor. Once, Marx felt himself nudged from behind as he was working on the bottom; engrossed in his task, he merely reached behind him to brush away the intruder, then quickly jerked his hand back. The touch was like sandpaper, which experience told him meant one thing: shark. Turning his head, Marx found himself staring directly at a large hammerhead, only inches away. For some reason, perhaps because of Marx's abrupt movement, the intruder swam lazily away.

Another hammerhead, however, wasn't frightened as easily. It ignored the divers' shouts and defensive arm-waving; twice, its fins sliced Marx's air hose as it swam by. Since the hammerheads could not always be frightened away, Marx was finally forced to add another job title to the variety of skills possessed by his crew: shark guard.

"The necessity of posting a guard slowed our work considerably," Marx recalled later in describing a particularly pesky hammerhead, "but the only alternative was to kill the shark. Fearing that its blood would attract other sharks, I preferred to get on with the job rather than invite out-and-out warfare with a shark gang." The decision didn't please one of Marx's chief divers, a burly Jamaican named Caynute Kelly. Without Marx's knowledge, he lured this hammerhead to the surface where the water was clearer (and no doubt where Marx could not see what was happening) and drove a spear through its head. Wise in the ways of the sea, Kelly then heaved the still-thrashing carcass into a nearby skiff to avoid the carnage that spilled blood surely would have caused.

With each major find, press reports touched off a deluge of sightseers; at times, the crowds at the excavation site were so thick that Jamaican police had to be called out to restore order. At the end of 2½ years, because of the extensive discoveries he and his divers had made, Marx decided that it was time to halt the expedition and devote full time to cataloging the treasure trove of artifacts, while the details of discovery were still fresh in his mind. Certainly, the work at Port Royal started by Link and continued by Marx stands as a monumental achievement in the world of marine archaeology. When the Jamaican government completes the large museum in which it plans to display many of Port Royal's artifacts, visitors who could not share the divers' thrill of discovery may at least see the results of exploring an important city of the drowned world.

The Sea of Lost Ships

Never had the world seen such treasure. It began to flow in the decade after Columbus planted the flag of the Spanish Crown at San Salvador, a tiny rivulet of treasure that at first inched eastward across the then-uncharted sea lanes of the inhospitable Atlantic: heirloom gold from Hispaniola, silver from Cuba, pearls from Margarita Island. During the next three and one half centuries, as Spain's exploration, conquest and colonization extended deeper into the New World and across the Pacific to the Philippines, the rivulet welled to floodstage: emeralds from Panama, gold and jewels from Mexico, an Inca king's treasury from Peru; silver bars, minted coins, platinum, diamonds, exotic goods from the Orient.

At first, the ships sent by Spain to haul the riches home were frail craft, woefully unsuited for the hazards of navigating a hemisphere unknown to Europeans until Columbus. After all, most of the ships had been designed for the quieter, familiar trade routes of the Mediterranean. Caravels such as Columbus' own flagship were sturdily built, highly maneuverable and of shallow draft, and were therefore ideal ships for exploration. But they were far too small for hauling the increasingly heavier cargoes of treasure that the New World would soon provide. Carracks, on the other hand, were virtual floating warehouses. Developed by the Portuguese and Dutch for the long, slow voyages around Africa to the East Indies, the carracks had a capacity of 1,500 tons and could accommodate a thousand or more passengers. But as deep water sailers, in all but the slightest zephyrs they were floating disasters.

The crews of the Spanish Crown's ships were, at the outset, an unlikely lot—international soldiers of fortune, escaped convicts and runaway slaves, dreamers, discredited aristocrats. They shared but one common trait—a thirst for adventure and easy riches. Freed by an ocean's span from tattered pasts, they thought they had found treasure as well as adventure in the lush Caribbean, with its sun-splashed islands and balmy weather and carefree life.

Even after Spain's early New World experience brought about the production of better ships—the trim, heavily armed fighting galleons, for example, and their roomier, cargo-carrying sisters, the *naos*—and even after New World riches lured more polished and better trained crews, the Caribbean's Utopian setting proved to be a continually fleeting illusion, its tranquility a deceptive and sometimes disastrous disguise.

The keels of even the stoutest of the Crown's ships were as poor a match for jagged fingers of coral as were their hulls for teredo worms, the hungry borers that could make sieves of thin timbers in a matter of days. Even less adequately prepared were the galleons and *naos* for the capricious hurricanes, awesome and frightening storms that came rampaging out of the Caribbean to destroy a ship—or an entire *flota*—often leaving not a single survivor to lead salvors to the spot.

To Spain, however, the maritime losses of the New World were no more alarming than casualties of war. They were losses to be guarded against, to be sure, but they would not be a deterrent to exploration. Spain's conquistadores, being human, certainly were no less immune from the temptation of greed than any previous (or future) colonizers. Yet in the wealth of the Indies, and on the mainland beyond, lay the key to a pressing national need as well: after two hundred costly and weary years, the armies now under King Ferdinand and Queen Isabella had at last defeated the Moors at Granada. That conflict resolved, the Crown began shaping plans to mold Spain into a major, influential, worldwide power. With the national treasury decimated by war and in need of restocking to finance expansion, the lure of American riches became an overpowering priority, whipped up by the religious and national fervor that the period had welded as one.

And so, year by year, the transatlantic trade increased, as did the disasters; at first, most of the sinkings involved individual ships, traveling alone or in twos and threes with only modest cargoes aboard. But later, as the mighty armadas were formed and as treasure was pried out of the New World, entire fleets were to perish. Battered by storms, scuttled by pirates, ravaged by enemy navies, their hulls began piling up on the floor of the Spanish Main, soon to be covered by layers of sand and mud.

As if foretelling troubles to come, Columbus' own flag-ship, the caravel *Santa Maria*, was among the first victims—but, ironically, her grounding and subsequent sinking were caused by none of the violent factors that were to destroy future ships. On a balmy, calm Christmas Eve in 1492, only two and a half months after the Admiral had reached the New World, Columbus noted in his logbook that he had departed L'Acul Bay that morning and was approximately one league off Picolet Point, at the head of Cap Haitien, Haiti. Finishing the entry, Columbus went to sleep about 11 P.M.

On deck, Juan de la Cosa, master of the flagship, peered into the darkness, making certain that he maintained a safe dis-tance from the 16-mile-long barrier reef to port; he could easily determine the reef by the whitecaps that crashed against it. But la Cosa, too, was sleepy from an earlier pre-Christmas celebra-tion, and at 11:30 P.M. he turned the watch over to the ship's helmsman, a teenage boy. About midnight the tiny caravel, sailing eastward toward Caracol Bay and gently buffeted by winds that whipped off the Haitian mountains and swept across the Cap Haitien plain, eased aground on a reef.

Awakened by his crew, Columbus decided that the damage certainly was not severe enough to abandon the vessel, and he ordered a longboat lowered into the water. It was his plan to use the *Santa Maria*'s winch to pull the flagship free. But la Cosa, after boarding the launch, seized the opportunity to abandon the Admiral and rowed instead in the direction of the *Nina*, not far away. The *Nina*'s crew proved loyal, refusing to let la Cosa or his officers aboard, but during the delay the *Santa Maria* worked herself more securely onto the reef, and was now slowly capsizing. At first, Columbus refused to give up hope that his ship could be saved. But hope dwindled as dawn neared. Finding the *Santa Maria* listing even more pre-cariously at daylight, he dispatched a crewman to the nearby island to enlist help from the local king, Guacanagari, upon whom Columbus had bestowed many gifts. The king re-sponded; hundreds of Haitian natives rowed out to the *Santa Maria* that morning, the first Christmas celebrated in the New World, and carried back all that was considered of value. Four hours later, the *Santa Maria* sank in a shallow-water grave.

Four and one half centuries later, in 1954, the first ma-jor effort to find her was begun. By then, of course, the histori-cal value of the little caravel had skyrocketed astronomically. The salvage attempt followed an arduous research program that involved, among others, Samuel Eliot Morison, author of *Admiral of the Ocean Sea*, the definitive work on Columbus.

Many hurricanes had swept Haiti in the period since the *Santa Maria*'s foundering; even if the exact location had been noted in Spanish records, chances are the wreckage would no longer be at the same spot. (One salvage crew, working another wreck elsewhere in the Caribbean, found parts of this hulk as much as four miles from the site where it had foundered. Though a few parts of the ship and her cargo had sunk deeply enough in the sand to gain protection, storms over the years had literally tumbled the rest of it from site to site.)

Armed with a magnetometer and metal detectors, Edwin Link and a group of associates launched the *Santa Maria* salvage effort in 1954, working from Morison's research. Their search, concentrated on the most promising reefs around Cap Haitien, turned up an anchor, hand-forged in several sections, which was identified as being of the Columbus era. The anchor was exhibited first by the government of Haiti, and later was turned over to the Smithsonian Institution.

Santa Maria—A Jinxed Wreck?

Link's second attempt to locate the caravel was begun six years later, in 1960. This time the Caribbean rejected him, and to anyone who is skeptical of superstitions of the sea and of so-called "jinxed ships," Link's experience might prove cause for reconsideration. Just as he prepared to make an underwater search aboard his new *Sea Diver II*, a passing freighter veered off course nearby and rammed a reef. The ship did not sink immediately. Instead, it drifted, as if ordained by an unseen force, to the exact spot where Link was working, then plunged to the bottom.

Link was searching with his magnetometer, an electronic instrument that records the presence of large metal objects. "Naturally," he observed later, "with that freighter lying right there, the magnetometer was useless in looking for the *Santa Maria*. For all we knew, it might have settled right on *top* of her." The odds of the freighter accident happening? In Link's estimate: "About a million to one."

If this mishap seems too unlikely to be attributed to chance, consider what happened during a later *Santa Maria* salvage attempt, in 1972. A few years earlier, Fred Dickson, a former Yale swimming champion and sometime treasure hunter, had formed an organization called the Santa Maria Foundation, whose sole purpose was to locate the remainder of the four century old caravel. A Philadelphia executive, Dickson had followed accounts of earlier *Santa Maria* expeditions with great interest. The historic ship had become his sole hobby, a personal obsession—and, like Link, he intended to search for the *Santa Maria* in a scientific manner.

Over a period of five years, whenever Dickson could break away from his office for a few weeks, he went to the wreck site and dug a series of underwater trenches in the search area beneath the Cap Haitien reefs, which teams of diver associates then scoured for clues, however remote. If too much time elapsed between visits, the Caribbean's shifting sands would fill the trenches, and Dickson would be forced to dig them anew. In 1972, however, the painstaking research seemed to be on the verge of paying off: twelve feet down in the coral, Dickson found fragments of Spanish pottery, the remains of a rudder clamp, copper spikes, bits of wood, and other artifacts dating from Columbus' time. But were they from the *Santa Maria*? Fred Dickson was never to know the answer. On November 11, 1972, he leaped from his dive boat—and as he struck the water, his face mask snapped back against his head. Feeling only minor pain, however, Dickson continued to dive for awhile, then surfaced and asked for assistance. He died several hours later of a fractured skull.

Experts with knowledge of diving equipment later said that the possibility of such a mishap was statistically miniscule; one called it "a freakish, million-to-one accident." But it had happened, and the *Santa Maria* search was cancelled. Later, Dickson's associates announced they would return to try again, but they also conceded that the project would mean a new beginning, since within weeks, even days perhaps, Dickson's trenches would again be filled with sand. Thus, the gallant little caravel that helped open an entire hemisphere remains as great a salvage challenge as ever.

In Columbus' day, when Indies treasure accounted for an insignificant percentage of the cargoes being shipped home to Spain, explorers made only cursory attempts to salvage any ships that were lost. But it soon became apparent that the New World held riches of enormous value, that a long and dangerous transatlantic voyage lay between the loading of the treasure in the New World and the unloading in the Old. Divers therefore became a vital part of Spain's New World operations as early as 1503—eleven years after Columbus had landed at San Salvador.

Spain maintained crews of Indian and Negro divers on alert status at all major ports in the Caribbean: Havana, Veracruz, Cartagena and Panamá. Whenever a sinking occurred, or whenever one seemed imminent, divers were rushed to the site by the fastest sailing ships. Because most New World ship losses occurred in shallow waters, diving bells were not widely used, nor were they needed. Most native divers, having lived a great part of their lives in the sea, had become proficient breath-divers.

In addition to the divers in port, Spain included diver teams aboard her ships, especially during the later years when large armadas were formed. As collateral duties, the divers performed underwater repairs on hulls; because most ships were habitually overloaded, they had plenty of work to do, patching cracked hull timbers and caulking bulging, leaking seams. Many divers did their work while the ships were underway. This was incredibly dangerous, of course, and on at least one occasion it prompted a reward of considerable esteem. In 1578, the admiral of a *flota* recommended to the king that a man who had been responsible for saving a cargo worth 12 million ducats be given a title of nobility. There is no record that the diver was thus elevated, though the fact that such a recommendation was made underscores the tremendous value the Spanish Crown placed on its divers.

The year that divers were first employed, 1503, coincides not incidentally with the establishment by Spain of the *Casa para la Contratación y Negociación de los Indias*, or Indies Bureau of Trade. This bureau was to control, with almost absolute authority, every aspect of Spain's New World commerce and navigation for centuries to come. As Spain moved farther and farther into the New World, first throughout the Caribbean, later into Mexico and Central and South America, the Bureau's power grew. Not only was it assigned to supervise the regulation of sailing dates, permits for loading and unloading of cargo, and the establishment of routes; it was also given almost unlimited civil and criminal jurisdiction over all personnel involved. Except by order of the king himself, no vessel could load or unload or leave port without a permit from the Bureau of Trade, and those who violated its sweeping authority faced severe penalties.

To Spain's credit, the Bureau remained surprisingly free of graft and corruption until the later years of New World occupation. Seville archival records indicate that its efforts to amass data on tides, currents, winds, depths, land formations and reefs throughout the Caribbean were indeed impressive. Considering how many ships were lost in spite of this information, it is obvious that the cost to Spain in lost treasure would have been tremendously greater had the Bureau been less dedicated.

From the outset, ship captains were commanded to collect data at regular intervals along their routes, and doing so must have seemed a petty and useless annoyance at the time. As a result of this information, however, the Bureau was able to establish a series of guidelines, which formed the basis of an increasingly rigid set of maritime orders and policies that were issued through the centuries. The chronological sequence of these orders reflects the varying nature and quantity of treasure cargoes, as well as variance in treasure routes. An understanding of this sequence, then, is of considerable help to the modern salvor who might find a shipwreck, but who is otherwise helpless to place it in a proper time perspective and thus determine its salvage value.

The most significant single order of the Bureau was the establishment of the armada, or fleet of armed warships. As word quickly spread of Spain's trickle of riches from the Americas, first the Barbary Coast pirates—and later, freebooters sailing under the flags of England and Holland—began to infiltrate the eastern edge of the Atlantic, attacking the unarmed freighters with repeated success. At first, it was necessary to provide armed escorts for the Spain-bound galleons only as they neared home port. But in 1522, the Bureau decided that accompanying armadas were not enough and that the returning caravels themselves should be armed. At the same time, it decreed that no ship of less than 80 tons should cross the Atlantic alone.

The Spanish Armadas

Three years later, finding even these precautions inadequate, the Bureau directed the formation of armadas to convoy returning ships the entire distance from the New World to Spain. Cargo ships were to cross in numbers of no less than six, and were to be escorted by four heavily armed galleons and two *pataches*, the latter being faster and heavier cargo vessels than the caravels (which disappeared from the Atlantic trade by 1575).

In 1543, the Bureau changed the rules again: now, all Indies trading vessels must be of at least 100 tons, and were to leave Seville in fleets of ten or more twice yearly. The sailing dates selected were March 1 and September 1, each date figured to allow the ships to reach the New World on favorable currents, load their treasure cargoes, and set sail for home before the hurricane season in the Caribbean. Though the armadas sailed westward six months apart, they sailed home together as one large *flota*. But by 1565, when it became apparent that the loss of one annual armada could cause almost irreparable financial damage to Spain's worldwide expansion, the fleets were divided into two.

Embarking from Spain in the late spring, the two fleets sailed together down the coast of Africa and to the Canary Islands, loading supplies and water, then continued westward on the Equatorial Current to the Antilles. Here they separated. The "New Spain" armada sailed for Veracruz by way of Puerto Rico, Hispaniola and Cuba, discharging supplies enroute. Meanwhile, the "Tierra Firme" armada followed a southern route, unloading cargo and picking up treasure at Cartagena, into which the wealth of South America had been funneled, and then continuing to Porto Bello in Panamá. Porto Bello was the receiving point for treasure that had been shipped to the Pacific side of the Panamanian isthmus from the west coast of South America by a third fleet, the "South Seas" armada, and then transshipped overland by mule train.

Meanwhile, the "New Spain" armada at Veracruz had loaded treasure transported there from Mexico and Central America, as well as manufactured goods from the Orient, which had been carried across the Pacific to Acapulco in galleons and transported overland from there to Veracruz. Cargoes at last loaded, the two major armadas then sailed separately for a rendezvous at Havana. From Havana they returned to Spain, first threading their way north through the Straits of Florida (which lie between the Florida mainland and the Bahamas) with assistance from the northward-flowing Gulf Stream, then turning eastward for the long and perilous crossing of the Atlantic, which took from seven to nine months.

Though the schedules were changed in detail from time to time by the Bureau of Trade, the well-planned trade routes linking Old and New Worlds remained essentially intact until the end of the period of Spain's colonization.

In 1565, the Bureau assigned two large war galleons to protect each cargo fleet, a pattern that was to remain essentially unchanged for more than three centuries. One galleon, commanded by an experienced naval captain, was designated the *capitana*, and her commanding officer was responsible for the safe navigation of the *flota*. The second galleon, the *almiranta*, carried the *flota*'s admiral; it was he who took charge, who had absolute authority, when an attack was imminent. The fighting galleons had but one purpose: to protect the cargo ships at all costs. For this reason, the Bureau of Trade in 1572 decided that eastbound galleons should carry but one cargo, treasure. Previous experience in battle had proved that cargo strewn about a galleon's deck greatly hampered deck activities during battle—and treasure, while of enormous value, took up little room; it was customarily stored in vaults just below the captain's or admiral's cabins on the galleon's poop deck. The *capitana* and the *almiranta*, then, above all other ships, draw the attention of the treasure hunter.

In the later years of Spanish conquest, graft and corruptions crept steadily into what had been a remarkably clean, if occasionally overburdened, maritime operation. Throughout the centuries of occupation, the Bureau of Trade was obviously aware of the enormous temptation that the treasure cargoes presented, even to wealthy and aristocratic ship captains and passengers, and it resorted to a number of devices to prevent pillage of the Crown's property. Divers, again, played a key role. Serving as early-day customs inspectors, they were assigned to check hulls of returning galleons even before the ships had docked. Attaching boxes of smuggled goods to the keel (by hiring the services of less honest divers on the other side of the Atlantic) had become a favorite tactic. Foiled by the discovery of this hidden loot, a few unscrupulous captains took to tossing heavy boxes of treasure overboard before port was reached, arranging to have them retrieved later. Smugglers eventually became even more ingenious. On one occasion, a Crown diver found that an enterprising captain had replaced the lower part of the rudder with one made of solid silver; what unmasked the fraud was the fact that salt water had eaten away the protective paint during the months of crossing the Atlantic.

No one knows, of course, how much illegal treasure—that not listed on ships' manifests—crossed the Atlantic, or went to the bottom, during some three centuries of Spanish occupation of the New World. However, considering the billions of dollars worth of legitimate cargo carried during those centuries, and the hundreds of millions of dollars of cargo that was lost, even a small percentage would amount to a sizable fortune. Whatever the amount, it adds a special aura of mystery—and potential "bonus profits"—to modern treasure hunting.

Less than half a century after Columbus, with treasure continuing to be pried out of the New World and with problems of administration of the new territory multiplying rapidly, Spain established two great New World viceroyalties. Each produced its own brand of treasure, and by 1810 the yearly output from America had increased to about $35 million. Records of these viceroyalties and their specific treasures provide today's treasure salvor with yet another important clue in his search, especially when he considers the geographic location of wrecks and from which viceroyalty their cargoes came.

The major silver producer, for example, was the viceroyalty of New Spain, which included Mexico, Central America and, after 1565, the Philippines. This viceroyalty operated the lucrative mines of Mexico and Central America. Silver was cast into ingots until 1536, when a mint was opened in Mexico City, after which it was minted into coins for shipment. Thus, silver coins found in a Caribbean wreck most likely indicate that the vessel foundered after 1536. (Such clues are not totally reliable, however. A favorite trick of some treasure hunters, one perfectly legal though highly exasperating to a competitor who arrives later on the scene, is to "salt" a shipwreck with coins or other artifacts found in another location. If the unsuspecting finder begins an expensive salvage on a worthless wreck, he eliminates himself as a competitor elsewhere, at least temporarily.)

Far wealthier, however, was the Viceroyalty of Peru, whose boundaries stretched for nearly the entire length of South America's west coast. Its colonizers first worked pre-Columbian mines of silver, gold, tin, copper and mercury that Pizarro found in operation when he arrived, but later opened new mines that eventually yielded more treasure for the Crown than the New Spain and later viceroyalties combined.

How much of this vast treasure was lost? Where is most of it to be found today? The answers to these questions involve many factors. Most important is whether a stricken ship was eastbound or westbound. From extensive research that produced *The Treasure Diver's Guide*, treasure expert John S. Potter estimates that fully one-third of the galleons lost in the Caribbean were on westward crossings. Though they were heavily laden, their cargoes were mostly perishable items, supplies for the New World settlements: wines, cognacs, clothing, foodstuffs, glassware, paper. Most of these items, while of historic value, would have deteriorated over the years.

An exception would be an estimated million dollar's worth of quicksilver, lost en route to Mexico, where quicksilver was used in refining silver ore. Quicksilver does not deteriorate with time, but it is doubtful that even the best-equipped salvage expedition could retrieve it from where it must have sunk, into the bottom of crevices and sand pockets. Even westbound ships that carried no valuable cargoes, however, are worth locating today, if only for the money, jewelry, silver dining sets and other items carried by officers and passengers.

"Nearly any westbound wreck," says Potter, "can be counted on for between $2,000 and $25,000." Such wrecks are most frequently found off the Canary Islands, the Antilles, Puerto Rico, southern Dominica, Cuba, Venezuela, northwest Yucatan, and the southern coast of the Gulf of Mexico.

By any standard of measurement, however, the greatest treasure potential of the New World armadas are the wrecks of the Spain-bound galleons. Of these ships, Potter writes:

Between 1500 and 1820 about 17,000 eastward crossings from the Americas brought back nearly twenty billion dollars in treasure. In the average year fifty ships transported $50,000,000 between them. If this silver, gold and precious stones had been equally distributed each of them would have carried $1,000,000 and every unsalvaged wreck of a returning ship would be piled up with loot. But that was not the way things worked out. Treasure values on homeward-bound freighters varied from nothing to nearly $10,000,000. What a ship had aboard depended upon the year, the voyage, and the function.

Because most sinkings occurred in relatively shallow water, and because native salvage crews were stationed not far away, Spain managed to locate the cargoes of a considerable number of her lost ships. However, it is obvious that not every doubloon or treasure trinket was reclaimed even from those wrecks immediately salvaged—and many ships were not located at all. And so, in the century and a half since Spain lost its influence in the New World, the Caribbean has continued to be the world's number one Mecca for diving adventurers with dreams of riches in their heads.

Captain Phips' Super-treasure

It was just such a roving, adventurous American, a Bostonian named William Phips, who made the greatest treasure recovery to occur in the Caribbean between the colonial period and Kip Wagner's salvage of the 1715 Plate Fleet near Cape Canaveral in the present century. Phips' story is all the more remarkable because it unfolded in the 17th century, long before scuba, magnetometers and other helpful salvage aids came on the scene.

Born in frontier Maine in 1651, Phips rose from humble origins. A shepherd until he was 18, he later served as a ship's carpenter's apprentice. Still later, largely as the result of marriage to a rich widow with influential connections, he attained the captaincy of several vessels, one of which took him to the Caribbean for the first time. Like many men before and after, Phips immediately was afflicted with treasure fever; giving up his shipboard position, he took up treasure hunting full time. Although several wrecks he located in the Bahamas did not yield vast amounts of treasure, their salvage was sufficient to pay Phips' expenses . . . and to whet his appetite for more. As he roamed the Spanish Main, Phips repeatedly heard varying accounts of a Spanish *flota* totaling more than 31 ships, which had been caught in a hurricane in the Straits of Florida in 1641. Most of the ships, staggering under the storm's fury, got no further, and foundered on reefs along the Florida peninsula. According to contemporary accounts read by Phips, Spanish salvors reached most of the ships immediately; the *almiranta* of the armada, however, managed to survive. For more than a week she drifted aimlessly, then finally sank on a reef presently known as Silver Shoals, about 90 miles north of Hispaniola.

Efforts by the Spanish to locate the vessel, Phips learned, had proved fruitless, and he decided to begin a search himself. Needing money, he went to London, where he waited 18 months for an audience with King Charles II, whom he hoped to interest in financing an expedition in return for a percentage of the spoils. The king finally agreed to see Phips, and was impressed enough with the salvage plan that he provided a ship and crew. In 1685, an empty-handed Phips was back in London. Although he had spent months working a wreck near Nassau that turned out to be worthless, had quelled a mutiny among his disappointed crew, and had not a farthing to show for all of his effort, his persistence was apparently undaunted. Though King Charles had meanwhile died, a private group of backers, apparently mesmerized by Phips' bubbling en- thusiasm, sent him sailing back to the Caribbean—with not one ship, but two, plus an even larger staff of divers.

One day months later, as the expedition was working the reefs near Silver Shoals, one of Phips' divers descended to bring up a sea fan that he wanted as a souvenir. Seconds later, he surfaced, shouting excitedly. Half buried in the sand about 40 feet down was the wreckage of a Spanish galleon. To Phips, there was no doubt; the hulk was the missing *almiranta*, sunk a half century before.

This time his persistence paid off. Over the next several months, despite periodic attacks by marauding pirates, Phips salvaged more than 27 tons of treasure, including silver, coins, gold, chests of pearls, and scores of leather bags containing pre- cious gems. All told, the treasure was worth more than $3 mil- lion at today's values. To Phips, it was worth even more; so delighted was the British Crown that it appointed Phips as the first royal governor of the Massachusetts colony.

Although Phips' was the largest and most lucrative sal- vage of the Spanish Main by a non-Spaniard until the 20th cen- tury, as an outsider he was by no means alone in the salvage business. Particularly toward the end of the Spanish domi- nance of the New World, as internal strife and corruption wea- kened Spain's well-run salvage network in the Caribbean and as ships of other nations began filling the vacuum left by Spain's diminishing influence in the sea lanes, the era of the "wreckers" dawned. Experienced, well-equipped free-lance salvors who stationed themselves at strategic points along the Florida Keys and southward throughout the Caribbean, they kept their ears tuned to reports of ship sinkings, racing to the scene in their fast boats to recover the spoils.

During the 1800s, as America's maritime trade in- creased, coastal schooners carrying cargoes of rum, cotton or molasses to frontier ports along the Gulf of Mexico began to make more trips along the east coast of Florida. They faced the same hazards of storms and lack of proper navigation aids as had their predecessors, the colorful galleons and *naos*, and many went down. Only with the advent of steam and the con- struction of lighthouses and other aids did maritime disasters become less frequent. The 20th century has added its share, nevertheless: tankers sunk by German submarines in World War II, cargo ferries plying the route from Miami to Key West, pleasure yachts ripped asunder by hurricanes in the days before the U.S. Weather Bureau learned to predict such storms with reasonable accuracy. As a result of these disasters there are probably more shipwrecks, mile for mile, along the shoals and reefs of the 150-mile-long Florida Keys than anywhere in the world. Though none of the latter wrecks offers the staggering wealth of the Spanish Armada era, their cargoes nevertheless mean profits at the scrap yard, particularly if they consist of large amounts of steel, copper, aluminum or other metals. (Ironically, it is the ferrous metal cargoes of these later ships that often play havoc with the sensitive magnetometers of today's treasure hunter; even the most sophisticated device has difficulty differentiating between a valuable 1700 Spanish galleon and a worthless World War II Navy practice torpedo.)

Twentieth Century Treasure Discoveries

In the first half of the 20th century, no major treasure find—at least none of the scope found by William Phips—was reported anywhere in the Caribbean. Although this time gap may be difficult to understand, since the presence of treasure was well known and its lure was overpowering, many factors were responsible. Until perhaps three decades ago, treasure hunting was still largely a haphazard, chancy, hit-or-miss proposition. Far more wrecks were discovered by accident than by design, and technology had not yet provided the means of retrieving the treasure in the deepest reaches of the few wrecks that had been located. The value of research—the gold mine of the Seville archives, for instance—had not been fully appreciated. And perhaps most importantly, the postwar underwater boom generated by the invention of the aqualung had not yet occurred.

But when the treasure-diving boom did finally arrive, it was as spectacular as a bolt of lightning. In the early 1950s, when the Wet Revolution was just getting underway, a rugged, veteran hard-hat professional diver named Art McKee was already on the scene in Florida. Most of today's treasure hunters joined the underwater gold rush from other, unrelated trades and professions; McKee was one of the few with a salvage career already behind him. He had been working underwater since the early 1930s. If credit for generating interest in modern treasure diving can be placed on the shoulders of a single individual, few professional salvors would vote for any other man. In terms of diving time, McKee is probably the oldest and most experienced salvor anywhere, and although by his own admission he is considerably less than a millionaire, the systematic salvage techniques he pioneered, the persistence that led to the discovery and recovery of an entire fleet of Spanish ships, and the relentless pursuit of adventure he considers as exciting as treasure itself would surely earn him a charter membership in any treasure salvor's Hall of Fame.

During his boyhood, McKee, like many youngsters, was a devoted reader of treasure stories, though he did not discover the lure of the sea personally until he was a teenager. During summer vacations from high school in Florida, he worked as a lifeguard at a New Jersey beach resort. One day learning that a salvage company was looking for a boat tender for an older hard-hat diver, McKee applied and got the job. Later, when the diver became too ill to work, McKee, though he had not a day's experience, volunteered to replace him. Clad in the cumbersome canvas diving suit and equally awkward metal helmet of the period, he entered a liquid world that instantly overpowered and awed him. "At that moment," McKee now recalls, "I knew there would be no other life for me ever."

The addiction grew even stronger a few months later when he was hired by another salvage company to search Delaware Bay for an anchor lost by a passing tanker. While walking along the murky floor of the bay, he literally stumbled into the remains of an early 18th-century English merchant vessel, whose broken hull had disgorged hundreds of broken rum bottles and potsherds. It was not treasure, but it sent McKee's adventurous spirits soaring. Following graduation from high school in 1934, he got a job as recreation director for the city of Homestead, Florida. On weekends and during vacations, he began diving on reefs off the Florida Keys that he felt, from research, offered substantial profits in the form of cargoes of metal that had been buried with modern ship sinkings. One day in 1937, while moonlighting as a salvage diver on a water pipeline then being laid from Miami to Key West, McKee was approached by a local fisherman who told of finding "an odd-looking pile of stones" not far offshore in shallow water. The fisherman's story piqued McKee's interest. The sea floor of the area was flat, shallow, and swept by frequent hurricanes. What would a "pile of stones" be doing there?

At first opportunity, McKee donned a diving suit, descended to the spot, and immediately located the pile. Suddenly, as his fingers tugged at the growth of coral that covered one of the "stones," his eyes widened. Underneath was, very clearly, a cannonball. Digging quickly into the sand nearby, he found four smaller objects, flat and round; a jeweler friend later was to identify them as silver coins of a much earlier period. Another dive yielded still another coin, this one gold and dated 1721. No modern ship carried cannonballs, McKee knew, and only a freak circumstance would place a coin more than two centuries old at almost the same spot. The coin pinpointed the period; the cannonballs suggested that the vessel had been a warship. In McKee's mind, there was but one answer: a Spanish galleon.

For the next few weeks, McKee pored through every local reference book he could find, visited museums, wrote the Library of Congress in Washington. The research turned up a blank. Finally, only half expecting a reply, he wrote the director of the Archives of the Indies in Seville, Spain. To his surprise, the mail a few weeks later brought him a bulky package containing copies of several hundred pages of archival documents. From them, the missing pieces of the mystery began falling together.

In May, 1733, a treasure armada consisting of 21 ships had sailed from Veracruz under the command of General Rodrigo de Torres y Morales, arriving in Havana in early July. In the Cuban city, a twenty-second ship joined the fleet, and preparations for the homeward voyage to Spain—including the loading of 20 million pesos, nearly all of it in Mexican silver—got under way. In early July, the heavily loaded armada set sail and soon began threading its way northward through the treacherous Straits of Florida. The winds shifted abruptly on July 14. Fearing a hurricane's approach, General Torres y Morales ordered the armada to change course and return to Havana. In those times, such an order was considered an act of desperation; in all but the calmest weather, the chances of a sailing ship reaching Havana after being committed to the channel were extremely rare. Most captains would choose to risk a hurricane instead. Though the newer galleons were far more suited to the task than their predecessors, they were at best clumsy, lumbering craft, hard to maneuver in tight places, and they were completely at the mercy of the wind. In the Florida Straits, their progress was hindered by two additional factors: the narrowness of the channel, which is barely 50 miles across at the widest point, and the steady six-knot flow of the current northward. Fighting the current in calm weather was difficult; buffeted by a storm, it was nearly impossible.

During the long, terrible night that followed, the hurricane began dashing Torres y Morales' ships apart one by one, driving their battered hulls and dying crews against the jagged reefs of the Florida Keys.

According to later accounts, the *capitana*, the *Rubi Segundo*, went aground at Key Largo in the Upper Keys, most of her crew and passengers reaching shore at Upper Matacumbe Key. At this point, records of the disaster begin to differ. According to one account, a Spanish salvage crew, arriving a few days later, managed to refloat the *capitana* by jettisoning all her heavy cannon and cannonballs (which, to McKee, explained the pile of "stones" he had found). Other records stated that the *Rubi Segundo* broke apart and sank off Key Largo. All narratives agreed on one point, however: that the Spaniards carried out a thorough job of salvaging most of the ships of the 1733 fleet within the next year or two, recovering all but 4 million pesos worth of silver and ingots the armada carried. (A peso in that period was a unit of value measurement, not a coin.) But by 1937, when McKee began searching for the lost ships of 1733, that meant about $6 million at current values—well worth the years of toil he had vowed to devote to the salvage.

For the next decade—until after World War II—McKee spent almost every waking hour tracking down clues to the 1733 wrecks and salvaging their hidden cargoes. Within another five years, he had been involved in the discovery and salvage of almost 75 wrecks throughout the Keys, including English frigates, pirate vessels and slavers. In his explorations, McKee found a total of 21 iron cannon; hundreds of cannonballs, bar shot and grapeshot, cutlasses and swords and daggers; and thousands of utensils, tools and items of pottery, china and glass. As for actual treasure, the 1733 ships yielded more than one thousand silver coins as well as other riches. One of many large silver ingots McKee recovered is now in the Smithsonian Institution; dozens of other items are displayed in the Fortress of Sunken Treasure Museum operated by McKee on Plantation Key. A 17-foot anchor, one of the largest ever recovered in the Caribbean, stands in front of the building.

In the days before the scuba boom and the horde of amateur salvors in the Keys prompted regulation by the State of Florida, salvaged treasure was considered to be personal property. But McKee's successes could not be kept secret, and news of his finds touched off a flurry of competition for the armada's wealth. During the late 1950s and early 1960s, McKee found himself besieged by well-meaning but meddlesome pirates clad in wetsuits; once he found himself defending a wreck with a loaded shotgun. Today the 1733 wrecks have nearly all been located and their cargoes recovered, although artifacts and coins are still found occasionally. A favorite hunting place is the pile of ballast stones in the rotting hull of each sunken ship. Because Spanish customs inspectors found it difficult and time-consuming to sort the ballast of each ship returning to Spain, these rock piles had become a favorite hiding place for the contraband of smugglers. For this reason, a sunken Spanish wreck often continues to produce treasure long after the amount indicated on its cargo manifest has been returned to the surface.

The Mystery of the San José

One galleon of the 1733 fleet remains a mystery to this day. She was the *San Joseph y Las Animas*, popularly known as the *San José*, a merchant vessel in the stricken treasure fleet. For decades the *San José* has been a continuing target of both amateur and professional salvors, including Art McKee himself, as well as the focal point in a furious legal battle.

The *San José* made headlines in 1968 when Tom Gurr, an experienced Florida treasure hunter and president of Marine-Tech Salvage Company, announced he had located her remains, after ten years of research that conclusively identified her. Contemporary accounts of the 1733 disaster that Gurr had found indicated that the *San José* had been wrecked off Plantation Key and had then settled on a sandy bottom 30 feet deep, between Davis and Little Conch reefs. Spanish salvors had managed to save only a small amount of her treasure before she slipped into deeper water and finally sank out of sight altogether. From his research, Gurr was reasonably certain he had the right ship. But one further clue—her name—ended all doubt in his mind. In his archival studies, Gurr had found an entry in the journal of an Edward McIver, chief mate of an English brigantine who had watched the 1733 armada sail from Havana. One of the ships, McIver recorded, was "New England built, of three decks, 36 guns, and mounted two teer ports, no wast, 900 tons." This British origin, Gurr believed, would explain why a ship operated by the Spaniards would have carried a name of English spelling, *Joseph*, rather than the Spanish *José*.

By mid-October, 1968, Gurr and associates had recovered about 2,000 pieces of silver and a few gold coins, in addition to a variety of jewelry, including thirty gold rings and hundreds of silver rosary beads. Valuable finds continued to surface in the months that followed: 18 large silver serving platters, pewter plates, cutlery, pistols, swords, projectiles, and a lead water pump dated 1728.

The rate of treasure recovery highly pleased Gurr. But he had not expected the rocky legal shoals over which the *San José* was to drag him throughout the next several years, a donnybrook that was to greatly influence the entire field of treasure salvage in Florida. Because the *San José*'s wreckage lay more than four miles beyond the coast of Florida, he assumed that Florida, controlling only that portion of coastal waters within a three-mile limit, had no jurisdiction. Therefore, he began salvage of the vessel without obtaining a permit. One day while aboard his salvage boat, the *L. R. Parker*, Gurr was approached by a boatload of officers of Florida's recently formed salvage law enforcement patrol, who shouted through megaphones that he was violating Florida law by diving on the *San José*, which lay below. When they asked to board the *Parker*, Gurr refused, replying that he was outside the three-mile limit and immune from their jurisdiction. When one of the patrolmen tried to board the boat anyway, one of Gurr's men fired a shot into the water near the patrol boat.

The shot proved only a momentary deterrent, and within days, Tom Gurr was served with a warrant formally charging him with violating the state's salvage laws. For weeks the case, and a civil counter-suit filed by Gurr's attorney to challenge the state's sudden assumption of authority, rattled through Florida's courts. Finally, in a historic decision, Circuit Judge Aquilino Lopez, Jr. ruled in favor of the State of Florida. The three-mile limit did indeed apply, he wrote in the decision—but the three miles was to be measured not from the coast itself but from the outermost edge of the state's barrier reef. Since in some areas the reef extends 10, 20 or even 30 miles from shore, this meant that Florida now could lay claim to virtually every salvageable wreck along the state's Altantic and Gulf coasts. The court impounded everything Gurr had recovered, and the lot was turned over to the state. Though work on the *San José* has been continued by other salvors, working with Florida salvage permits, it may be years before the last elusive artifact is recovered, and the mystery of the ship solved once and for all.

Although the Tom Gurr case is perhaps the most celebrated in Florida salvage history, Florida salvage law itself—on which many other coastal states have since patterned their own—dates to the period of Art McKee's work on the wrecks of the 1733 fleet. Until McKee arrived, treasure hunting was being conducted on such a small scale that Florida had no need of funds for regulating salvage activities. After the 1733 fleet discovery, however, when hordes of untrained amateurs began descending on the state's reefs, often destroying valuable historical wreck sites with dynamite, concerned Floridians demanded action. In 1958, they got it. In that year, the Florida legislature, in a landmark act, proclaimed the three-mile limit for the first time and simultaneously established administrative machinery within the framework of state government to regulate all salvaging.

In effect, Florida works on a partnership basis with treasure salvors, taking 25 percent of the proceeds off the top and leaving the salvors with the remaining 75 percent. Both exploration and recovery are closely regulated by a permit system. A salvor wishing to search for a wreck must first convince the Florida Board of Archives and History of his financial capability, good character, and experience. He must also post a

$5,000 bond. This entitles him to an exclusive franchise, valid for one year over a designated exploratory site. If his search convinces him that salvage is worthwhile, he may then apply for a recovery permit, which requires another bond; this time the amount is increased to $15,000.

State archaeologists accompany each salvage operation to record and assist in recovery of artifacts. Recovered items of monetary value are stored in bank vaults, while those of historical value, after being treated to insure their preservation, are sent to the state Division of Archives, History and Records Management in Tallahassee. At year's end (though some salvors grumble that bureaucratic red tape stretches that year to two, three or more) the recovered treasure is divided; the state's share is placed on display in state museums and the salvor's share usually is auctioned to meet expenses of his business.

Although many treasure hunters complain about inequities of the system, Florida's salvage laws are actually far more lenient than those of many foreign nations or of other states. Among the many small nations of the Caribbean, treasure hunters often find themselves forced to pay enormous bribes to remain in business, even after meeting statutory treasure permit fee requirements. In most of the European nations that have established salvage laws, treasure recovery is encouraged, but the diver must pursue it with a highly adventurous heart, for all of what he finds belongs to the nation involved. In the United States, Texas allows absolutely no treasure salvage at all; on Padre Island, off whose coast many ships are known to have been wrecked, it is against the law to even possess salvage equipment. But in Florida, Texas or elsewhere, no law says that a diver cannot at least *look* at a shipwreck, and most jurisdictions tacitly ignore the adventurous loner who is after only a doubloon or two as a souvenir. For many divers, that is reward enough. But for others it is only a beginning, as the present flurry of major treasure diving indicates.

Salvage of the 1715 Plate Fleet

If the inspiration for the boom can be traced to Art McKee, it was Kip Wagner's highly publicized and financially successful salvage of the 1715 Plate Fleet that propelled treasure hunting into the world of serious, sophisticated and very big business, as related briefly in the opening chapter of this section of *The Golden Sea*. Wagner graduated from beachcomber to treasure hunter on the day he picked up a tarnished coin, later found to be more than two centuries old, on an east Florida beach. A builder and astute businessman, Wagner pursued his treasure with patience and planning. It was fully ten years after that fateful day—after immersing himself in research and after assembling a professional team—that he finally ventured into the surf beyond which the ships of 1715 tantalized him. From the outset, Wagner sensed that the coin, and others he was to find, were clues to an enormous fortune, yet he also suspected that the task of retrieving it was too great for one man alone.

In the intervening years, Wagner consulted often with a neighbor and friend, Doc Kelso, a practicing physician in Vero Beach and a local history buff. They decided that extensive research was necessary before attempting the salvage operation. A noted authority on Spanish coinage verified that the coins Wagner had found were valuable, had been cast during the early days of the Spanish colonial mint in Mexico City and were, in his opinion " . . . the most important finds from a Spanish Plate Fleet ever made in Florida, both historically and numismatically, as the future will prove." Wagner then contacted Dr. Mendel Peterson at the Smithsonian Institution; the archaeologist replied that such a fleet had indeed perished in 1715, but cautioned that available records indicated it had gone down not on the mainland east coast of Florida, where Wagner was looking, but 200 miles away in the Florida Keys.

Wagner, however, continued to play his hunch. Meanwhile, Kelso devoted a summer vacation to examining records of the Spanish period in the Library of Congress. One book, *Armada Espaniola*, published in 1900, gave a graphic historical account of the 1715 fleet's disaster but was of little specific value in leading searchers to the site. Finally, Wagner ran across something of much greater value. Published in 1774, it was a nautical chart drafted by the English cartographer Bernard Romans, and in the margin near present-day Cape Canaveral was a notation: "Opposite this River, perished the Admiral, commanding the Plate Fleet 1715 . . . the rest of the fleet, 14 in number, between this and the Bleech Yard." Excitedly, Kelso telephoned Wagner from Washington, and before the conversation ended, both knew that at long last they had pinpointed their treasure. From previous research and from Kelso's knowledge of the history of the area, it was clear that "this River" could mean only Sebastian Inlet. The "Bleech Yard" was an early reference to a peninsula a few miles south near the mouth of the St. Lucie River, where Spanish crews often stopped to camp during their homeward voyages, to wash salt-encrusted sails before the long transatlantic crossing.

In 1949, two boys who had been swimming about 75 feet offshore told Wagner they had spotted the wreckage of a ship, in about four feet of water. Hastily assembling a group of friends as the forerunner of a company that was to grow into a major enterprise, Wagner set up camp near the site. Planning their assault as engineers, they rented a bulldozer and began shoving sand from the beach into the shallow water toward the reported wreck, thus building a causeway from which to work. The wreck was there, all right, but by the end of summer the only "treasure" it had given up was a single copper coin. The summer had cost $12,000 and an unlimited number of frayed nerves. Years later Wagner was to learn that the wreck held a value none of them had realized at the time; it was but the superstructure of a richly laden ship farther offshore.

In the winter that followed, Wagner pursued his research with renewed interest, and from Dr. José de la Pena, director of the Archives of the Indies, came an incredible three thousand microfilmed pages—copies of documents relating to the 1715 Plate Fleet sinking. For the first time, Wagner pieced together a full account of that disaster:

The convoy consisted of 12 ships. Five were units of the New Spain Armada, commanded by Captain General Don Juan Esteban de Ubilla. Six were of the Tierra Firme Armada, under command of Captain General Don Antonio de Echeverez y Zubiza. The 12th was a lone ship, the French frigate *Grifon*, that had sailed from Havana at the same time; the Spaniards, fearing the *Grifon*'s crew would entertain notions of piracy, had forced this vessel to accompany the Spanish armada. (Ironically, only the *Grifon* was to survive the hurricane that followed.)

On the night of July 31, cruising northward through the Straits of Florida off Cape Canaveral, the ships were struck by a hurricane of savage fury. Of 2,500 officers, crew members and passengers, little more than half managed to reach the coast alive, and the ships themselves were quickly dashed to pieces against the reefs. Among them the ships carried an estimated 14 million pesos in treasure.

To the Spaniards, the loss of an entire armada was unthinkable, for it meant the loss of almost an entire year's national treasury, including the so-called "King's Fifth"—the 20 percent of New World riches that the Crown reserved for itself. Almost immediately after news of the disaster reached Havana, salvage teams were dispatched. No less interested was an Englishman, Henry Jennings, who had gained considerable notoriety as a free-lance privateer sailing under the flag of various nations. Assembling a fleet of five vessels and 300 men, Jennings arrived at Cape Canaveral on the heels of the Spanish, and only after a pitched battle with the rightful defenders of the treasure did he withdraw. Since Spain and other major world powers only two years earlier had signed the Treaty of Utrecht, which outlawed privateering, Jennings thus became the first major figure in the golden age of piracy.

The Spaniards' salvage work on the 1715 derelicts continued well into the following year, though new storms, currents and tides pushed all but one-third of the treasure beyond their reach. Thus buried under a blanket of mud and sand, the lost ships of 1715 were to slumber for more than two-and-a-half centuries.

Spanish records indicated where the salvage base camp had been established, and Wagner decided this was the logical place to begin his search. After only a few days of systematically digging throughout the area, he began filling his makeshift tent warehouse with the first valuable clues: ceramic and porcelain shards, musketballs, coins, pieces of silver. First in a rubber inner tube, later on a surfboard into which he had cut a peephole, Wagner began drifting over the nearby reefs. Both survey methods were extremely slow, but as experienced salvors know, nothing is more exasperating than to learn later that a valuable wreck has been missed in haste. Not far offshore from the old Spanish beach camp, Wagner looked down one morning from his surfboard onto a suspiciously dark clump on the sea floor beneath the clear water. Breath-diving to the spot, he discovered the clump to be a cluster of cannons. Nearby lay a ship's anchor, its shape barely recognizable beneath a two-century-old cloak of coral. Wagner surfaced, shouting with elation; he had found the first of the 1715 fleet's lost ships.

Inspired by a pelican he had seen soaring over the area, Wagner next rented an airplane and circled the reefs at near stall speeds, hoping to spot more of the telltale dark clumps. He saw several, each a new bit of evidence of the ships. (At very low altitudes, airplanes are usually an inefficient means of searching for wrecks, since they are generally too fast. Helicopters are slower, but the down-wash of their rotor blades disturbs the sea surface. As yet another example of salvor ingenuity, Teddy Tucker once tried using a balloon tethered from a boat off Bermuda; it paid off with the locating of several wrecks.)

A few days later, Wagner's friend Doc Kelso presented him with his first set of scuba diving equipment. Though Wagner had never taken a diving lesson in his life, and though he was approaching an age at which most men begin eyeing the calendar of retirement, he knew it was the only way to work on "his" ships. Before sunset, he had become a self-taught aquanaut. Word now was quickly spreading of Wagner's finds. In perhaps the wisest move of his life, Wagner applied for and was granted an exclusive exploratory lease by the State of Florida, to an area reaching 50 miles along the Atlantic coast from Sebastian Inlet to Fort Pierce. He was also granted salvage leases for specific sites. The leases legally protected Wagner, and the cluster of participating companies and associates he would soon gather to assist in the gigantic undertaking, from the free-booting wreck "pirates" he felt would soon come sniffing around.

Wagner launched his search with a dream, an iron will, and an inexpensive metal detector. When the project ended years later, with millions of dollars worth of silver, gold, ingots, jewelry and other items of treasure resting safely in Florida vaults and museums, he would head a monolithic salvage organization that was perhaps larger and more complex than any in history. The Real Eight Company, Incorporated, was chartered on April 17, 1961, with Wagner as president, and in the half decade following it grew to encompass a small fleet of ships, dozens of employees skilled in a wide variety of fields, and thousands of dollars worth of the latest in salvage equipment. At the outset, Real Eight was a privately held corporation. But after six years, when it became apparent that even the periodic auction of artifacts recovered was insufficient to meet the spiraling costs the project had encountered, the company went on the public market, offering 250,000 shares of stock through a New York brokerage. Money was not enough, however; Real Eight also needed the talents of salvage specialists whose names had become legend elsewhere—especially those who had invented equipment adapted for the specialized work that the salvage of the 1715 fleet demanded. Rather than invest in a $30,000 magnetometer, for example, the company invited Mel Fisher, a veteran California skin diver and treasure hunter who had achieved notable success as a Florida salvor, to come in for a share of the profits. In addition to owning a magnetometer, Fisher had invented a device—quite by accident—that had revolutionized the salvage industry. He had been bothered by the fact that, although on some wreck sites the water on the sea floor was turbid, because of the nature of its composition and the currents, water near the surface was usually quite clear. Wasn't there some way, he wondered, to send the clearer water down below, so that the divers would be afforded better vision? Fisher, a tinkerer since boyhood, pondered the problem, and finally came up with a solution.

Fashioned from aluminum tubing, it was a U-shaped pipe that was fitted on hinges over the transom of his salvage boat, the *Dee-Gee*; when in the "down" position the tube encircled the boat's powerful propellers. The *Dee-Gee* was anchored in place, the "blaster" (as he called it) was lowered into the water, and the engines were started. The device did exactly what Fisher had hoped . . . and far more. Functioning like a gigantic whirlpool, within seconds it chewed out a hole in the ocean floor almost twenty feet deep. Until then, the most important excavation tool of treasure hunters had been the airlift, an airpowered device, hand-held, that gently scooped up bottom material with a vacuum-like action.

Salvagers still consider the airlift as an important tool, since it becomes increasingly efficient at greater depths; Fisher's blaster is limited to surface operation, because it gradually loses power as water depth increases. But in shallow-water operation, Fisher's invention greatly cut down on costly "bottom time," was used considerably in the latter stages of the 1715 fleet salvage, and is considered a standard piece of equipment in the salvage field today.

Although salvage continues periodically on the 1715 Plate Fleet ships, the work of Real Eight is completed. The company itself has disbanded, and Kip Wagner, his dreams fulfilled manyfold, has passed away. But in terms of systematic planning, organization, inventiveness, caliber of personnel, depth of research, and, certainly, dollar value of recovery, the work of Wagner and Real Eight stands as a monumental achievement in the field of salvage, and as a model for future treasure hunters to follow.

The evidence of the ten year undertaking may be seen at the Real Eight Museum of Sunken Treasure, opened in 1968 at Cape Canaveral, where a major share of the salvaged fleet's treasure is on permanent display. Many other items were sold during the operation to meet expenses and are in various museums and galleries throughout the world. The prices brought by just a few of these artifacts at a single sale underscore the enormous appeal of treasure hunting. In an auction held in February of 1967 by the Parke-Bernet Galleries, a shell-encrusted crucifix, 3½ inches high, sold for $2,000, and a 2-inch plain gold cross went for $1,900. Bidding rose to $7,500 for a single 9-pound round gold ingot, and a 43-pound silver bar fetched $4,000. Prices for individual coins ranged from $10 for tiny cobs to more than $300 for *ochos reales*—pieces-of-eight—in good condition. Bidding was especially brisk for many items of well-preserved, undamaged porcelain of the K'ang-hsi Dynasty of China. Wagner considered it "miraculous" that such delicate china could have survived the perilous route: first, from mainland Asia to the Philippines, then across the Pacific to Acapulco aboard a Manila Galleon, by mule-back over the Mexican mainland to Veracruz, across the Caribbean to Havana in another galleon—and finally, to the bottom of the sea in a 1715 hurricane, to lie there for two and a half centuries until a modern-day salvor recovered it. By far the most valuable single item salvaged, however, was an intricate gold medallion that had served as a Spanish general's badge of office. It was auctioned for $50,000.

Though Kip Wagner's work is now history, and Art McKee's present profits originate not on the Florida reefs but in the pockets of paying tourists who stream to Plantation Key to view relics of his past achievements, the era of treasure salvage they pioneered is just beginning. Treasure hunting is continuing at a furious pace, not only in the Florida Keys and the Caribbean, but everywhere in the world where man has shipped his goods in the holds of ships.

Ever more tantalizing, for instance, are the Manila Galleons—larger, stouter, more heavily laden than the ships of the Spain-to-Caribbean armadas—that sank between 1565 and 1815 during the perilous 10,000 mile transpacific crossings between Manila and Acapulco. Although an estimated one out of every twenty of these galleons met disaster, and though the cargo on each ranged in value from half a million to three million dollars, and though most are in water depths accessible to modern salvage equipment, not a single Manila Galleon has been salvaged in modern times.

Of the two dozen sailing ships of Spain's Invincible Armada that sank off the coasts of England and the west coast of Europe in 1588, only a few have been located, even fewer salvaged. Yet each was a floating treasure trove: chests of gold, jewelry, boxes of delicate silverware, all of it intended by King Philip II to be presented to his conquerors of the British Empire, as a reward for their feats of daring. Other ships of the Spanish Empire lie buried off the coasts of Spain and Portugal, each a potential fortune to its lucky finder.

The North Atlantic is another graveyard of lost ships. A subject of several salvage efforts, for instance, has been the liner *Andrea Doria*, which sank in 240 feet of water on July 26, 1956, after colliding with the steamer *Stockholm*. The *Andrea Doria* carried an estimated $1 million in money and jewels in her safe. Despite the depth, a number of divers have reached her hull, though the valuables have never been recovered. Two of the first were Peter Gimble, the New York department store heir and adventurer, and Kenneth MacLeish, then of *Life* magazine. In 1973, two Navy divers, Don Rodocker and Chris DeLucchi, made a much-publicized salvage attempt, using a pressurized underwater habitat, but were beaten back by the triple hazards of depth, extreme cold and swift currents.

In the eastern Atlantic, 112 miles off Kinsale's Head in southern Ireland, the torpedoed World War I liner *Lusitania* has rebuffed salvage efforts for more than a half-century. She lies 315 feet down, exceeding the safe working depth of scuba, but well within the range of increasingly efficient deep recovery salvage equipment. Rumors that the *Lusitania* carried cargo far in excess of the value listed on her manifest occur period-

Mile for mile, the Caribbean is the richest treasure hunting area in the world.

This Symbol ⬆ indicates location of sunken vessel.

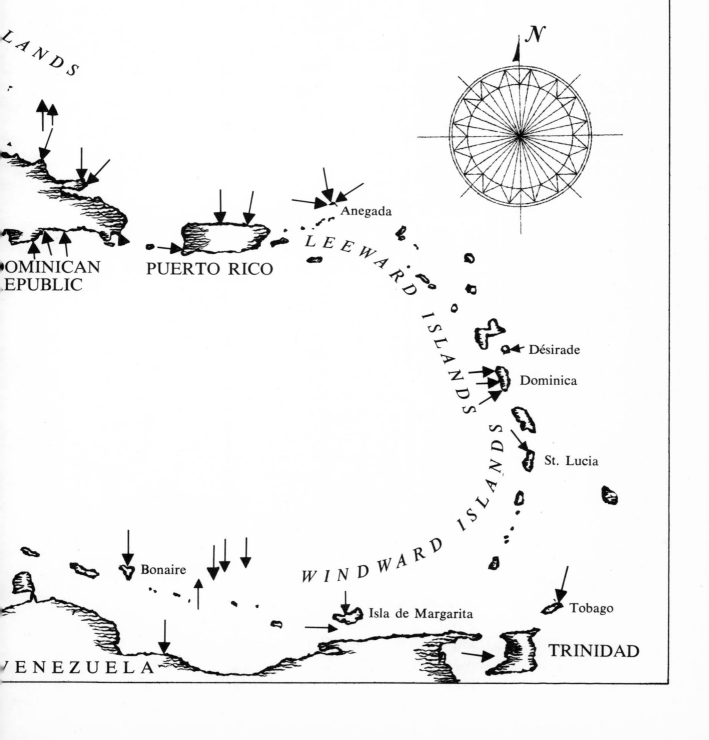

CARIBBEAN

N

LANDS

DOMINICAN
REPUBLIC

PUERTO RICO

Anegada

L E E W A R D   I S L A N D S

Désirade

Dominica

St. Lucia

W I N D W A R D   I S L A N D S

Bonaire

Isla de Margarita

Tobago

VENEZUELA

TRINIDAD

ically; it has been estimated, however, that at today's scrap metal prices the copper ingots and brass sheeting in her holds alone is worth more than $1 million.

Recovery of the *Atocha* Treasure

In shallower seas around the world, however, particularly those of the Spanish Main, the activity of treasure hunters continues at an accelerated pace. Thanks to new equipment, major wreck recoveries, which once occurred only every few decades, now have become an almost monthly staple for news-hungry headline hunters. And in 1971, the headlines described a shipwreck that, after the years of work it will certainly require, may become the undisputed grand champion of all time. The vessel is the *Nuestra Señora de Atocha*, the *almiranta* of an armada of 17 ships struck off Florida by a hurricane, with the loss of ten of the vessels, on September 4, 1622. The *Atocha* was one of the most heavily laden galleons ever to sail the Spanish Main. Because of a series of administrative delays within the colonial Spanish administration, two years had elapsed since any wealth at all had moved eastward to Spain from the New World, and the *Atocha* was especially fitted with extra heavy armament to protect her doubled cargo of treasure. When she sank, all hands perished with her.

Although immediate salvage efforts were launched by the Spanish on the *Atocha* and on two other treasure galleons of the Tierra Firme Armada, the *Santa Margarita* and the *Nuestra Sēnora del Rosario,* a second hurricane struck the area a month later, leaving only a portion of the *Atocha*'s cargo to be eventually found by contemporary salvors. Estimates of her value vary considerably. The most conservative is around $2 million. Mel Fisher, president of Treasure Salvors, Incorporated, who announced in 1973 that the wreck had been found, later produced the results of exhaustive research indicating that its treasure may be as high as $138 million.

For years a procession of treasure hunters prowled the Florida Keys in a vain search for the *Atocha*. During lulls in the salvage of the 1715 Plate Fleet, Fisher took up the search himself; his Treasure Salvors, based in Vero Beach, was to become even larger than the Real Eight Company with whom he had joined forces. Fisher's *Atocha* expedition typifies the big-business approach to modern treasure work, and he is himself the stereotype of what Hollywood might look for as the model of a treasure hunter. Born in Hobart, Indiana, he had tinkered with diving rigs of his own design a full decade before scuba came on the scene; his first helmet, which he made when he was only ten, consisted of a five gallon paint can weighted with the melted-down remains of his boyhood tin soldiers. World War II duty on the French Riviera, where he discovered salt water diving, whetted his adventurous appetite, and he moved to California after the war to open the West Coast's first diving shop, in Redondo Beach. In nearby San Diego, he joined the world's first skin-diving club, the Bottom Scratchers, but even its offering of kelp diving and spearfishing seemed too tame. In the mid-1950s he formed his own club, Shark Underwater Adventurers, whose two membership requirements may suggest Fisher's devil-may-care attitude: a prospective member first had to kill a shark with his bare hands, then spear a fish with a mouth large enough to put his own head into.

Eventually, Fisher moved to Florida and set his sights on the fabled galleons of the Spanish Main. After a number of successful recoveries, capped by participation with Kip Wagner in the salvage of the 1715 Plate Fleet galleons, he decided the time had come to devote full time to seeking the *Atocha*. Research of previous expeditions had indicated only that the *Atocha* had sunk in "the Matacumbes," a reference all assumed to mean either Upper or Lower Matacumbe Key, about midway along the string of islands stretching 150 miles south from Miami to Key West. By now, Treasure Salvors had become one of the world's largest marine salvage companies, operating six ships, with a staff of 50, including a professional archaeologist—and, perhaps most important of all, equipped with a proton magnetometer developed by Fisher's friend Fay Fields. Magnetometers today are the most important tool in wreck research. The more inexpensive models are frequently unreliable, however, and not many salvage companies—Treasure Salvors being an exception—can afford the better models that cost $30,000 or more.

For two years Fisher's small fleet of ships cruised monotonous grid patterns off the Matacumbe Keys without finding a trace of the elusive *Atocha*, or even the slightest clue that might lead to her whereabouts. His company's funds sorely taxed by the long, expensive search, Fisher was almost ready to give up and admit he had lost the battle. On a hunch, however, he sent his archaeologist, Dr. Eugene Lyon, jetting to Seville, Spain, to make one last attempt to find something in the archives that would turn their luck. Two weeks later, beaming, Lyon was back in Florida.

Earlier salvors, Lyon explained, had overlooked one important fact in their *Atocha* research. While all available records agreed that the ships of 1622 had gone down off the "Matacumbes," this Indian word then meant not just the present Upper and Lower Matacumbes, but the *entire* chain of islands, from the Florida mainland to the Marquesas Keys beyond Key West.

Wrecks of Spain's Manila galleons are scattered about the Philippines.

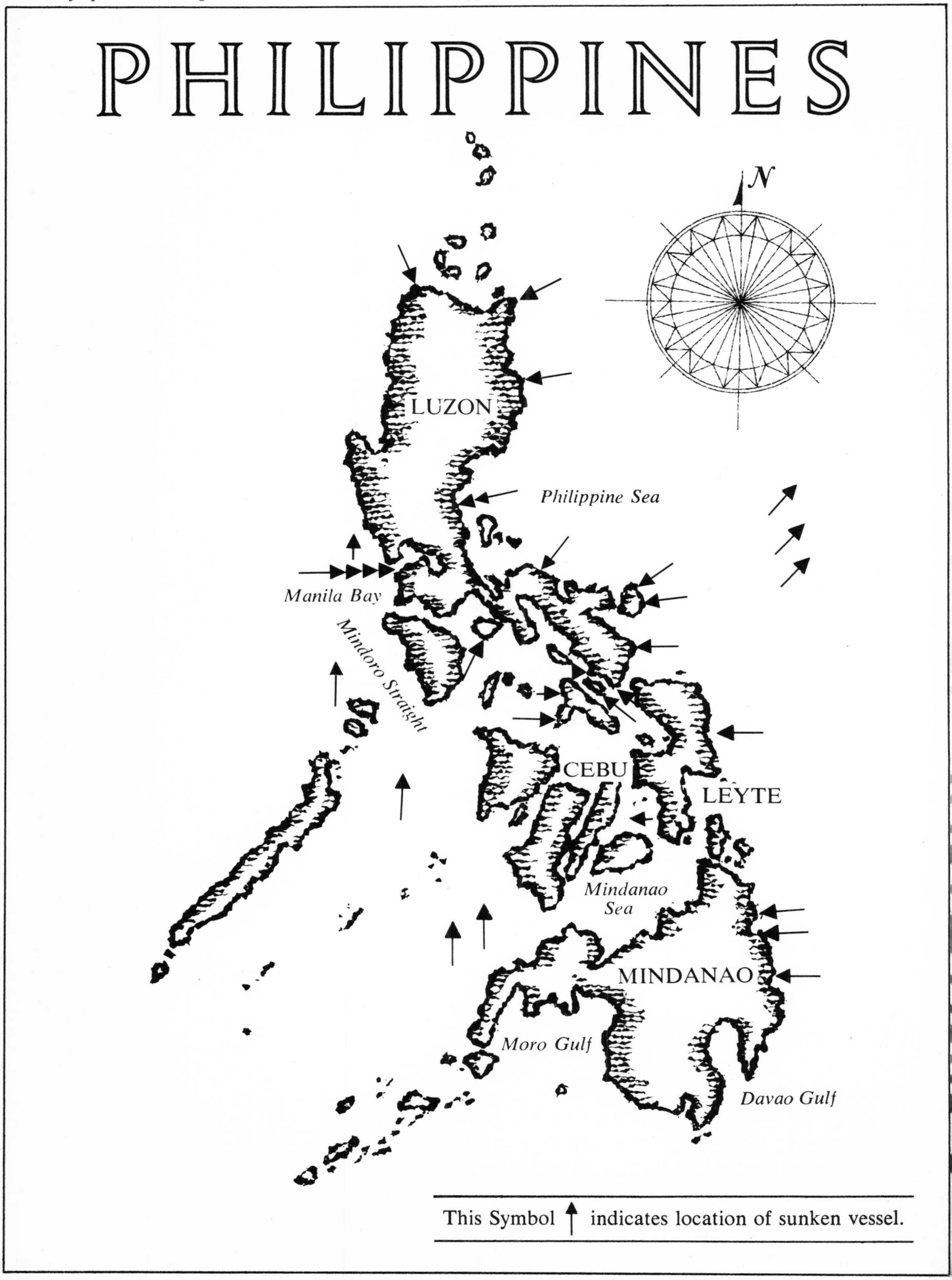

PHILIPPINES

N

LUZON

Philippine Sea

Manila Bay

Mindoro Straight

CEBU

LEYTE

Mindanao Sea

MINDANAO

Moro Gulf

Davao Gulf

This Symbol ↑ indicates location of sunken vessel.

For many nights, the lights in the offices of Treasure Salvors burned past midnight as Fisher and his associates attempted to reconstruct, from the new evidence and from previous knowledge of winds, tides, currents and the 1622 fleet's sailing instructions, where the actual sinking might have occurred. Lyon's discovery in Seville had opened a new avenue of possibility, but Fisher now faced the prospect of searching not in an area only 30 miles long, but one that had suddenly stretched to an imposing 200 miles. Finally, deciding to gamble one last time, he spread a map of the Keys on a table and pointed to the Marquesas Keys, fully 200 miles away from where he had been hunting. A few days later, Treasure Salvors began packing for the move from Vero Beach to Key West, where Fisher eventually established headquarters aboard the *Golden Doubloon*, a full-sized wooden replica of a fighting galleon anchored in the Key West harbor. Once again, his ships set out on their wearying, monotonous cruises along the close-spaced grid lines that had to be followed if the *Atocha* were ever to be found.

On a windy day in June, 1971, Mel Fisher at last hit paydirt: his magnetometer zeroed in on a heavy iron anchor buried deep in the sand off the Marquesas Keys. A jubilant Fisher recognized it as being of the armada period. Still, it was by no means final proof. Even after divers continued to bring up new evidence that the wreck had been a capital ship—several cannon, cannonballs, arquebuses, muskets, swords, each an indicator that a military unit had been aboard—he resisted the temptation to publicly announce his find. That did not come for fully two more years, in July of 1973, when the serial numbers on three silver ingots from the wreck were compared to the numbers on manifests of the armada researched at Seville. None of the serial numbers had been found in the manifests of either the *Santa Margarita* or the *Nuestra Señora del Rosario*, but all were listed on the *Atocha*'s manifest. The celebration aboard the *Golden Doubloon* that night was one of the most memorable in the history of Key West.

Full-time salvage of the *Atocha* will extend for at least a decade, perhaps much longer. According to his own estimate, however, Mel Fisher expects eventually to recover no more than half, perhaps only a quarter, of the reported millions aboard her. The main wreck is scattered over an area at least a half-mile square; stray pieces may have been tumbled as far as ten miles. Even after a decade, however, the adventure surely will not end. For Mel Fisher and others like him, the memory of accomplishment, of disappointments and discoveries, and of reliving a rich and tumultuous period of history will linger forever. And no amount of Spanish gold could ever buy that.

The Treasure Ships

In romantic fiction, there is a clearly predictable sunken treasure ship. It lies upright in very shallow water, guarded by a school of sharks or a terrifying octopus. Its wooden hull is intact, its sails flutter in the current, perhaps even a skeletonized crewman still stands faithfully at the helm. In the real world of treasure hunting, that image vanishes the instant the would-be salvor pokes his head beneath the surface. Though finding sunken riches can be a rewarding adventure, it is also grueling work and the trail to success if often strewn with disappointment. After lying submerged for only a few years, wooden ships elude the seeker; nothing destroys wood faster than salt water, and in shallow areas, shifting bottom sands soon cover over all remaining debris.

In recent years, however, a variety of new and relatively inexpensive equipment, together with the experience of many successful salvage expeditions, have made the adventure available to almost anyone with enough time, a little capital . . . and an abundance of patience. Improved diving equipment has proved immeasurably helpful. Now that humans are able to descend below the traditional 600 foot mark in safety, entire new areas of the sea floor have opened to the treasure hunter. It may seem inconsequential that the diver of the next few decades may be able to descend to 1,000 feet instead of 600, for instance, yet the additional 400 feet of "working room" opens an estimated 10 *million* square miles of the United States continental shelf to him—and it is on this "wet shoulder" of the continents that most sunken ships are found. The experienced salvor approaches his task with planning and precision. He researches thoroughly and, only after carefully determining his strategy, does he begin the search. Abundant clues are at his disposal to help determine which wrecks are worth salvaging. Dates found on coins, for instance, the design of cannons or anchors, even the shape and style of pottery discovered at a wreck site— all these help guide him in his quest. And if he is fortunate, they may add huge riches to his deep water adventure.

The discovery of a gold or silver coin, like these in the Shetland Islands, can become the clue to a rich harvest.

Some ships have foundered and sunk in the deep ocean but most that have perished lie in relatively shallow water along the coastlines of the continents where shoals, reefs and storms sent them down. By far the richest area for the treasure hunter is the Caribbean, including the historic Spanish Main, the crescent-shaped coastline extending northwest from the northern coast of South America to the Gulf coast of Mexico. Generally, the shipwrecks of the Mediterranean and along the shores of Europe are valued primarily for their

historical significance. Those in the Caribbean and along the trans-Pacific routes of Spain's treasure-laden galleons are worth millions in intrinsic value. The red symbols on this

map are intended only to indicate the vast sections of the world's oceans where treasure is to be found; detail maps showing more precise locations in the Caribbean and the Philippines

are found in the preceding pages. Centuries of future searching will barely diminish the potential for the determined treasure hunter, since the total of wrecks runs into the thousands.

PACIFIC OCEAN

South
China
Sea

INDIAN OCEAN

one-half billion dollars in treasure remains
ged in world areas of major ship sinkings.
d by the symbol: ▲
ines trace important global trade routes.

NOONAN

A treasured find is a sunken shipwreck as well preserved as the hulk of this 2,500 year old vessel discovered near the Mediterranean island of Cyprus.

Magnetometers and other devices to detect metal are important in salvage work; encrustation of metal objects like this cannon can easily deceive the eye.

With a school of tropical fish and a curious ray for an audience, a team of treasure divers methodically "works" a sunken wreck to bring its artifacts to the surface. A vital tool of the salvor is the airlift (left). Where mud, sand and stones are to be cleared away, it is used to suck the sediments and expose the treasure, like that at the top right, buried underneath. Lacking such specially-designed tools, some unthinking treasure seekers have destroyed many valuable wrecks by the use of dynamite and other careless meth-

ods. *As salvage technology provides increasingly effective equipment, however, hunting treasure is growing more productive and more fun as well. Once a wreck has been probed both by airlift and by hand, the task of bringing valuable artifacts to the surface remains. Smaller, lighter objects can be surfaced by hand, but those such as cannons and heavy anchors require mechanical assistance. One simple but reliable method is the use of barrels (overleaf) which are filled with air from the diver's tank for buoyancy.*

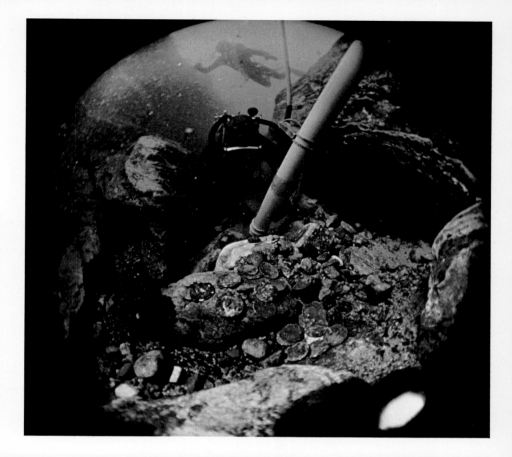

Because of a phenomenon called stereotropism by which organisms are attracted to solid objects, wrecks soon become busy communities of marine life.

The diver in the foreground wears a lightweight Electrolung, which recycles its breathing gas supply, thus permitting quieter, longer work while in the sea.

Metal objects such as this sword soon become encrusted with growth which must be hand-chipped away, removed with light drills, or chemically cleaned.

*Hardly disturbed since they were sunk in a stunning American naval air atta[ ]
in 1944, a fleet of Imperial Japanese Navy ships lies on the bottom of the P[ ]
cific's Truk Lagoon. The three-inch deck gun below is in only five feet of w[ ]
ter; 32 crewmen were fatally trapped in the sinking of the submarine at rig[ ]*

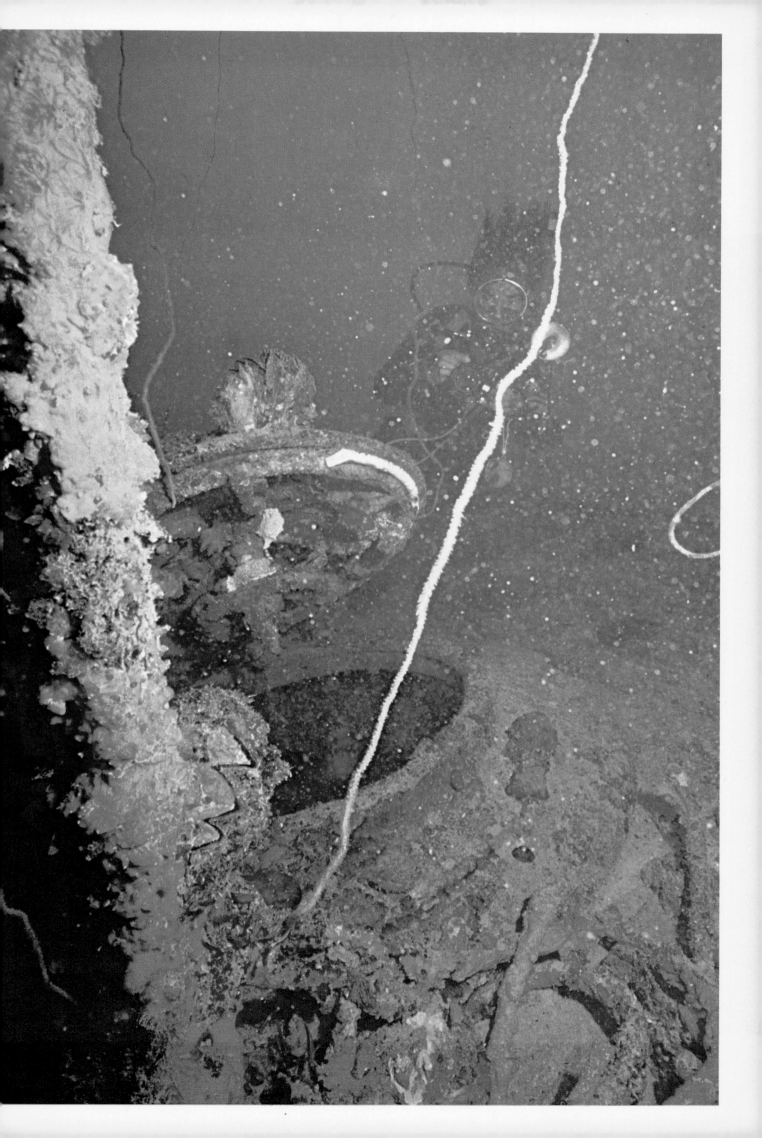

Rivers of Gold

Historians have written that the hardy Argonauts who streamed to California's rich Mother Lode gold country in the 19th Century picked the rivers, streams and mountain valleys clean of treasure before moving on a few years later. Modern-day diving gold hunters have proved otherwise. Wearing rubber suits to protect them against the chill of Sierra rivers, they have developed a number of effective, simple tools to extract new riches from the pockets the Forty Niners missed. Being a heavy metal, gold settles into hidden crevices that often evaded the reach of conventional gold miners who, before the advent of scuba, had no way of prospecting for it in deep rivers. To the Space Age adventuring aquanaut, however, it's Gold Rush time all over again.

A handful of handsome gold nuggets is the diver's reward for underwater prospecting in the North Fork of the Yuba River of the High Sierra.

Dates on coins are one of the most valuable clues to identifying a shipwreck; finding of a single coin is usually inspiration enough for an arduous search.

Not all the sea's sunken riches are man-made; pearls, like this basketful harvested on the Caribbean island of Margarita, are an enduring natural treasure.

The Sea and Survival

For all their collective value, the greatest treasures in the sea are neither Spanish doubloons nor jeweled chests of pirate booty nor tons of other valuable cargoes that have gone down in the ships of man. They are the life-sustaining resources of food, minerals and fresh water of which the ocean is the greatest supplier and the most spacious storehouse on earth.

In the sea, for instance, is found every mineral known to man, and some are found nowhere else. From the sea, in a never-ending cycle of evaporation, rainfall and the downward rush of rivers and streams, comes 97 percent of the world's water supply. And in just one of the sea's animals forms alone, the millions of tons of microscopic zooplankton which Jacques Cousteau once appropriately called "living soup," is enough potential energy to sustain every human now on the globe.

The supply of neither ocean food nor ocean mineral is inexhaustible, and the compounding effect of pollution on seafood is now well established. Yet the enormous resources of the ocean's storehouse have actually increased over the millennia as the earth continues to reshuffle her component materials and life forms in a direction ever seaward. Despite their profusion, however, man has quite literally tapped only the surface of their utilization. A land-oriented creature, he has, until recently in the span of his existence, found in the deep forest and lush meadow all the food he required. Fresh water flowed past his feet. And until he began yearning for more than mere subsistence, minerals were of little use to him.

As a result, man has only just begun to fully understand, appreciate and catalog the wealth of the seas, and to develop the tools for its orderly and productive harvest. Though world income from fishing (including whaling) now exceeds $8 billion, for instance, and though in some countries such as Japan it represents a major share of the gross national product, the more than 55 million metric tons of seafood it produces represents but three percent of the world's food supply. Fishery production doubled in one recent decade, but it is still a trifle. Perhaps more surprisingly, three-fourths of the production is harvested by only 14 nations. And except for a few minerals such as salt and magnesium—and lately, petroleum—the ratio of mining on land to that in the sea is perhaps even more disproportionate.

But this attitude of restraint is at last coming to an end, as end it must in a world whose mushrooming population is straining the resources of the continents. The age of what one writer has called the "Great Ocean Business" has dawned. Within a few decades—by the beginning of the 21st century, certainly—the serious business of mining the sea's minerals and harvesting its crops promises to surpass in intensity even the feverish excitement and financial investment of the space race of the 1960s and early 1970s. The boom of course will open vast new opportunities for men who work in the sea. Already, the "Great Ocean Business" has spawned an array of inventions especially designed for the task: "factory ships," pioneered by Russia and Japan, that can catch, process and can tons of seafood without ever returning to port; instruments that locate entire schools of fish through the miracle of sonar; computers that reach 22,000 miles to a satellite in Outer Space for signals that help guide ships home to port; pressurized cylinders in which men can live and venture out to work at great depths for weeks at a time.

The activity has also placed a new word in the marine lexicon: *oceanology*. "Oceanography" simply will not suffice any longer. By strictest definition, oceanography is that branch of geography dealing with the ocean; in recent years, especially since universities began conferring degrees with that title as well as in sub-disciplines it represents, oceanography has been broadened to mean learning what is in the depths, the ocean's chemistry and physics, the dynamics of its movements, and the nature and relationships of the biological communities within the ocean environment. *Oceanology* is the next logical step: the coupling of technology to this body of knowledge, so that the ocean's resources can be harvested for man's good.

The major thrust of underwater development in the remainder of the 20th century will probably be aquaculture.

Today, "fish farming" accounts for only about 10 percent of the world's seafood harvest, or about 3,700,000 tons of finfish, one million tons of oysters and other shellfish, and 300,000 tons of products derived from seaweed. Despite its small size, however, aquaculture is far from new; both France and Japan have been cultivating oysters and mussels for three centuries, and some kinds of shellfish were raised in captivity by early Greek and Roman civilizations.

Britain, Australia and the United States have commercial oyster industries, and in the Philippines there are shrimp beds as large as 25 acres. So far, however, shellfish aquaculture, because of its economics, has been stimulated by Epicureanism rather than by a desire to assist the millions of marginal people on earth who lack the protein the sea might provide.

As a sea farmer, modern man is similar to a Stone Age creature. He hunts his food as randomly in the vast seas as his ancestors hunted wild game in the forest. Only recently has he attempted to isolate those species of marine animals that will become the sea's cows, pigs and chickens. Deep ocean technology may help determine which may be best "corralled," domesticated, and turned out in almost assembly-line fashion for dinner tables as have generations of Texas Longhorn steers and Rhode Island Red chickens. It took centuries of trial and error for man to determine which of the land's wild animals could be most easily tamed and most profitably raised. In the sea, about which we still know considerably less than we do about the land, biologists have been pressed into overtime duty to produce some answers. The sea's major "livestock" may be an animal not yet even discovered. Suggests James Dugan, the late diver and underwater explorer: "The pig of the sea may well turn out to be the deep-water invertebrate that grows to 80 feet long. Observers in bathyscaphes report big mounds and craters on the deep ocean floor, indicating the presence of large burrowing animals not yet identified."

Ashore, most of the human race exchanged forest hunting for barnyard food production centuries ago. The reason was much the same as that existing in the sea today: man found only a small number of the animals suitable to his needs. Despite the fact that the stock of the ocean fishery is enormous—an estimated 400 billion tons of organic life is produced each year—only about 60 of the 30,000 species of fish are caught commercially, and man has little control, in the deep sea, over the delicate environmental conditions that can cause sudden—and economically disastrous—shifts in biological populations. On two occasions, for example, sudden temperature shifts in the Humboldt Current off the coast of Peru, believed to have been caused by weather patterns that failed to stir up bottom nutrients, resulted in a near-catastrophic decline in the important Peruvian anchovy industry.

Aquaculture will continue to be a costly venture for years to come, and economics is the major argument of critics who point to the topheavy cost/benefit ratio of the industry as it struggles along in its embryo stages.

While the argument is based on valid statistics, it fails to consider the ingenuity generated by terrestrial experience in agriculture. So-called "miracle wheat" and "miracle rice," for instance, emerged from the demand for greater yield per acre, but more important, this demand emerged because of the life-sustaining needs of more than one third of the earth's people. Increasingly, man has managed to squeeze more production out of the soil of the continents. In Orange County, California, as another example, citrus production in the decade of the 1950s continued to spiral each year even as more and more orange groves succumbed to the blade of the bulldozer.

Land-Sharing Fish Farmers

Aquaculturists argue that the same technology can apply in the sea, especially when the demand for seafood becomes more critical. But they also admit that the problems may be even more acute than on the land. Unlike land farming, which can be done in areas of low-cost land, aquaculture must be done in the most expensive zones of all, the coastal margins. Despite the size of the oceans, all but a small percentage of their area is a biological desert; 90 percent of all marine life exists along the continental margins and in a few deep-ocean areas where currents bring along vital nutrients. Increasingly, however, world populations are migrating to the seashores, and land costs there continue to spiral. In the United States, more than half of the population lives within 50 miles of the coast, and by the year 2000, it has been predicted, the figure is expected to reach 80 percent. Clearly, then, if aquaculture is to be conducted economically, it must not only increase yield but must share this expensive real estate with other users. In Washington's Puget Sound, for instance, a productive salmon seafarm shares space with Navy fueling activities within the boundaries of the 235-acre Puget Sound Naval Supply Center. Together, the younger salmon "ranch," operated by Domsea Farms, and the older petroleum operation make up a highly unlikely but nevertheless successful partnership. Hidden amid the low hills ringing a small bay on the Sound are 34 large tanks, each with a storage capacity of 50,000 barrels of oil. In just one month, the Navy loaded and unloaded 400,000 barrels of fuel, all with no apparent adverse effect on salmon penned in nearby waters. By strict enforcement of anti-pollution guidelines that the Navy has established at Puget Sound, a thriving fish farm can be operated in an area where costs of private land ownership might be prohibitive.

The Domsea project also illustrates, in a small way, the enormous capital risks of fish farming. Even utilizing the government-owned harbor area, suggests Jon Lindbergh, vice president of Domsea and deep-diving son of aviator Charles Lindbergh, the farm represents an investment of several hundred thousand dollars and five years of planning. The farm's two million fish consume 8,000 pounds of feed per day, and this spirals to 20,000 pounds per day just before harvest. With such high costs, Lindbergh points out, raising the protein-rich salmon must be aimed at a very narrow gourmet market, not the millions of needy whom it might benefit at a later date when such farming becomes economically feasible.

Other examples of this land-sharing concept abound. In San Diego, shrimp, Maine lobsters and Florida pompano are being raised in the warm water discharge of a local power plant. Normally, the water of San Diego Bay would not support these species, but a long-range experiment of the Limnos Corporation indicates that they not only thrive in the effluent but grow three times faster than they would on their native East Coast. "What we are doing," explains Dr. George Schumann, marine biologist who heads the project, "is giving them a perpetual summer."

At Moss Landing in central California, scientists have found that clams and scallops, grown in pens near another power plant, mature in 1 year to 15 months instead of the four years required in a natural ocean environment. And in the Gulf of Mexico, biologist Sammy Ray, director of Texas A & M University's marine laboratory at Galveston, Texas, is experimenting with growing oysters by dangling them in sacks from offshore oil platforms. Development and other causes of pollution have affected inshore oysters in the area, Dr. Ray explains, but offshore, his seedlings seem to be thriving. "After a time in the water," he says, "the platforms become artificial reefs, attracting many marine creatures. We place oyster spats (seedlings) in mesh sacks, suspend them from the platforms, and they devour the nutrients that come floating by." Building platforms especially for the oyster project would be prohibitively expensive, he adds.

There are less innovative and equally successful programs for exploiting the sea around the world, but most of the models of aquaculture can be found in Japan. There, in the Inland Sea, oysters are cultivated in hanging farms. At one place in Kesenneuma Harbor, huge floats made of concrete "balloons" hold up oyster wires 6 to 25 feet long; each float supports 200 or more wires, and each wire holds as many as 18 dozen oysters. The oysters are suspended above the bottom, where predators such as the starfish lurk. In Chiba, Japan, is one of the world's largest abalone farms, and Matsu Bay is famous for its scallop farms. Japanese aquaculturists are successfully raising salmon and trout in Okachi Bay, corraling them in huge sleeves of pipe frame and netting anchored at a depth of 60 feet. The fish are fed daily through feeding chutes in the sleeves, by diver "cowboys."

One large Japanese company, Seto Island Sea Marine Stock Farms Association, operates four large ocean farms, including one at Kaimura that covers nearly three acres. Incorporated in 1963, the company has produced bold evidence of its faith in sea farming as a wave of the future: at a special school, employees who once functioned as commercial fishermen are now being trained as scuba divers.

The disadvantages of high site-cost to the fish farmer are at least partially offset by the laws of physics of the sea, which assist in producing much greater yields of food per unit of "pasture" than on land. Being denser than air, seawater supports fish; they do not require bones as large or strong as those of terrestrial animals and therefore expend less energy in moving about. Being cold-blooded, neither are they as susceptible to cold and the ravages of weather; though fences of some kind are needed to keep them from straying, the sea farmer is not saddled with the costs of barns, coops and heating devices. According to one estimate, a space the size of an acre can be expected to produce 100 pounds of beef on dry land but will yield more than a ton of fish in the sea. Shellfish, even more sedentary, have an even greater productive capacity; an acre will yield about 100 tons of mussels or oysters. Carrying this a step further, if a body of water the size of Long Island Sound could be utilized entirely for mussel fishing, its 1,000 square miles could produce a quantity of protein equal to three times that of the present world seafood catch. Shellfish production in Japan's Inland Sea in recent years has become an enormous industry.

The critical problem in fish farming is reducing hatch mortality. Many fledgling aquaculture experiments, marginally financed at best, fail to survive their first year because large numbers of young die either as a result of insufficient knowledge of the reproductive systems, or from outside influences such as pollution.

Pollution is a global problem. Since the mid-1960s, it has also become a global concern. For centuries, man was deceived by the vastness of the seas; its 350 million cubic miles seemed a logical and unlimited garbage dump. We have now at last realized, hopefully not too late, that even small amounts of chemicals and other pollutants dumped in the ocean have far-reaching and long-lasting effects. Even minute traces of DDT, concentrations far too small to be directly toxic, result in great damage as they are passed along from organism to organism in the marine food chain. Except for a very few materials sealed in tunnels or compacted deeply in land pits, all waste from man's activities sooner or later goes back to the sea, and there are now bodies of water on earth so contaminated they may not be "safe" in the lifetime of the present generation.

Investigating Pollution of the Sea

Until the science of oceanography achieved pop status after World War II, followed by the more recent boom in oceanology, scientists found it difficult to even guess at the rate of oceanic pollution, since no baselines existed. Fortunately, it is now the policy of most nations, including the United States, to study an area in considerable detail before allowing the start of any development that will affect it. The controversial trans-Alaska pipeline is an excellent example. Resulting mainly from environmentalists' objections, the first large-scale environmental impact study in history was ordered before permits for the project were issued. At a cost of several million dollars, scientists of many disciplines studied the entire route of the projected pipeline, as well as water quality in the Arctic Ocean to the north and the Gulf of Alaska to the south. It was comparable to the situation that might have occurred if scientists had taken samplings of the water of San Francisco Bay in the mid-19th century, so that the real impact of subsequent tanker spills and development could then be measured.

If pollution does occur as a result of the Alaskan pipeline (as surely it will, for very little that man does is absolutely pollution-free), scientists will at least have a yardstick on which to measure the damage.

On an even larger scale is a project called GEOSECS, conducted by scientists of the Lamont-Doherty Geological Observatory of Columbia University. At an estimated cost of $4 million and three years of time, GEOSECS scientists are taking water samples at 50 different levels of the sea, from bottom to surface, at 120 ship stations around the world. For the first time, data will provide a complete chemical cross-section of the Atlantic, Pacific and Indian Oceans, and scientists hope to determine from this how various sections of the oceans are affected by their circulatory systems. GEOSECS scientists are particularly interested in interpreting the age and movement of the various radioactive isotopes that have resulted both from natural processes and from the fallout of nuclear activities.

Whether for the benefit of fish farmers, ocean miners or merely recreation-seeking divers, the deep ocean undoubtedly will become one of man's major research laboratories in the future. It is in the great depths, undisturbed by currents or surface weather, that a great abundance of evidence lies, which will help scientists piece together a history of the oceans and how man's presence has affected them. GEOSECS researchers believe, for instance, that in some areas of the deep ocean may be found samples of water that have moved not an inch in more than ten centuries.

When man achieves the technology that will permit him to explore there safely and at reasonable cost, the sea floor will also become a rich hunting ground for the aquaculture experimentalists. Along the coasts of the Persian Gulf, for instance, there live people who have never tasted seafood. Yet tons of oysters teem undisturbed on the floor of the gulf. In exploring the bed of the continental shelf in the Indian Ocean, Jacques Cousteau reported seeing "mile upon mile" of crustaceans, in places so thick they obscured the seabed itself. It has been suggested that if means could be found to cultivate and harvest these crustaceans inexpensively, the protein they represent would go a long way toward solving hunger problems of neighboring India.

At present, man relies mostly on organisms near the top of the marine food pyramid for the seafood he harvests. The bottom of that cycle begins with phytoplankton, the minute plants that drift on currents along with their free-swimming animal cousins, the zooplankton. Together, they constitute the ocean's plankton, vast swarms of rich pasture land for larger organisms higher in the chain—invertebrates, fish, and larger vertebrates, including mammals. Abundant numbers of animals are required at the base of the pyramid, to support the predators above (which usually become fewer and larger near the top). Roughly ten times more food is required by the animals on one level than on the next level down. In other words, it takes about one thousand pounds of sea plants to feed 100 pounds of plant-eating fish, which in turn may serve as food for ten pounds of fish-eating fish. Viewing this complicated pyramid, many scientists have wondered why man cannot harvest directly from the more abundant lower levels of the pyramid— the plankton. During his 1947 drift aboard the raft *Kon Tiki*, Thor Heyerdahl called plankton "good eating." The mammoth blue whales, largest creatures ever to live on earth, find it so; each must consume several tons of tiny, shrimplike krill daily just to meet the energy demands of its huge body. Female baleen whales suckle their young with a soupy milk produced from digested krill, and since each baby whale weighs two tons at birth, the nutritive value of such is quite evident.

Krill are found mostly in cold Antarctic waters, where they swarm in schools that are sometimes several miles wide. Viewed from the air, their reddish mass gives the sea a blood-like effect. Whales are far better hunters of krill than man, however, and if scientists are to test their theory that krill may furnish an answer to mass food demands on earth, they will require some assistance. There have been some successes, however. The Soviet trawler *S.S. Knipovich* has reported krill catches of up to six tons in half-hour trawls. If the dreams of one engineer come true, man may emulate the whale in harvesting this vast crop of the sea; he has designed—on paper—a whale-like submarine that would gulp down tons of krill through huge baleen-like strainers mounted on its bow, sending the result through chutes to deep freeze storage tanks in the hold. Meanwhile, biologists are trying to determine a way that the body shells of krill can be removed easily before storage, to prevent the rapid decay of their flesh that occurs when they are not deshelled.

Those whose tastebuds balk at the thought of "krillburgers" may instead prefer one of the many dishes produced from algae and other plants of the sea. Seaweeds, particularly kelps, have been harvested for food and other purposes for many centuries. The ancient Chinese grew, harvested and dried several smaller species as a delicacy, and today seaweed culture is a major food industry in Japan. Monks of the Middle Ages believed kelp was a good cure for stomach illnesses; to prepare it for eating, they first boiled strands to form a jelly and then sprinkled on sugar. The ancient Romans used a kelp extract to dye their clothing.

Kelp is not a major food source in the United States, but as a commercial product of many uses, it is a major industry on the West Coast where thick offshore forests grow. Harvested by large boats with lawnmower-like paddles mounted on their sterns, kelp is used as a base for more than 100 industrial products. Because it contains a unique substance called algin, it is used as a suspension agent for materials that would otherwise stick together; a kelp derivative prevents a cupcake's icing from sticking to its cellophane wrapper. In recent years, kelp has been studied for possible uses in medicine. Two researchers at Scripps Institution of Oceanography have discovered, for example, that seaweeds have certain properties not found in any land plants; it is possible that in the unique chemical composition of these fastest growing of all plants on Earth, there might be found extracts that would prove valuable in the manufacture of pharmaceuticals.

The California kelp beds have provided a valuable lesson in what happens when man tampers with the marine ecosystem. Because of kelp's many uses, one official of the California Department of Fish and Game estimates that each square mile of kelp forest is worth about $1 million. It was with considerable alarm, therefore, that marine scientists in the late 1950s learned that the coastal beds had suffered a marked decline in size over the previous 20 or 30 years. A noted marine biologist and environmental engineer, Dr. Wheeler North, was retained by the state to study the situation. At the time, commercial fishermen were blaming kelp harvesters for the kelp decline; Dr. North found, however, that by mowing the top three or four feet of the forests, growth was actually stimulated, because this permitted more life-giving sunlight to penetrate into the tangled kelp jungle below. Were outfall sewage plants to blame? No, Dr. North argued; most samples of marine life he had studied actually thrived in sewage. Finally, he found the answer, and its origins dated back more than a century.

Before the imposition of federal laws, the sea otter was hunted almost to extinction on the west coast of North America. Though the otter made a valiant comeback under protective statutes early in the 20th century, its population today is far below what it once was. One of the otter's choice food delicacies is the spiny sea urchin; in turn, this prickly marine animal finds kelp just as delectible. When the sea otters began disappearing, the kelp-eating urchins multiplied. Soon, even the fast-growing kelp could not regenerate itself fast enough to stem the rate of decline.

Based on these findings, Dr. North then mapped out a control program to reduce the urchin population. As he continued to seek a long-range solution among various chemicals that would kill urchins but not other marine life nearby, he recruited teams of volunteer divers who spent several weeks pursuing an interim remedy: they killed thousands of urchins by pounding them with hammers. (One may wonder what some future diving archaeologist will deduce from the rusting frames of thousands of these spent hammers along the sea floor of coastal California.) Today, the West Coast kelp beds are flourishing once again, and the incident serves to prove that while man can disastrously alter the delicate ecosystem of the sea, he can also replace and rebuild.

While man's manipulation of the underwater environment involves risks and must be preceded by careful studies of what effect it will have, certainly it will be the bold innovators using the latest in marine technology who will achieve major breakthroughs in sea farming in the coming decades. Just as the laboratory produced better fertilizers and the factory turned out more efficient threshing machines, so must science and technology marshal their talents for the benefit of Neptune's farmers. For instance, ocean fish farming will require improved forms of inverted irrigation; blowers, perhaps nuclear-powered, will be needed to force nutrients up from colder, richer bottom areas to poorer surface layers.

A research project sponsored by the Lamont-Doherty Geological Observatory, at St. Croix in the Virgin Islands, has put together a working model for possible future application on a major scale. St. Croix was chosen because, only a mile offshore, the sea floor plunges abruptly to depths of 3,000 feet or more. A pipe has been inserted into deeper water at the drop-off and, using conventional power, rich bottom nutrients are sucked up to the surface. Satisfied Lamont-Doherty scientists found that plankton production in the upper layers of water increased thirty times as a result; as a spinoff, they now believe that the cold bottom water may somehow be utilized as a natural air conditioning system for the entire island of St. Croix.

Chemical nutrients will also be introduced to fish farms by more conventional means, and the "ranch hands" will have sea jeeps, miniature submarines and remote underwater television to keep an eye on things. Engineers are experimenting with various types of electronic "fences" that will serve as underwater corrals, preventing livestock from straying and predators from entering.

As on the land, means must also be found to transplant the sea's crops, but success in this area rests as heavily in the arena of politics as it does in the science laboratory. About 60 years ago, for instance, a British biologist named Walter Garstang transplanted several tons of plaice, a commonly harvested European fish, from coastal waters near Holland, where food for plaice was scarce, to the more plentiful open sea near Dogger Bank in the North Sea. Within a year the plaice, which no longer face extensive competition for food, were reported growing three times faster than they had off Holland. But Garstang's work ended at that point; Dogger Bank is in international waters, and neither Garstang nor his country had any legal control over fishermen of other nations who came to reap the profit of his labors.

Artificial reefs are another form of man's ingenuity in stimulating the production of fish farms. Fish and other marine creatures tend to avoid barren sea bottoms; even where reefs do not exist, the greatest concentrations of life are found where the bottom is rocky. By developing artificial reefs, however, scientists have created vast biological communities where none existed before. Japan is a leader in this field. In California, the state Department of Fish and Game, at the behest of commercial and sports fishermen, conducted a number of successful artificial reef experiments in the 1950s—using old street car bodies, automobiles, concrete blocks and huge chunks of quarry rocks that were dumped at strategic locations. In every case, after a period of five years that it took algae to discover the reefs and to begin building the first link in the marine food web, entire new fish communities flourished.

Freshening the Sea's Salt Water

No less imaginative has man been in his attempts to produce fresh water from the sea. The need for this resource is great. World use of water for human consumption, agriculture and industry has risen astronomically in recent years. It takes about 10 gallons of water to refine a single gallon of gasoline, and 4,400 gallons to manufacture a ton of steel. A single ton of wheat requires 300,000 gallons of water between planting and harvest. By comparison, man's individual thirst is minuscule; the worldwide average of individual human water consumption is only 220 gallons per year. Considering that there are three billion such users, however, the scope of the demand for water is obvious.

Much has been said about a "water shortage" on Earth. The term is a misnomer, for water is perhaps the most abundantly recycled substance. The problem is not shortage, but finding the means of transplanting water from areas of perpetual plenty to areas of perpetual drought. Desalination, the conversion of seawater to fresh, seems a logical solution, but so far the cost of conversion plants and their operation is so high that, except for nations like Israel and Japan where need justifies the huge expenditures necessary, they are still considered to be in the experimental stage. (Emergencies are an exception to this rule; when Cuba's Fidel Castro cut off the supply of water to the U.S. Naval base at Guantánamo Bay, an experimental desalination plant at San Diego was disassembled bolt by bolt, shipped to Cuba and reassembled. It is still in use there.)

Several years ago, Professor John Isaacs of Scripps Institution of Oceanography proposed a novel solution to the water problem. At the time it was ridiculed as little more than an idealistic pipedream; today, however, it has not only been revived by two other serious scientific researchers, but has support funding from the prestigious National Science Foundation. Isaacs' idea was to tow icebergs from Antarctica to the west coast of North America, where they would be melted down to extract their huge amounts of fresh water.

Isaacs' critics might justifiably question the obvious huge costs of such an undertaking, but they could hardly deny its potential. Seventy-five percent of the earth's fresh water is locked up in icebergs, and 90 percent of those icebergs are located in Antarctica. As much fresh water is lost in the calving fringes of the Antarctic ice pack each year as falls on the continental United States in the form of rainfall. And unlike Arctic icebergs, which are jagged, those in Antarctica are flat with rather uniformly perpendicular sides; they float on the water like table tops. Some are as long as 100 miles, and the average depths of these bergs is about 900 feet.

To bring the icebergs to North America, Isaacs proposed a system of tugs, perhaps nuclear powered, that would tow them in train-like links at a snail's pace of one knot. The slow speed, he explained, would reduce melting during the long, ten month voyage; to protect the bergs further, it was suggested that they be wrapped in huge double sheets of plastic. John Hult and Neil Ostrander, two scientists at the Rand Corporation, have revived Isaacs' idea and are studying the realistic feasibility of it; the National Science Foundation, perhaps remembering how space travel also seemed like a pipe-dream less than a lifetime ago, has agreed to provide continuing funds.

In agriculture, fresh water may someday not be required at all. If a number of past and current experiments prove successful, man may bypass the conversion or transfer process altogether and use seawater for the enormous quantities of irrigation water needed for the world's land crops. At Scripps Institution of Oceanography, for instance, two researchers, Peta Mudie and Walter Schmitt, have reported success in experiments raising red table beets in seawater. The beets were first irrigated entirely with freshwater, then increasingly larger amounts of salt water were added. Not all plants are as tolerant to salt water as beets, but further research indicates that perhaps crossing the less tolerant plants with varieties that accept seawater may produce new strains that can be irrigated directly from the sea.

Much earlier in history, a group of Carmelite monks reportedly grew tomatoes, corn and grains by watering them with seawater on the Atlantic coast of Spain. And in 1949, Hugo Boyko, an ecological adviser to Israel, raised 180 species of plants in the Negev Desert by irrigating them with salt water drawn from an oasis. The brackish water contained about .3 to .6 percent salt.

For all the problems salt may cause agriculturists, it remains a multi-million-dollar industry around the world. About one million tons of salt, the sea's fourth most abundant mineral, is extracted from the seas of the earth each year, and the supply, even at that rate, probably never could be exhausted; there are about 166 million tons of salt in each of the oceans'

350 million cubic miles.

Just as he tilled the sea to augment his terrestrial food supply, early peoples turned increasingly to the sea for minerals other than salt. The Phoenicians produced purple dyes from the Murex snail, and the homes of many early civilizations were cemented together with a mortar made of crushed seashells mixed with beach sand. (Despite the advances of modern chemistry, the seashell still serves the builder well. In Faxa Bay, Iceland, local residents produce 50 tons of cement daily from seashells found on nearby beaches; there, they are in a partnership with Nature, whose pounding surf saves them the trouble of crushing the shells.)

On a large and productive scale, however, development of the sea's mineral treasures has only just begun, and man is still learning about the location and nature of their supply. A cubic mile of seawater contains about 175 million tons of dissolved chemicals of all sorts, worth more than $5 billion if it could be recovered and used. Much of it cannot be, although there have been periodic attempts to retrieve some of the more glamorous minerals, such as gold. Following World War I, for instance, the brilliant German chemist and Nobel laureate, Dr. Fritz Haber, devoted ten years of his life and considerable sums of his country's money to an experiment to take gold from seawater. Haber, a respected scientist who had learned to extract nitrogen from air, which greatly aided Germany's war effort when its supply of nitrate from Chile was cut off, suggested marine gold mining as a means of paying his country's war debt. Haber did indeed succeed in his scheme, but the cost of the small amount of gold recovered was about five times that of its value.

Meanwhile, the Great Ocean Business involving less glamorous minerals continues at a quickened pace, and until someone finds the clue that eluded men like Haber, they'll have to be content with the billions of dollars of profits from commodities such as magnesium, manganese, and oil.

When scientists aboard the 19th-century research vessel *H.M.S. Challenger* discovered mineral-bearing nodules on the ocean floor, they were quite aware of their value. But since there was no way at the time to recover them, the curious little lumps became mere notations in scientific record books. Lately, however, nodules have become the target of a complex, incredibly expensive deep-sea treasure hunt. The nodules, formed by precipitation of metal ions in the water, carpet areas of the ocean bed in concentrations of 50,000 tons per square mile, with the best known grades found in a triangle between Southern California, Hawaii and Panama. Viewed on surface consoles of underwater TV cameras, they seem no more exciting than clumps of potatoes (which indeed they resemble), yet recent efforts to mine them have touched off an international scramble of unparalleled fervor.

At issue is the question of who owns the nodules, as well as all the other minerals lying on or below the seabed in international waters that are beyond the legal jurisdiction of nations. High level international conferences of a specially designated United Nations committee began on a yearly basis in 1971 to resolve the question, but undoubtedly the dispute will not be settled for years to come.

Offshore oil, of course, is another key card in the big game of international mineral politics. It is also presenting engineers with increasingly thorny problems, for they are the technologists who must design the equipment to retrieve the oil, safely, from depths about which man only a century ago knew almost nothing.

Only a quarter-century ago, there was not a single offshore oil platform in the entire world. Today there are thousands; in the United States, offshore oil accounts for 18 percent of the total annual production of oil, and 6 percent of all natural gas. And in the seas, still not explored or produced, are vast oil reserves believed to be far greater than all those on the continents combined.

From the beginning, the oil industry formed a partnership with the diving fraternity, and without the talents developed from years of descending into the liquid world for science or recreation, vitally needed submarine oil would still be lying untouched beneath the ocean floor where it was formed millions of years ago. The need for human, deep-diving skills will be no less great in the years ahead. Because man is approaching the limit of the means of extracting ocean oil from surface apparatus, tomorrow's production will originate *underwater*. In elaborate manned pumping stations and control centers, perhaps as deep as 10,000 feet, oil will be found, pumped and transported to storage ashore completely unseen by even the most sharp-eyed seagull skimming along whitecaps above.

Except by descending in tethered capsules or submarines, human divers today cannot even begin to approach such depths, of course. But, viewing the great explosion of technology the Great Ocean Business has touched off, few would venture to bet that they never will.

The Tomorrow Sea

In the beginning, the oceans were the territory of a hardy few, the daring explorers like Magellan and Cook and Columbus whose surface pioneering linked the hemispheres and opened new global transportation routes. Exploration of the depths came much later; it was not until barely a century ago that the first major oceanographic expedition, involving the British corvette *Challenger*, got underway. Today, the adventure of probing the deep is racing ahead and, within the next few decades, men will be working, playing and doubtless living in the deep sea as effortlessly as they now do on land. In the name of science, industry or recreation, they will build cities on, in and below the sea, flanked by aquatic versions of all the supporting elements of terrestrial communities: airports, factories, power plants, hospitals. Increasingly, the deep sea is being tapped for the material goods that will fulfill man's physical needs as it has always been a source of fulfillment for his aesthetic and emotional demands. Man is enjoying a new kinship with his mammal counterparts in the depths, the whales, dolphins, sea lions and walruses. In the sea of tomorrow, they will be his fellow explorers. Tomorrow's deep sea world will be a home, a farm, a factory, a realm of high adventure. Already food, minerals, fresh water and medicines come from the sea. In the lowly sea squirt, for instance, a grape-sized, bottle-shaped animal, contemporary medical researchers believe they have found a substance that may arrest and possibly eliminate human skin cancer. And from tiny crabs, found to be possessed of fantastic memories, may come other information that will be useful in the study of the human brain. Man has few answers even yet to the enigmas of the seas; in fact, he doesn't even know many of the questions. But he is learning, and quite rapidly, aided considerably by increasing interest in the oceans. Quite possibly, he has learned more in the past three decades than in all previous centuries of ocean study put together. And with an array of intriguing new devices at his disposal, he stands today at the threshold of the most exciting unexplored frontier on our earth.

In an underwater living experiment near Belize, divers wearing Electrolung rebreathing equipment prepare to re-enter their sea floor habitat.

The increasing use of submersibles in undersea research and exploration, like the Navy's spherical glass vehicle Nemo (left, opposite page and overleaf), has hastened the development of a fleet of auxiliary and service craft. Submersibles operate efficiently underwater, for instance, but often encounter problems in launch or recovery when seas are rough at the surface. To overcome this hazard, the Navy has developed a maneuverable platform to recover or launch submarines underwater. Designated LARP, it is towed to a specified site, then is sunk by flooding its pontoons with water. Once below, LARP is maneuvered into position by scuba divers working at

an instrument console (overleaf). Operators of LARP risk dangers of the deep much as aircraft pilots do in the open sea. Because they are not in a closed capsule but in the open ocean on LARP's deck, they are often visited by curious, harmless fish, but there is also a possibility that a more ferocious creature may come wandering by. Usually, however, the columns of air bubbles and the size of LARP are enough to frighten the intruder. Larger versions of LARP are on the drawing boards of tomorrow's undersea frontier; some will be capable of lifting tremendous payloads from great depths, and technologists foresee a bright future for them in deep salvage work.

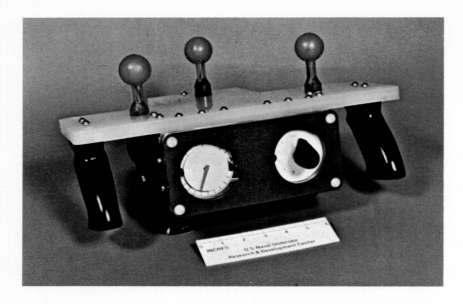

(Left) Console of Navy's LARP. (Below) Divers approach Nemo. (Opposite page) Some submersibles are being developed strictly for sport. The Perry Cubmarine, for instance, is used for hunting sharks. In 1971, using the vehicle, a contestant in the United States Open Shark Tournament bagged a 16-foot, 1,340 pound tiger shark near Palm Beach.

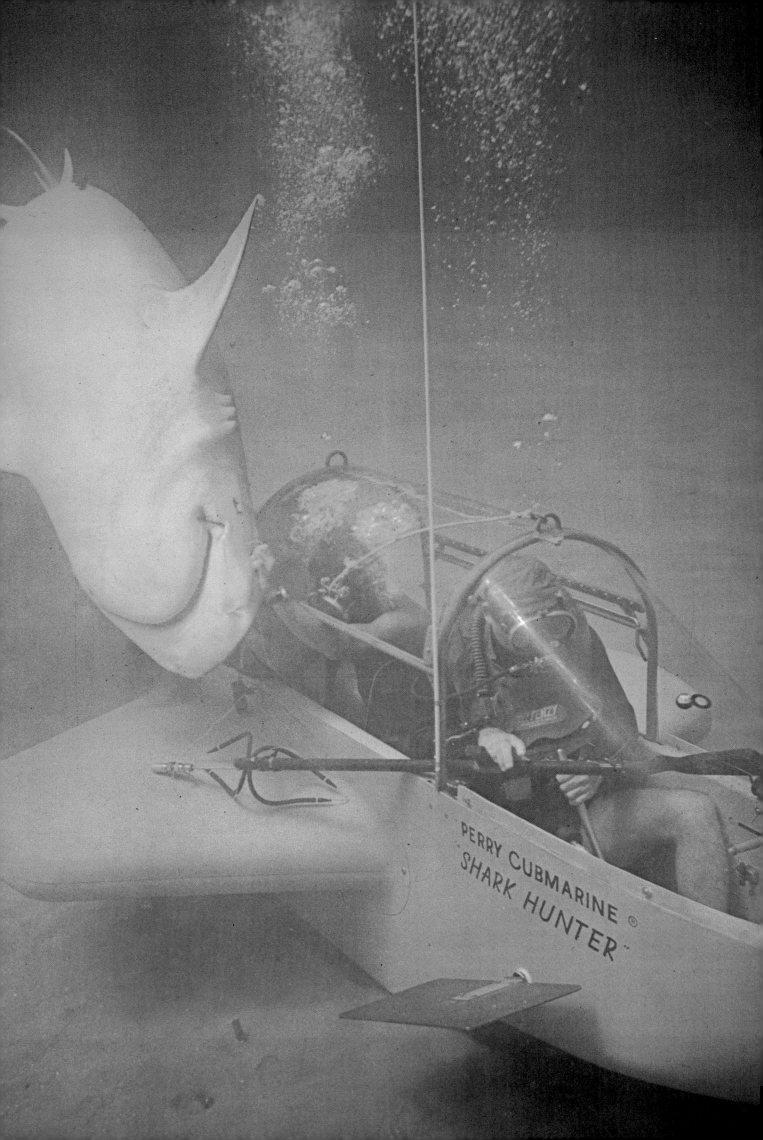

Exploring the sea for science, this diver uses a specially-designed plastic box to collect samples for study; care must be exercised not to harm the specimens.

Research on many over-fished seafood resources such as this giant Maine lobster is providing vital data for their continued existence in the world's seas.

Two divers swim over the spectacular Wall of Andros in the Bahama Islands.
The photograph suggests the type of terrain of tomorrow's farms in the sea.

Huge schools of fish such as this one photographed in the Palau Islands may one day be bred and harvested as seafood on underwater farms; to avoid time-consuming ascents and descents, the ranchers will live temporarily in pressurized habitats like the Hydrolab, bottom, which has many "topside" amenities.

The lightweight radio pack used to track this killer whale obviously doesn't impede his frolicking. He leaps as well with it or without it.

A mammal cousin of the killer whale, this sea lion has been trained by the Naval Undersea Center to recover objects at great depths in the sea.

Killer whales, pilot whales and sea lions have joined the porpoise in training to assist man's underwater exploration. Notable successes have been reported by the Naval Undersea Center in the use of whales (left) and sea lions (opposite page) in recovering lost torpedoes and missiles in depths from which retrieval by humans would be both risky and prohibitively expensive. The animals first locate the sunken objects, then fit grappling devices for hauling them to the surface.

Marine mammals which have long intrigued scientists, these porpoises at Hawaii's Sea Life Park are undergoing research because of their deep-diving capability. They are taught first to swim through an instrumented hoop (opposite page) which records physiological data such as blood pressure; other instruments carried in a body harness (lower photograph) record depth and duration of the animal's dive.

The Challenge of the Sea

One day in 1974, a fantastic structure that seemed a figment of Jules Verne's wildest daydream began rising out of the sea near the island of Okinawa. Now completed, it floats partly above water and partly below, towering two stories over a 117-square-yard submerged hull that is anchored fast to the Pacific floor by 16 giant chains. A floating bridge connects it with Okinawa's Motubu Peninsula, 1,300 yards away. By using mechanisms controlled through a computer, the entire structure can be raised or lowered as much as 50 feet, thus hiding it from the wrath of typhoons, or allowing visitors to peer through undersea windows at the parade of marine life along Okinawa's abundant shoreline.

The floating island-city, a monumental engineering accomplishment, is named "Aquapolis." It was built by the Japanese government (at a cost of $38 million) to symbolize a six-month-long International Ocean Exposition, which the host country called "a celebration of the seas." But beyond mere symbolism, Aquapolis was the first real-life "city of the sea," and a practical prototype of full-scale ocean communities of the future.

Predicting the future has been one of mankind's favorite avocations since Babylonian times, perhaps earlier, and centuries of enlightenment have not diminished enthusiasm for predictions; someone has pointed out that while the United States has an estimated 20,000 practicing astrologers, it has only 2,000 degreed astronomers. In the case of the sea, however, envisioning tomorrow requires neither Tarot cards, I Ching nor palmistry. One need look no farther than today's science laboratory and production factory for a realistic appraisal of how man will work, play and live in the sea that he is only beginning to utilize.

Within a few decades—perhaps as early as the year 2000—even cities as imaginative in concept as Aquapolis may be as dated as yesterday's log cabin. Cities will be built not only on the sea or in it, but below it. Some will be designed to meet economic demands and to alleviate crowded conditions on the continents. Others will exist simply to lift the spirit of man.

In *Future Shock*, Alvin Toffler suggests the wide range of "city specialization" that the new era of ocean exploration will bring about, and compares it favorably with the specialization of retirement cities, medical centers, "company towns" and the like, which are found in many nations. In the sea, some cities will be devoted to science, others to medicine, others to industry, still others to recreation.

Cities, however, represent but one phase of technology's bold push seaward. Roomier, deeper-diving, less expensive submarines will be developed to link the cities and supply them. Today, man develops the ocean's resources almost by remote control; tomorrow it is logical that he will bring entire industrial complexes into the sea. Technology will also include sophisticated equipment for a wide range of work tasks: herding fish, navigating underwater, recovering long-lost archaeological treasures in the depths of the sea.

Certainly, man will learn to alter his ocean environment for his own benefit. In one of the most startling proposals, an American physicist has seriously suggested damming the Arctic's Bering Strait to warm the Pacific and redistribute rainfall; by so doing, he contends, parched Southern California could be turned into a rainforest. Less grandiose are schemes to control hurricanes and suppress ocean fog.

Though the very thought may appall environmentalists, scientists are exploring ways that the ocean can be used safely, as a disposal area for man's staggering annual waste. In one study, Massachusetts Institute of Technology is attempting to turn potentially harmful sewage into a useful fertilizer by bombarding it with electron beams; the method, say MIT scientists, could destroy viruses and bacteria in other substances to be disposed of and could also deactivate harmful detergents.

Very importantly, the sea will be used as a major source of food, altering the nutrition of millions, and as a source of mineral riches. In these quests and others, man will be assisted by his mammal friends—the whales, dolphins and sea lions.

Even if some of the more dramatic predictions do not

materialize, the opening of the oceans will certainly create a host of new professional and avocational specialties, new academic curricula, new life styles, and a new and challenging era for esthetic expression.

Futuristic forecasts of how we will soon live and work in the sea no longer are limited to the imagery of science fiction writers. Today they also originate from the laboratory and university. "Within fifty years," says Dr. Fred Speiss, director of the Marine Physical Laboratory of California's Scripps Institution of Oceanography, "man will move into and onto the sea—occupying it and exploiting it as an integral part of his use of this planet for recreation, minerals, food, waste disposal, military and transportation operations and, as populations grow, for actual living space."

From a purely economic standpoint, it is unlikely that any one segment of society can underwrite the tremendous costs of moving into the sea by itself. More likely is employment of a "systems concept" by which industry, government and universities will share in the research, technology and eventual development. In recent years, this has been the pattern of ocean exploitation, a co-mingling of the know-how of academicians, scientists and industrialists toward common goals. The first use of the sea was as a supplemental food source and for transportation. Later, the sea became a battleground, a scientific laboratory, a new frontier for adventure. Now the need is not merely economic, but a matter of survival. Today's explorers will be followed by tomorrow's colonizers, who will bring all the trappings of their civilization with them. There is no reason to build a city in the sea, for instance, and leave the facilities normally associated with a city far away on the land. To provide needed energy, sea cities would probably be best— and most economically—served by floating or sea-floor power plants. Factories that employ the sea-dwellers could likewise be located in watery suburbs. And why not airports?

"Airports need to be near people, yet they occupy huge tracts of land near the cities that people need for other purposes," points out Dr. Athelstan Spilhaus, a noted engineer, inventor and so-called "father" of the United States' federal Sea Grant Program. "Airports are under fire for aircraft noise, and in some places planes are restricted in use of power on takeoffs and landings that either increase the hazard of flying or increase the cost of the aircraft. Couldn't airports join the complex at sea?"

In the United States, 53 percent of the population now lives within fifty miles of the coast, and projections say that by the year 2000, the figure will increase to 80 percent. Weighted under this crush of population, the coastal zone has become the most valuable, over-used and ecologically threatened real estate on the continents. So far, however, man has broadened the coastline only by extending it inland. He has not broadened it much by extending it to sea. "We come inescapably to the fact," reasons Dr. Spilhaus, "that any land-use involves sea-use; the sea has space to offer us, particularly space near the shores."

An outspoken advocate of developing offshore regions around the world, Dr. Spilhaus contends that by employing the "systems concept," the costs of expanding seaward would not be unreasonable, and that present technology has provided the means of guaranteeing that such development would not be environmentally harmful. Prototypes for many of the offshore facilities suggested by Spilhaus and others already exist or at least are now on drawing boards, and as often as not they are adapted from tools developed for scientific research of the sea.

For instance, the novel stabilized floating instrument platform, FLIP, has suggested to Richard Salter, a researcher at the Rand Corporation, how nuclear power plants can safely be moved offshore. Operated by Scripps Institution of Oceanography, FLIP is a strange looking, 355-foot-long research ship that is towed horizontally and then up-ended vertically so that it becomes a stable in-sea work station; with all but about 25 feet of its length submerged in the ocean, FLIP rises and falls less than 3 inches in 30-foot swells. Salter sees no reason why a 300-foot-long power station modeled after FLIP could not be built. Towed to an offshore site and then tethered to the bottom by cables, Salter says, the facility would be virtually invulnerable to earthquakes, a potential danger cited by many environmentalists in their opposition to land-based nuclear power plants. A typical plant would consist of several bottle-shaped modules, each capable of generating 250,000 kilowatts. Three clusters of seven vessels would be able to produce 5 million kilowatts, or enough electricity to service a city the size of Los Angeles.

The principle of FLIP, which ironically attracted almost no interest when included in a broad-ranging prospectus of significant ocean studies drawn up for the decade of the 1960s by the National Academy of Sciences, has now become a much-copied model for ocean-based facilities. Looking ahead to a time when political events may force a withdrawal of Americans from military posts overseas, for instance, the Pentagon has seriously considered building prefabricated airfields that could be flown across thousands of miles of sea, then set down, piece by piece, on remote sites over a FLIP-like platform.

One of the men assigned to study the feasibility of such seagoing airfields, John Craven, now has extended the idea to include entire cities. A brilliant naval engineer who for a decade served as chief scientist in the U.S. Navy's Special Projects Office, Craven later was to become director of marine affairs for the state of Hawaii. Like Spilhaus, he is a believer in the influence of the sea on human destiny. He was involved in several underwater living experiments and research on the continental shelf during the administrations of Presidents Kennedy and Johnson, and says he was influenced in his "sea city" ideas by the watery environment of his new post in Hawaii. Like Japan, Hawaii is of course "ocean oriented," and in the early 1970s, Craven, remembering FLIP, began a campaign to get the island state to build a vast floating city complex off the coast of Oahu. Craven's idea was that the city, a symbol like the later Aquapolis on Okinawa, would help draw attention to two major events upcoming in Hawaii, both centennials: that of the United States, in 1976, and that of Hawaii's discovery by Captain Cook, in 1978. The unique city would be built entirely on a series of floating tubes sunk into the sea. Its residents would commute to Oahu via hydrofoils or air-cushion water taxis. Furthermore, Craven insists, such a city could be built at a cost competitive with those now being built on the land, and would be the hub of huge complexes that would involve all city-related facilities such as power plants, industries and recreation areas.

Craven believes that the state of ocean technology already is sufficient to enable man to make a major thrust seaward to meet his housing, economic and esthetic needs. Among his predictions, forecast in an address to the American Institute of Architects:

Marine mammals can be domesticated for entertainment, for work, for service, and for the saving of life; men can live in the ocean at depths of 600 to 1,000 feet, at the pressure of depth, for extended periods; submersibles can dock and be undocked beneath the surface of the sea and free from the forces of waves and weather; low-cost plastic submersibles can be built to operate at depths of 1,000 feet or greater; low-cost structures can be built to carry equipment and possibly men to depths of 20,000 feet.

Craven's futuristic city idea, first publicly proposed in 1970, drew a whirlwind of praise from Honolulu newspapers. It also attracted the interest of Kiyonori Kikutake, a noted Japanese architect, who had been dreaming of his own floating city for several years. A holder of several awards for creative esthetics, Kikutake says his design was inspired by a small sea creature, the *Velella*, whose dangling tentacles provide stability in the water in very much the same way that FLIP's submerged hull does on a much larger scale.

By coincidence, Kikutake had accepted a visiting professorship at the University of Hawaii not long after Craven moved to Oahu. In talks to his students, the Japanese "futurist" continued to enumerate the reasons why he felt such a floating city was no mere architectural pipe-dream but a practical solution to shrinking elbow room, not just in Hawaii, but throughout the world. Man, he said, is multiplying at a frightening rate, although the land he lives on has grown hardly at all; by minute degrees, in fact, it is even disappearing in some places. The sea, on the other hand, is capable of responding to the constantly shifting emotional, psychological and esthetic demands of the human condition.

Kikutake's proposed city dwarfs Craven's by comparison. Craven foresees a city only large enough to serve as a usable model for larger cities to come, in the same way that Okinawa's Aquapolis served to call attention to Ocean Expo '75. Kikutake's, on the other hand, would be mammoth, perhaps sixty miles square, developed outward from a central core to serve a population density of 200 to 300 persons per acre. That's a lot of people in a small area. Kikutake is a believer in the principle set forth by architect Paolo Soleri: that preservation of environments is best accomplished by extremely high density, with residences given easy access to central or surrounding parks.

In Kikutake's city, family residences would occupy horizontal slices in cylindrical towers, each slice with space available for a father and mother and two children. Moving belts and escalators would assist travel about the city. The entire complex would be built in modules. If for any reason a city outlived its usefulness, the modules could be taken apart and towed to another site for reassembly.

Craven was anything but dismayed by the competition represented by Kikutake's arrival in Hawaii in 1971. In fact, when the two men finally met to compare notes, Craven was impressed by the possibility of what he had foreseen merely as a working model being expanded into a full-fledged "working city."

In blueprinting his own version, which also employs a modular concept, Craven estimated that the cost of each module would run about $10 million. An ideal community would consist of twenty modules, bringing the total price of such a city to about $200 million. As building costs go these days, Craven points out, that kind of price tag is not as outrageous as it may seem. "A reasonable budget for the foundations of a small floating city," he says, "would be only a couple of times as big as the budgets for projects that are built four or five times a year in Hawaii nowadays."

Neither Craven's nor Kikutake's city nor a combination of them yet rises dramatically from the western seascape of Honolulu. Yet the fact that they could generate the kind of support they did among hard-headed engineers and architects suggests that cities like them may become a reality long before man has previously imagined.

Elsewhere in the world, other sea cities, perhaps not as sweeping in concept but still larger than anything presently afloat have begun moving through the stages of raw idea to drawing board to funding to actual construction. Scripps Institution of Oceanography, for instance, has received a half-million-dollar grant toward building a full-scale oceanographic platform, using the FLIP principle, that would be large enough to accommodate a helicopter landing pad and numerous scientific facilities on top. The 200 by 100 foot rectangular platform would be towed to a working site in modules, then assembled; Scripps scientists say several modules could be fitted together to form a mini-city.

And in Britain, where population density already is creating problems of land use, the "sea city" idea has resulted in a large-scale model of what could become a community in the ocean for 30,000 persons. Designed by the Pilkington Glass Age Development Committee, a body set up to investigate the feasibility of this and other far-seeing projects, the city would offer all the amenities of mainland living. It would be located on the Haisborough Tail, a shoal area 15 miles off the east coast of England, where the water depth does not exceed 30 feet and the tidal range is no more than 4 to 7 feet. The main structure of "Ocean Venice," as it is called, would be a 16-story amphitheater built on piles and protected by an encircling breakwater.

The outer structure would enclose a lagoon containing clusters of floating man-made islands and would be broken only at the southeast corner, to provide a narrow harbor entrance. Altogether, the city would measure 4,700 feet by 3,300 feet. Unlike either Aquapolis or the designs of John Craven or Kiyonori Kikutake, however, the massive city itself would not actually float but would be anchored by concrete pilings. Its designers admit that Ocean Venice might not be built until the early part of the next century, if at all. But they say it *could* be built today with existing materials and present methods. In fact, a step in a similar direction already has been suggested for Toronto, Canada, where a scheme to extend the downtown area seaward onto a massive pontoon-and-raft foundation, has been broached. While this is not an open sea project, the idea is the same—conserving valuable land by building on water.

As development of the ocean's resources accelerates,

proposals for "sea cities" will generate much greater economic incentives. "It is probably not economical for an individual activity—oil refining, for example—to move out to sea as a single activity and in the short time available to meet our urgent demands for energy," says Athelstan Spilhaus. "But if we join uses in a systems concept with a common kind of underpinning, moving out to sea is feasible. The total cost of such a sea complex would be less, and the social, environmental and economic gains more, than the sum of the individual components."

Living and Working in the Deep

Science already has provided ample evidence that undersea and in-the-sea living can be not only safe but esthetically appealing. Just as man must live on the continents to study land creatures, so he must live in the sea if he is to learn more about the complex system of life that exists there, a system whose environment he wants to share on more than an occasional visiting basis. Already, many prototypes for full-scale undersea laboratories exist. In Hawaii, for instance, the Makapuu Oceanic Foundation has developed a 70-foot long laboratory capable of housing up to 22 men in a comfortable, "shirt-sleeve environment" for long periods. Named the Aegis, the million dollar habitat consists of two pressurized cylinders joined by a control sphere in the center. One of the spheres contains laboratory facilities, the other, living quarters—including bunks, an infrared oven for heating food, and a freezer. "What we have," explains Gosta Fahlman, general manager of the foundation's experiment, "is a complete working and living facility. The temperature is kept warm enough for a shirt and shorts, and a hatch at the bottom allows the scientists to go into the water and bring back lab samples. There's no reason why the Aegis could not become the predecessor of entire inhabited villages on the ocean floor; certainly, we have the technology to start building them now."

The first human experiments in living under the sea began in September, 1962, when a Belgian diver, Robert Stenuit, remained below for 26 hours in a chamber anchored at a depth of 200 feet. During eight of those hours, Stenuit emerged from the chamber to explore the sea around him. He breathed a gas mixture of 3 percent oxygen and 97 percent helium, and 88 hours were required for decompression when he emerged. Only a week later, two French divers, Albert Falco and Claude Wesley, swam down to a giant chamber held on the bottom with 34 tons of pig iron at a depth of 36 feet. The experiment was the first of two in a project called Conshelf, sponsored by Jacques Cousteau.

The technology for extended dives relies on a theory developed by a U.S. Navy physician, Captain George Bond, who in 1957 carried out a series of "saturation diving" experiments in a dry-land, simulated chamber in New London, Connecticut. Tests first made with monkeys and later with human volunteers proved it was feasible to breathe a mixture of oxygen and helium for long periods without ill effects, though long periods of decompression are required before emerging into the normal open-air environment.

The U.S. Navy itself conducted three saturation diving experiments, called SeaLab. In the final phase, a porpoise named "Tuffy" joined the human participants; he was trained to carry tools and other objects from the surface to divers working and living below. During SeaLab, America's two-way thrust into both Outer and Inner Space was joined; one of the 30 men involved—in teams of 10 men, each of which stayed down 15 days—was former astronaut Scott Carpenter. SeaLab II was conducted in water 205 feet deep. The final SeaLab experiment, involving a habitat sunk to 600 feet, unfortunately had to be cancelled because of a fatal diving accident.

A later series of experiments, named Tektite, was the first to draw together cooperative efforts of federal agencies, private industry and universities. During Tektite I in 1969, four diver-scientists spent a record-breaking two months working and living 50 feet down on the floor of Great Lameshur Bay, St. Johns Island, Virgin Islands. Universities furnished the manpower, the federal government paid most of the bill, and the hardware—the habitat itself—was designed and built by the General Electric Company. Tektite II, on the same site, began in 1970 but on a much broader scale. It lasted seven months and involved teams drawn from 60 scientists, aquanauts, engineers and doctors. One team consisted entirely of women.

In pressurized tanks on land, successful saturation dives have been made to depths exceeding 1,000 feet, and today's engineers insist that the ultimate depth at which man may be able to work will be considerably deeper. The deep-probing decades of the 1950s and 1960s also saw a proliferation of manned submersibles. Unlike their military cousins, however, most of the science-seeking subs were financed by private industry— and because they were very costly to operate, most spent far more time in dry dock than in working the depths. Yet through that trial-and-error period, a versatile array of undersea vehicles was born. The decades ahead no doubt will see the development of special-purpose submersibles rather than those designed for all-around tasks. Notes Dr. Jerry D. Stachaw, a Navy scientist who was active in developing transparent-hulled submarines: "The emphasis has shifted from just going down into the ocean depths and being there to going down to do something specific. This will lead to the development of many kinds of submarines, in strange configurations, to carry out very special missions."

As one example, the Japanese have developed a huge, tracked submersible whose lines suggest anything but the conventional submarine. In fact, it looks more like a jetliner mounted on tank tracks; designed for shallow depths, unmanned, it is used to cut trenches in the ocean bottom and in cable laying operations.

Stachaw compares the current generation of submersibles to automobiles of 30 or 40 years ago. "Eventually," he says, "submersibles will become more reliable and less expensive, just like motorcars." In addition to the "work subs," he believes that within a few years factories will produce a variety of inexpensive, efficient undersea runabouts tailored for the weekend hydronaut.

The Future of Glass Subs

Meanwhile, designers of submersibles are turning more and more to the world of glass and acrylics for materials that can be produced at low cost, that can withstand great pressure and that will resist the corrosive effect of salt water. The idea of a glass submarine usually provokes laughter from laymen, yet glassmaking techniques of the past few years have made the material well suited for a host of exotic applications, including deep-diving sea craft. Glass is one of the oldest of manufactured materials, with the oldest known example dated at around 7000 B.C. Elastic and unbreakable glass is a common reality today. Remarkably, glass becomes *stronger* when subjected to great depths, because its molecular composition toughens under pressure. Anyone who has ever attempted to crush a fragile egg can understand the resistance of a glass sphere to water pressure. It takes a tremendous hand squeeze to break the egg shell if pressure is exerted evenly all around it; glass or acrylic spheres resist water pressure the same way.

The potential advantages of using glass submarines and habitats are so great that considerable effort is being directed at perfecting them. Studies of these materials in prospective hull designs began independently in Navy laboratories several years ago. So far, they have resulted in the development of a spherical glass pressure hull 56 inches in diameter for the submersible *Hikino* and a 44-inch hemispherical enclosure for the Navy's *Deep View*. Shark studies at depths of 100 feet have been conducted by the Navy's *Nemo*, a submersible acrylic capsule that provides 360-degree visibility for its two occupants. Designed to reach a depth of 600 feet, *Nemo*'s hull is 2½ inches thick, boned with a special acrylic adhesive atop a cylindrical metal support-equipment module that contains life support, ballasting, communications, anchoring and ancillary systems. Underwater illumination is provided by lights mounted on the base of the submersible. The tethered sphere is cable-controlled from the surface, and a normal dive lasts about two hours.

The Smithsonian's novel *Johnson Sea Link*, named for its designers and donors, Edwin Link and J. Seward Johnson, also uses acrylics for its 66-inch observation control sphere. The *Johnson Sea Link* is a 23-foot, 9½-ton, five-man submersible designed to dive to 1,000 feet and to submerge for as long as 48 hours.

Other future undersea devices in various stages of development by both private firms and national governments involve a wide variety of deep sea hardware: sea floor excavators, fork lifts, vacuum cleaners for oil slicks. Much of the equipment is designed to assist man in working underwater. It is likely, for instance, that more modern, transportable tools will be required to repair and maintain sea-bottom pipelines and terminals that will be built to extract and transport marine minerals such as oil. For deeper work, engineers must develop better diver-to-diver and diver-to-surface navigation and communications systems. One firm already has announced the development of a wrist device, no larger than the wrist radio of Dick Tracy comic strip fame, that will home in on a strategically placed underwater pinger and give the diver accurate bearings by emitting clicks.

As technology pushes deeper, new vistas will open for the treasure diver and for those who hunt wrecks because of their archaeological importance. Many wrecks of great historic value now lie in very deep water. Although they are presently unreachable because of depth, the deep water, usually colder than that at the surface, also functions as a preservative.

Confident that the future of marine archaeology lies in deep water, the Aluminum Company of America and the deep-sea salvage firm of Ocean Science and Engineering have jointly invested considerable sums of money in a ship designed from the keel up specifically for deep-water tasks. Named the *Alcoa Seaprobe*, the 243-foot vessel looks like a floating oil derrick. The pyramid rig rising 125 feet above the deck is used to suspend drilling pipe through a "doughnut hole" well in the hull. The pipe also can be used to conduct sea water under high pressure to the bottom to operate hydraulic actuators, jets and valves.

Attached to the bottom of the pipe is a pod—somewhat like a small, unmanned submarine—that is equipped with sonar, television cameras, lights and strobe photography equipment. Signals to and from the pod are transmitted through a cable attached to the outside of the pipe. In use, *Seaprobe* can remain over a submerged wreck without drifting, by employing fore and aft thrusters that compensate for tide or currents. The location of the underwater object is confirmed by the electronic "eye in the sea," then the derrick is used for recovery.

In one test, the ship recovered a Navy acoustical device, weighing 15 tons, from a depth of 2,233 feet near Eleuthera Island in the Bahamas. Ultimately, *Seaprobe* will be able to recover objects of up to 200 tons in water more than a mile deep.

And Robots, Too, of Course

One of the future's most capable deep-sea performers will be the underwater robot, a tireless, obedient servant that is undisturbed by cold or pressure, that is immune to bites of sharks or venom of sea snakes, that has sight, vision, hearing and strength far superior to the human's. The U.S. Navy has begun experiments with a swimming underwater camera, nicknamed "Snoopy" by its handlers. Next in line is "Super Snoopy." This robot's movements will be controlled entirely by a human diver wearing a duplicate diving suit and a spacious helmet; the diver will follow the robot's movements on a TV monitor or by eye and will give it "orders" by turning his own head or moving his arms and legs. Each movable part of the robot will be keyed to a similar part of the diver, so that when the diver reaches for an object he sees on the TV screen, Super Snoopy will duplicate the movement—for real.

Aiding the Snoopies will be various underwater work platforms, such as the Navy's Cable Controlled Underwater-Recovery Vehicle (CURV). CURV-1 made history in April, 1966, by clamping its iron jaw shut around a long-lost H- bomb off Palomares, Spain, and bringing it up from a depth of 2,850 feet. Modern versions of CURV can retrieve heavy objects from depths of 7,000 feet, and CURV IV, which will work at 20,000 feet, is expected to be operational by the year 2000.

Will all of this mean that the human diver will be retired into obsolescence in the future? Not at all, insists Rear Admiral O. D. Waters, Jr., who served as Oceanographer of the Navy in the late 1960s when the deep-sea engineering program was accelerated. He believes there will always be exploratory work that can best be performed by a thinking, imaginative man on the scene. Just as the most sophisticated computer is a helpless collection of wires and tubing without human programing, so will human talent be required to run the marvelous machines of the sea in the future.

Year by year, diving technologists are pushing downward the depths at which they can safely work. Saturation div-

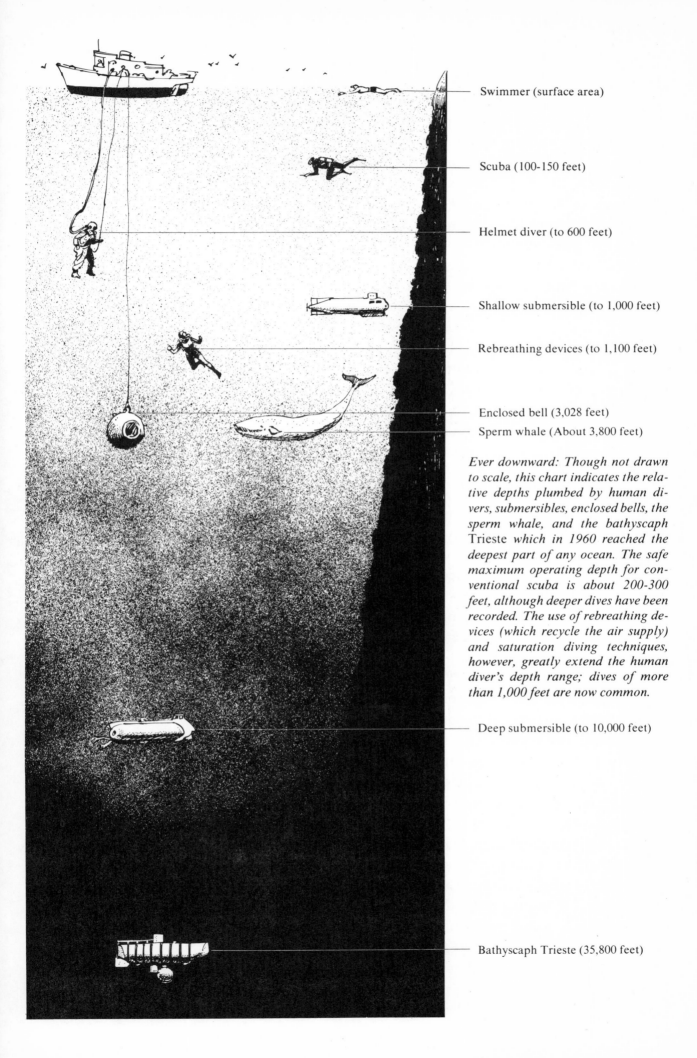

Swimmer (surface area)

Scuba (100-150 feet)

Helmet diver (to 600 feet)

Shallow submersible (to 1,000 feet)

Rebreathing devices (to 1,100 feet)

Enclosed bell (3,028 feet)

Sperm whale (About 3,800 feet)

Ever downward: Though not drawn to scale, this chart indicates the relative depths plumbed by human divers, submersibles, enclosed bells, the sperm whale, and the bathyscaph Trieste *which in 1960 reached the deepest part of any ocean. The safe maximum operating depth for conventional scuba is about 200-300 feet, although deeper dives have been recorded. The use of rebreathing devices (which recycle the air supply) and saturation diving techniques, however, greatly extend the human diver's depth range; dives of more than 1,000 feet are now common.*

Deep submersible (to 10,000 feet)

Bathyscaph Trieste (35,800 feet)

ing methods, developed by Dr. Bond and others, have already extended the diver's depth range beyond 1,000 feet. The Bond method works on the principle that body tissues, once saturated for a given depth with the proper mixture of inert gas, require the same amount of decompression time whether the diver stays at that depth for a day or a month. Once his tissues are saturated, the diver lives in a habitat in which the pressure is the same as that of the surrounding water. The chamber is periodically resupplied by other divers or, in the case of Sea-Lab, by a helpful porpoise.

So far, saturation diving is the most advanced technique of long-range undersea exploration. However, scientists are not yet satisfied that even this advanced state of technology will be sufficient for the kind of tasks coming up in the future, when ocean exploration probably will be assigned the kind of priorities and funds previously allotted to the space program and nuclear energy. The next logical step, one already tested successfully with dogs and other animals, is a quantum jump that only a few years ago would have sounded like a Buck Rogers fantasy. Someday, man may be able to breathe not air when he is in the sea, but fluid.

This technique involves pumping an oxygenated saline fluid through a diver's lungs, providing inside pressure equal to that outside. Since no inert gas is absorbed, this permits instant return to the surface without decompression. With development of mechanical assistance devices and improved communications, Dr. Bond believes that a 3,000-foot depth can be reached by the saturation method, and that a three-mile depth by fluid breathing is possible before the 21st century.

Cousteau's *Homo aquaticus*

One of the first proponents of "liquid breathing" was Jacques Cousteau, who developed the concept of *Homo aquaticus*. Costeau theorized that through surgical alteration, diving man will be able to resist pressures at depths exceeding 4,500 feet, will move to this depth mechanically and freely, and will surface again just as quickly with no decompression at all. To accomplish this, Cousteau said, "We will have to fill our lungs with an incompressible liquid. Then a whole new generation of man will be born, perhaps even in underwater hospitals where, upon birth, he will be operated on much in the manner of space experiments." Cousteau pointed out that in the latter experiments, progress already has been made: the taking of blood, for example, from beneath the left arm and circulating it through a regenerating cartridge on the belt. A surgically altered man would not be confined to water alone, Cousteau added; after surgery, he would use a regenerating cartridge to breathe air on the land.

Even as Cousteau was making this prediction, Dr. Johannes A. Kylstra of the University of Leyden was experimenting with "liquid breathing" techniques, using mice as subjects. In one experiment, he passed a mouse through an air lock into a pressure chamber filled with a liquid and a salt composition similar to that of blood plasma, which was charged with the same concentration of dissolved oxygen as the air. The mouse at first attempted to escape from the liquid, but was prevented from doing so by a grid placed just below water level. After several futile attempts to escape, the mouse settled down and began inhaling the liquid. One test mouse lived 18 hours, breathing only liquid. Its death resulted not from a lack of oxygen, but from an accumulation of carbon dioxide, a problem that researchers have not yet totally solved.

Other experiments have followed, one of the most recent being the development of a device at Drexel University in Philadelphia. Dogs have remained alive breathing only liquids. The "lung machine" resulting from research by Drs. Stephen Dubin and Gordon Moskowitz was designed not for an immediate application in aquaspace travel, but as an aid in certain types of lung surgery. The developers, however, suggest that it could be the forerunner of the kind of equipment envisioned by Cousteau and others.

The most immediate application of the liquid breathing machine will probably be in a medical technique known as lung lavage, or lung washing. This treatment is now used sparingly on patients with certain forms of chronic bronchitis, emphysema or cystic fibrosis. It has also been used to treat people who have inhaled radioactive dust. The problem with lung lavage as presently carried out is that it requires general anesthesia, as well as some tricky maneuvering with a foot-long tube that is used to seal off one lung while the other is flooded with saline solution. In breathing a liquid, the researchers point out, lung separation is unnecessary.

Despite the similarity between the tiny air sacs in mammalian lungs and the tiny plates that compose a fish's gill, a mammal cannot survive by breathing a liquid without the benefit of mechanical assistance. The second obstacle is the limited amount of oxygen in most liquids. Water, for instance, contains about as little dissolved oxygen as air at 70,000 feet. Fluorocarbon is used in the Drexel experiments, because this liquid holds as much oxygen at standard pressure as does regular air.

Whether bulky machines like that at Drexel University can be miniaturized to a size that could be back-packed by a diver in his deep exploration is yet another technological problem under study. In the far distant future, beyond even the most advanced imagery of today's scientific laboratory, perhaps underwater man will be born in the sea, and will have underwater surgery at birth, as Cousteau suggests. Far-fetched though this may sound, it should be remembered that in the thousands of years that man has been involved with the sea, most of the great technological advances have come swiftly, in only the past 50 years or so. It is not unreasonable to expect that the rate of advancement will accelerate even more in the next few decades.

Meanwhile, as man attempts to emulate the amazing deep-diving feats of marine mammals, he is increasingly enlisting their assistance. Of the thousands of forms of life in the sea, it is with his fellow air-breathers that man feels the closest affinity. First in his walks along the shores of the oceans about which he knew little, next as a seafarer confined to the sea's surface, finally as an underwater explorer, scientist and adventurer, man has marveled at the sea-going mammals' unique adaptation to an element from which he himself evolved but in which, for all his devices, he is still a trespasser.

For centuries, the whales, sea otters, walruses, sea lions and dolphins served man in the manner that land animals did. He killed whales for blubber and oil, walruses for their tusks and meat and hide, seals and otters for their fur. Though Western man generally excepted dolphins from slaughter, considering them his own image mirrored in the sea, hundreds of thousands of dolphins still die each year as they pursue tuna and other fish into commercial seine nets.

More recently, however, man has turned increasingly to his aquatic friends not for sustenance but for knowledge, for inspiration, and for assistance in his exploration of the liquid world. In the United States, in fact, federal law now prohibits the wanton killing or capture of any marine mammal, and the fishing industry and the federal government are investing tidy sums in an effort to protect dolphins from becoming the victims of purse-seine nets. Scientists have learned much about the walrus, the whale and the dolphin, and some of this knowledge can be used not only to extend the existence of these mammals in the sea, but to assist man as well.

It has been suggested that a combination of the best characteristics of several ocean mammals, a cross-breeding, would produce a more nearly perfect creature for exploring the oceans than can now be found anywhere on Earth. Consider a mammal that would have the dry-land mobility of the sea lion, the strength of the whale, the intelligence and playfulness and inventiveness of the dolphin, and the dexterity of the otter (the only sea mammal that uses tools). Short of this far-fetched scheme, which is of course biologically impossible, man must be content to learn as much as he can about his aquatic mammal cousins and to couple their capabilities with his own superior intelligence and power to reason. Certainly, man's admiration for the physiological and emotional capacities of marine mammals has created a fascinating body of science and literature, and considerable sums have been invested in finding ways that mammals can be trained to assist humans in the sea.

Marine mammals are indeed unique, not only from the humanistic point of view, but also from a pragmatic one. "As an engineer," says Dr. Athelstan Spilhaus, "I admire the whales because they gather, filter and concentrate the protein of euphasid shrimp far more efficiently than any machine man can devise. We should be breeding whales to crop the pastures of the sea as we breed domestic animals that live off the pastures of the land." In other ways, too, marine mammals are vastly superior to man in their environment. By utilizing new diving techniques, as described in this book, human divers are now able to descend deeper than 1,000 feet, but they have yet to lick the time-consuming problem of decompression on the way up. Depending upon how long they have been down, this can literally take days (as in the case of saturation diving). Many marine mammals, on the other hand, can plunge and return with no ill effects.

Man's Animal Assistants in the Sea

This deep-diving capability is of special interest to the Navy for recovery of objects on the deep sea floor, an activity that has become very costly when human divers or submersibles are used. Probably the first animal trained for this purpose was the common dolphin, or porpoise. Since then, researchers, particularly those in the Navy, have added other animals to the experiments. In a project called "Quick Find," for instance, scientists at the Naval Undersea Center trained a group of California sea lions to routinely recover objects at depths of 500 feet. The recovery system developed by NUC is remarkably simple. It consists of two or three men, a small rubber boat, a reel of nylon line, a pinger receiver, a grabber device . . . and a cooperative sea lion.

Bioscientists found that the eyesight of the sea lion is "dark-adapted," that is, it compares to that of a cat; although some sort of pinging sound was required to lead the animals near a target, they were guided entirely by their own vision in the last yards of approach, no matter how murky the water.

During early training in Hawaii, the sea lions were first "worked" in shallow water, and as they became more proficient, the target objects were placed in increasingly deeper water. Martin E. Conboy, leader of the project, explains that sea lions were chosen for the experiment because they adapt quickly to a training environment. "They can be captured wild, and within two or three weeks will submit to a harness," he explains. "Unlike porpoises, sea lions can stay out of water for long periods and move about on land; we decided they would be an ideal animal for transporting and recovery."

The harness enables a trainer to lead a sea lion about as one would a leashed dog. Once trained with the harness, the animal is then allowed to dive into the water when the boat has approached within about 100 yards of the "lost" underwater object. A "pinger" previously has been affixed to the target. The sea lion, once he locates the target, notifies the trainers by pushing a rubber disc mounted on the underside of the boat, and a "grabber" device is then placed over his nose. The animal descends once again, pulling a nylon cable that is attached to the grabber. Once at the target, he presses the grabber against it and claw arms automatically unfold and lock on. Aboard the boat, the human crew then merely reels in the object with the nylon line.

To test the effectiveness of the system as compared to how efficiently human divers might accomplish a similar recovery, the Navy in 1970 tried an experiment using both sea lions and humans, near the island of San Nicholas off the Southern California coast. In testing how well the seals had been trained, the Navy this time used a live rocket, fired across 2,000 miles of ocean from the Oahu Naval Ammunition Depot in Hawaii. An experienced Quick Find seal named "Turk" and two less experienced back-up animals were then flown from Oahu to the California site (scientists noted happily that they were not overly tired by the long trip). Next, all were taken to the recovery area aboard the naval vessel *USS Orleck*.

Two unexpected problems arose immediately. Though the Navy crew had scheduled the test in clear weather to increase chances of success, a pea-soup fog rolled in unexpectedly and the experiment was postponed for 24 hours; meanwhile, a buoy marking the rocket's location drifted away. "Everything seemed to be against us," Conboy recalls, "and if ever Turk had to do his best, this was it." Conboy's worry proved unnecessary. As perfectly as he had in several previous practice tests, the sea lion performed on cue, and the Navy soon had one very expensive missile back in its possession. In contrast with the simplicity and low cost of the operation, the Navy points out, human divers would have required a large support boat, special air breathing mixes—and a decompression chamber, medical van and medical officer standing by in case something went wrong. The Navy had carried out a landmark achievement. For the first time in history, a mammal other than man had successfully located an operational test device.

Though Quick Find's sea lions have performed well at 500 feet and some of them have been known to dive as deep as 750 feet, the Navy considers this far too shallow for an ongoing working program. Tests have therefore continued with other, deeper-diving mammals. In 1972, Navy scientists reported that two trained whales, a 1200-pound pilot whale named "Morgan" and a 5500-pound killer whale named "Ahab," had made routine recovery dives to 1,000 feet—twice the depth achieved by the Quick Find animals. On one recovery, Morgan reached a "working depth" of 1,654 feet.

Whales, being much larger, obviously are more expensive to maintain and more difficult to transport. The Navy has at least partially offset the second problem by letting them roam free in their own environment, the ocean, after training. Previous experience with dolphins had established that once they have become familiar with man, marine mammals very seldom bolt in the open sea. (An exception was a male porpoise trained at Point Mugu, California; scientists could overlook even this costly anomaly when they learned the reason—it was the porpoise mating season and a pod of female animals had just passed by.)

Unlike the smaller sea lions, whales offset the cost disadvantage by their capability of carrying heavier and more involved recovery equipment. The whale operations, called Deep Ops, employ the same basic recovery tools of Quick Find, with an important addition. It is a hydrazine gas generator device carried by the whale to the target; after finding the object, he first attaches a "grabber," then the gas automatically inflates a balloon that lifts the object to the surface.

Future experiments with even larger whales, the Navy hopes, may extend the range of deep-sea recovery to perhaps 3,000 feet or more.

The Navy pioneered research involving dolphins, and there is probably no aquatic mammal more closely identified with the sea in the public's mind. Intelligent, playful and inventive, dolphins have attracted man's interest for centuries, though it was not until the late 1940s that scientists discovered their amazing qualities and began studying them in earnest. Since then, the science of cetology has become a worldwide function, at a cost of several millions of dollars per year. In recent years, the Navy's specific interest has been in the ability of the dolphin to make rapid descents and ascents without harm to its body; Navy researchers believe that knowing how the animal performs this way may be of great assistance in improving human diving systems.

Like humans, dolphins (and all other mammals that

live in the sea) hold their breath during dives, and the air in the lungs is compressed, shrinking air chambers under the increasing pressure of depth. Research has shown, however, that the dolphin's body possesses a flexibility that Nature has denied man. "When the dolphin descends," explains Dr. Samuel Ridgeway, a research veterinarian at the Naval Undersea Center in San Diego, "his entire chest collapses, including all the air passages and cavities, right down to the tiny alveoli. At the same depth and pressure, man experiences a 'chest squeeze syndrome' that causes hemorrhaging from lung tissues." Ridgeway's research indicates that dolphins absorb very little gas in their blood during deeper parts of a dive, a built-in guarantee against the "bends" that affect human divers.

"By studying dolphins," Ridgeway explains, "we're not looking for ways that man can emulate them as a free diver. But the knowledge gained from research on their physiology may be of tremendous help in improving breathing equipment for man."

Sonar technicians are equally as fascinated by the dolphin's ability to "hear" through its jaw and to discriminate between small objects. Nautical architects are intrigued by its ability to streak through the water without creating a wake. And no chemist yet has been able to duplicate the oil that greases the hinge mechanism in the dolphin's jaw. The oil won't freeze below 30° F.; it resists oxidation, gumming and evaporation; and each animal possesses enough of it to lubricate a million fine watches. The most massive research, however, has been reserved for the dolphin's communication system, and if an ultimate breakthrough is achieved—the discovery of a way of actually "talking" to dolphins and getting them to "talk" back—man's exploration of the sea will have made a giant leap forward.

Can Dolphins Talk with Man?

Vocal communication between man and a non-human species is a goal sought by scientists for centuries. The inability of man to bridge the gap between himself and the animals with which he feels a kinship was once described by anthropologist Loren Eiseley as "the long loneliness."

"Man," wrote Eiseley "is separated by a vast gulf of social memory and experiment from the lives of his animal associates. He has entered into the strange world of history, of social and intellectual change, while his brothers of the field and forest remain subject only to the invisible laws of biological evolution."

For centuries, marine creatures were thought to be mute, and the oceans silent. During World War II, however, naval technicians who lowered instruments into the sea to listen for submarines were astonished to learn otherwise. The microphones picked up a bedlam of sounds, ranging from the crackling of shrimp to the quite noisy vocal repertoire of whales and dolphins, and scientists have been scrambling ever since to learn what all the sounds mean.

This is especially true in the case of the dolphin, whose intelligence rates perhaps higher than any other mammal besides man—and who, many scientists feel, would make the ideal, all-around work companion of man in the sea, if the "vast gulf" referred to by Eiseley could be crossed and some sort of mutual "language" established. Dr. John Lilly, who spent almost a decade trying to discover a means of man-dolphin communication, remains convinced that it can be achieved. Given enough time, effort and patience (and, certainly, money), Dr. Lilly feels, inter-species communication will be accomplished, will probably involve the dolphin, and will come about within a decade or two. But he adds that it will occur only if man humbles himself a bit, by abolishing from his mind a number of "interfering assumptions." Lilly lists a total of eight such assumptions, one of which is that "no animal is as intelligent as man."

In 1959, Lilly quit his job as Chief of the Section on Cortical Integration, Laboratory of Neurophysiology of the National Institute of Mental Health, and plunged into his theories with almost reckless abandon. A respected member of dozens of scientific societies, councils and committees, he had never practiced medicine; his entire medical career had been as a researcher. Much of the study, however, involved animal communication and vocalization, and when Lilly began reading what fellow scientists had learned about dolphins, he obtained a National Science Foundation grant and established a laboratory in the Virgin Islands to devote full time to this animal.

Dr. Lilly says now that inter-species communication was remote from his mind when he began his work; his interest was merely in trying to find out what the various sounds made by the dolphin meant. That dolphins could even mimic was unknown to him. "If anyone had told me in 1947 that a whale could mimic human words," he recalls, "I would not have believed him. But by 1957 I was forced to believe, through the experience of hearing one do it."

The dolphin he referred to was a male adult dolphin named "Elvar," which after a series of well-publicized voice experiments in Lilly's laboratory probably became the most famous marine mammal in history. For more than two years, Elvar was kept separated from other dolphins; in captivity, his daily companions instead were humans: Lilly, assistant Alice

Miller, and other researchers at Lilly's Communications Research Institute. Lilly instructed his staff that in speaking to Elvar, they should use only English words appropriate to the task at hand. And loudly enough, Lilly added, that Elvar could hear through the barrier of water. At first (although not within Lilly's earshot), CRI staffers complained of the foolishness of trying to elicit human speech from a small whale. "But by September 1961," Lilly remembers, "we were able to determine that Elvar was quite capable of producing sounds like those of human speech. We began to encourage him to shape definite and distinctive human words." Lilly wrote two best-selling books that described his years-long efforts. He insists that toward the end of the experiment, Elvar had indeed learned to "speak" a number of English words and responded to questions put to him by the human researchers.

Lilly's theories were far from universally accepted, and many scientists insist that trying to talk with animals is sheer nonsense. After a series of experiments that mostly involved Atlantic bottlenose porpoises in Florida, biologists David K. and Melba Caldwell of the Communications Sciences Laboratory at the University of Florida concluded that, although dolphins are extremely intelligent, their vocalization can hardly be called a language. "In our studies," they wrote in *Underwater Naturalist*, journal of the American Littoral Society, "we have found nothing suggestive of a dolphin language—nothing even indicative of the variety of notes found in a song bird. The whole idea of talking dolphins would be relatively harmless or perhaps even psychologically beneficial were it not for the time that has been lost by trained research personnel and their students who have lent some credence to the idea." True, the Caldwells say, dolphins make sounds, many sounds, but they are not nearly as complex as some scientists have suggested. The dolphin's whistle does have the potential for becoming a powerful research tool, but not in the "language" context, which the Caldwells suggest many accept because of "a communal need for fantasy."

As Lilly pursued his studies, other scientists—though not as generous as Lilly in their appraisal of the dolphin's intellectual capacity—trod parallel trails. Among them the gulf of opinion on dolphin communication yawned like a Grand Canyon. One of them, an acoustical engineer named John Dreher, suggests the dispute could be resolved if scientists could agree on what "language" really means. In his opinion, delivered at a national symposium of cetologists in Washington, D.C., language "is a series of symbols that appear in a time-ordered syntactic sequence and obey predictable rules." Whether the symbols are words, numbers, letters, signs or any sort of coded emissions is immaterial, he feels, "as long as they convey the information which will modify the actions of the sender or the receiver and cause him to obey pre-arranged rules."

It was in 1962 that Dr. Dreher, then conducting acoustics research for the Lockheed California Corporation, first became fascinated with dolphin communication. Aboard the research ship *Sea Quest* off the California coast one day, Dreher's staff had placed a series of hydrophones in the water to record the sounds of Pacific grey whales as they swam past on their annual 7,000-mile migration from the Arctic to calving grounds in lagoons of Baja California. Suddenly, Dreher noticed a herd of dolphins racing past. Obviously, they were interested in and curious about the underwater equipment that was unfamiliar to them; as the main herd swam to a safe distance, a "scout" came to investigate. Aboard, tape recorders preserved a whole range of sounds from the animals: squeaks, squawks, whistles. Having apparently determined that the underwater hydrophone would cause no harm, the scout raced back to the main herd and a babbling conference followed. The quite vocal "vote" of the school seemed to be unanimous; having thus decided that the looming hulk of the ship and its strange appendage of equipment dangling below was no predator, the dolphins resumed their normal and orderly course.

Your Language, Dolphin, or Mine?

The incident convinced Dreher that dolphins certainly communicate with one another. He is also convinced that if man could learn the code of their language, they could provide valuable assistance in his search of the seas, perhaps providing him information beyond the capabilities of any instruments. "In the lay sense, when we investigate another language, we hope eventually to crack the meaning of the 'code,' and there are highly skillful ways of doing this," Dreher reported at the Washington symposium. "Thus far, most of the language thinking has involved people, whether their target language is generated by a lone informant or by a vast library of written material; some degree of concept liberalization may be in order, therefore, before we tie the term 'language' to an infrahuman system. Casting aside, for the moment, if we may, the implication that 'language is something exclusively reserved for humans,' we now find it useful to apply the more basic yardstick of my definition of language."

While Lilly and others have attempted to teach dolphins to speak English, Dreher suggests that it is perhaps a bit pompous to expect them to do so. With a grin, he quipped to his colleagues in Washington: "The only gracious thing that

Man, as the king of beasts, can do is to attempt to talk to the dolphin in his own language."

That is precisely what still another researcher, the late Dr. Wayne Batteau of Listening, Incorporated, once attempted to do. Rather than train a dolphin to mimic and learn English, admittedly difficult because the dolphin isn't as physiologically blessed in the vocal department as humans are—Batteau wondered: why not devise a machine that would translate a man's voice into the kind of whistles a dolphin can understand, instead of the other way around? Working at Coconut Island in Hawaii with two dolphins, "Puka" and "Maui," Batteau developed just such a machine; before his death he claimed to have found a way to translate 22 English words into dolphin whistles. The whistles were not necessarily the kind the dolphin would normally emit himself, but were sounds that carried meaning to him which he could repeat more easily than English words.

To translate, Batteau dictated English words at one speed on his machine, then speeded up the equipment to the higher frequencies used by dolphins. As a control—to make certain that his experimental animals weren't merely mimicking—he trained each dolphin to pass along all 22 words to another. The next animal would prove it understood by performing a trick. Even when Batteau exchanged the order of the animals, they performed with a high degree of accuracy. Were they perhaps merely reacting to the sight of Batteau himself, standing at the edge of the pool? To find out, he crouched completely out of sight; the only communications link with the dolphins were signals transmitted to them through the water. Their response was just as impressive.

There is a third fascinating possibility in dolphin-man communication—a neutral language. It, too involves whistles, but in this case they are not the dolphin's, but man's. In several widely scattered communities of the world, there are tribes of people who communicate not only by language as we know it, but by whistles as well. One whistle language is used by the Mazataco Indians of Mexico. A second is used in the village of Silbo-Gomero, which is appropriately in the Canary Islands. One of the oldest whistled languages, in Kuskoy, Turkey, has been so perfected that such whistles can be heard up to five miles. That's a greater distance than even the human voice amplified over a loudspeaker can be heard, and is only about four miles less than the nine-mile vocal range of the sperm whale, which still fascinates scientists.

According to Dr. Rene Guy Busnel, a French zoologist who heads the Animal Acoustics Laboratory of the National Center for Zoo-Technical Research at Jouy-en-Josas, France, dolphin whistles and human whistles have amazing similarities. Not long ago, Dr. Busnel spent considerable time studying the whistled language of the inhabitants of a small French village, Aas, in the Pyranees. Like that of the Canary Islands, the Aas language is based on Spanish. Oscillograms taken by Busnel of the Aas whistles demonstrates that they are quite similar in frequency and amplitude to those of the dolphin and his whale cousins; frequency scales sometimes differ but there are examples of whistles, Busnel found, on the same wave lengths.

What prompted Busnel to report his findings at a conference on marine mammals was that the people of Aas do not use their vocal cords when whistling, of course, nor does their larynx move at all. Instead, the whistler first pushes the middle of his tongue back so as to provide flexibility for the tip of the tongue; thus forming a pocket of air in the back of the throat, the whistler can produce a great range of notes by moving the tip of the tongue only. The dolphin has no vocal cords. Busnel reminds us that the noises emitted from a dolphin's blowhole are not whistles but intermediate noises between whinnying, bawling, bleating, jabbering and grinding; in other words, they can't be defined in terms of our own vocalization. Yet by creating vibrations that modulate the passage of air, the dolphin is creating sounds almost as does the Aas whistler with his tongue.

Experimenting further, Busnel now believes that man could very closely imitate the whistled sound of the dolphin, thus avoiding the "pomposity," as John Dreher jokingly put it, of expecting the dolphin to learn man's language, or of requiring man to speak Dolphinese.

Lest this suggest an immediate bridging of the dolphin-man communications gap, however, Busnel adds a few words of scientific caution. While it is possible to make an analogy between delphid whistles and human whistled languages, this doesn't mean that man and animal will one day soon be able to sit down together around a conference table and indulge in complicated intellectual conversation. True language involves abstraction. We know that animals mimic; some birds, for instance, are adept at mimicking not only other birds, but animals and humans as well. But most do nothing *but* mimic. The repetition of sounds they hear has nothing whatever to do with their own behavior.

Busnel puts it another way: "The child who says to his mother, 'I am hungry, I am thirsty,' is still an animal. In saying 'Look what I did this morning,' he is becoming a human being."

At least Busnel's whistle language idea may be a place

to start. Perhaps one day, adroit teams of whistling Aas Frenchmen, Mexican Mazataco Indians or Canary Island Silbo-Gomeroans will become intrigued enough with the prospect of inter-species communications that they will join the widely divergent forces of science studying this most fascinating area of delphinology—and man and dolphin together will be able to break the "long loneliness" that has haunted man for centuries.

* * * * * * *

Man is a territorial animal. To exist, he must have frontiers to cross, and as each is crossed, there must be another on the horizon. Today, that frontier is the sea: beautiful and dangerous, elegant and strong, bountiful and capricious. Science and technology have opened the gates, have made this liquid world safer to explore, and the bounty it will return is limited only by man's vision, knowledge and boldness. Beyond mere material return, however—perhaps even more important than fuels, minerals and food—man needs the sea as an outlet for his restless spirit.

As in any exploration, the physical excursion will provide a catalyst for science and economic wealth. No growth, however, is meaningful without the application of a creative intellect. Science of the sea is not enough. Production of the sea's resources is not enough. To prevent the sea from becoming a jungled wasteland, man must apply reason and caution and purpose. Fortunately for man, the very nature of the liquid world stimulates creativity and inspires respect. Many a would-be plunderer, once he floats weightlessly and effortlessly amidst its great beauty, returns from the sea a zealous missionary.

Today, any human can become a man in the sea. He can explore tropical reefs, dive for ancient treasure, commune with his fellow mammals. But to progress far, he must also listen with a creative mind and thoughtful spirit. The sea is willing to share her secrets, if man is willing to listen. And if he listens well, he may learn far more about himself.

Picture Credits

i	David Doubilet
ii-iii	Steve McCarroll
iv-v	Jack McKenney from The Sea Library
vi-vii	Coles Phinizy
viii	Akira Tateishi from The Marine Art Center
31	Ron Taylor from The Sea Library
32	Peter Gimbel
33	Ron Taylor from The Sea Library
34	Akira Tateishi from The Marine Art Center
35	Valerie Taylor from The Sea Library
36	Carl Roessler from The Sea Library
37	top, Carl Roessler from The Sea Library; bottom, David Doubilet
38	Akira Tateishi from The Marine Art Center
39	Carl Roessler from The Sea Library
40-41	Akira Tateishi from The Marine Art Center
42	Ron Church
43	Carl Roessler from The Sea Library
44	top, Bernie Campoli from The Sea Library; bottom, Coles Phinizy
45	David Doubilet
46	David Doubilet
79	Natalka Czartoryska
80-81	Natalka Czartoryska
82	Robert Marx
83	Robert K. Vincent Jr.
84	top, Steve Fochios; bottom, Joseph W. Shaw, used with permission of University of Chicago and Indiana University
85	Frank J. Frost
86	Joseph W. Shaw, used with permission of University of Chicago and Indiana University
128-129	William Noonan
132	William Noonan
135	Flip Schulke from Black Star
136-137	William Noonan
138	Steve Shane from The Sea Library
139	Peter Stackpole from Time Life
140	top and bottom, Coles Phinizy
141	top, Flip Schulke from Black Star; bottom, Coles Phinizy
142	Coles Phinizy
143	top and bottom, Carl Roessler from The Sea Library
144	Al Giddings from The Sea Library
145	Coles Phinizy
146, 147	Akira Tateishi from The Marine Art Center
148	top and bottom, Coles Phinizy
149	Flip Schulke from Black Star
150	Bradley Smith
167	Al Giddings from The Sea Library
168, 169, 170	Naval Undersea Center
171	Perry Oceanographics, Inc.
172	Akira Tateishi from The Marine Art Center
173, 174	David Doubilet
175	top, Stan Keiser from The Sea Library; bottom, Paul Tzimoulis
176, 177, 178, 179	Naval Undersea Center
180	Coles Phinizy
181	top, Naval Undersea Center; bottom, Coles Phinizy
182	Daniel Audrerie from The Sea Library
195	William Noonan

Acknowledgements

We wish to extend our deepest gratitude to a number of persons and organizations who kindly provided material assistance, advice and encouragement during the research, writing and preparation of illustrations for *The Golden Sea*. In particular, the author extends his thanks to the distinguished marine archaeologist, Dr. Nicholas C. Flemming of Cambridge, England, who authored the excellent book on Mediterranean sunken city excavations, *Cities in the Sea*; to Treasure Salvors, Inc., Key West, Florida; to the staff of the Naval Undersea Center, San Diego, California; to Janet Rogers of Sea World, San Diego; to the medical and public affairs departments of Drexel University, Philadelphia, Pennsylvania; to Dr. Athelstan Spilhaus, consultant, National Oceanic and Atmospheric Administration, Washington, D.C.; and to Dr. James Wheeler North, professor of environmental engineering, California Institute of Technology, Pasadena, California.

Special thanks are also due to Don Greame Kelley, editor, *Oceans* magazine, for permission to refer to and quote directly from a number of articles in past editions of this excellent periodical of the sea, and for invaluable assistance in research.

The author also wishes to acknowledge the kind permission granted by the publishers of the following books and periodicals to reprint copyright material:

The Sea Around Us, Rachel Carson, Oxford University Press.

Life Magazine, Lieut. Don Walsh, "Our Seven-Mile Dive to the Bottom," Feb. 16, 1960.

National Geographic Magazine, Kip Wagner, "Drowned Galleons Yield Spanish Gold," January, 1965.

The Treasure Diver's Guide, John S. Potter, Jr., Doubleday & Co., Inc., New York, 1970.

Bibliography

Barada, Bill, *Underwater Hunting*, Doubleday, New York, 1971.

Bardach, John, *Harvest of the Sea*, Harper & Row, New York, 1968.

Bass, George F. (editor) *A History of Seafaring Based on Underwater Archaeology*, Walker & Co., New York, 1972.

Bass, George F., *Archaeology Under Water*, Frederick A. Praeger, New York, 1966.

Behrman, Daniel, *The New World of the Oceans: Men and Oceanography*, Little, Brown & Co., Boston, 1969.

Berlitz, Charles, *The Mystery of Atlantis*, Grosset & Dunlap, New York, 1969.

Berman, Bruce D., *Encyclopedia of American Shipwrecks*.

Blair, Clay Jr., *Diving For Pleasure and Treasure*, World Publishing Co., Cleveland, 1960.

Carson, Rachael, *The Sea Around Us*, Oxford Press, New York, 1951.

Cohen, Paul, *The Realm of the Submarine*, Macmillan, New York, 1969.

Cousteau, J-Y, (with James Dugan), *The Living Sea*, Harper & Row, New York, 1964.

Cousteau, J-Y, (with Frederick Dumas), *The Silent World*, Harper & Row, New York, 1953.

Cross, E. R., *Underwater Photography and Television*, Exposition Press, New York, 1954.

Davis, Sir Robert, *Deep Diving and Submarine Operations*, St. Catherine Press, London, 1951.

DeLatil, Pierre and Rivoire, Jean, *Man and the Underwater World*, Jarrolds, London, 1956.

Diole, Philippe, *4,000 Years Under The Sea* (Tr. by Gerard Hopkins), Julian Messner, New York, 1954.

Douglas, John Scott, *The Story of the Oceans*, Dodd, Mead, New York, 1952.

Dugan, James, *Man Under The Sea*, Harper's, New York, 1956.

Dugan, James, *World Beneath the Sea*, National Geographic Society, Washington, D.C., 1967.

Firth, Frank E. (editor), *The Encyclopedia of Marine Resources*, Van Nostrand Reinhold, Co., New York, 1969.

Flemming, Nicholas C., *Cities in the Sea*, Doubleday & Co., Garden City, New York, 1971.

Frey, Hank, and Tzimoulis, Paul, *Camera Below*, Association Press, New York, 1968.

Frey, Hank, *Diver Below!*, Collier Books, London, 1969.

Freuchen, Peter, *Book of the Seven Seas*, Simon & Schuster, New York, 1957.

Frost, Honor, *Under the Mediterranean: Marine Antiquities*, Prentice-Hall, Englewood Cliffs, N.J., 1963.

Greenberg, Jerry, *Underwater Photography Simplified*, Seahawk Press, Miami, 1969.

Gullion, Edmund A., *Uses of the Sea*, American Assembly, Columbia University Press, New York, 1968.

Hapgood, Charles, *Maps of the Ancient Sea Kings*, Harper, New York, 1954.

Haas, Hans, *Challenging The Deep*, William Morrow & Co., New York, 1972.

Idyll, C. P. (editor), *Exploring the Ocean World*, Thomas Y. Crowell Co., New York, 1969.

Lee, Owen, *The Complete Illustrated Guide to Snorkel and Deep Diving*, Doubleday, New York, 1963.

Loftas, Tony, *The Last Resource*, Henry Regnery Co., Chicago, 1970.

Marx, Robert, *Shipwrecks of the Western Hemisphere*, 1973.

Marx, Robert, *Sea Fever*, Doubleday, New York, 1972.

McKee, Alexander, *Farming The Sea*, Thomas Y. Crowell, New York, 1969.

McKee, Alexander, *History Under The Sea*, Dutton, New York, 1969.

Mero, John, *The Mineral Resources of the Sea*, American Elsevier Publishing Co., New York, 1954.

Ohrelius, Common der Bengt, *Vasa, The King's Ship* (Tr. from Swedish by Maurice Michael), Chilton Books, Philadelphia, 1963.

Pennington, Howard, *The New Ocean Explorers: Into the Sea In the Space Age*, Little, Brown & Co., Boston, 1972.

Peterson, Mendel, *History Under The Sea*, Smithsonian Institution, Washington, D.C., 1969.

Rackly, Hanns-Wolf, *Diving Into the Past: Archaeology Under Water*, Charles Scribner's Sons, New York, 1968.

Ramsey, Raymond H., *No Longer On the Map*, Viking Press, New York, 1972.

Rebikoff, D., and Cherney, P., *A Guide To Underwater Photography*, Amphoto, New York, 1965.

Schenck, H., Jr., and Kendall, H., *Underwater Photography*, Cornell Maritime Press, Cambridge, Md., 1954.

Schurz, William Lytle, *The Manila Galleon, Illustrated*, E. P. Dutton & Co., New York, 1939.

Shenton, Edward H., *Exploring The Ocean Depths*, W. W. Norton Co., New York, 1968.

Shepard, Francis P., *The Earth Beneath The Sea*, Johns Hopkins University Press, Baltimore, 1959.

Silverberg, Robert, *Sunken History, The Story of Underwater Archaeology*, Chilton Books, Philadelphia, 1963.

Smith, F.G.W., and Chapin, Henry, *The Sun, The Sea and Tomorrow*, Scribner's Sons, New York, 1954.

Stark, Walter and Brundza, P., *The Art of Underwater Photography*, Chilton Books, New York, 1966.

Stefansson, Vilhjalamur, *Great Adventures and Explorations*, Dial Press, New York, 1947.

Stenuit, Robert, *The Deepest Days*, Coward McCann, New York, 1966.

Tailliez, Philippe; Dumas, Frederick; Cousteau, J-Y, *The Complete Manual of Free Diving*, G. P. Putnam's Sons, New York, 1957.

Taylor, Joan du Plat, *Marine Archaeology*, Thomas Y. Crowell, New York, 1966.

Throckmorton, Peter, *The Lost Ships*, Little, Brown & Co., Boston, 1964.

Throckmorton, Peter, *The Unharvested Sea*, Little, Brown & Co., Boston, 1969.

Wagner, Kip., and Taylor, L. B., *Pieces of Eight*, E. P. Dutton & Co., New York, 1966.

Walford, Lionel A., *Living Resources of the Sea*, Ronald Press, N.Y., 1958.

Weiss, Malcolm E., *Man Explores The Sea*, Julian Messner, New York, 1969.

Index

Written by Joseph E. Brown
Edited and produced by Bradley Smith
Designed by Bradley Smith and
Don McQuiston
Graphics: Don McQuiston and
Debra McQuiston
Text Editor: Lee Massey
Production: Florence Kronfeld,
Helen Reed Smith, Iris Moses,
Sharon Weldy

This text is set in Times Roman,
the design of which was commis-
sioned by THE TIMES of London
and supervised by Stanley Morison
in 1931. The type was set
by Intertype Fototronics
System by Central Graphics of
San Diego, California. Color
separations, printing and binding
are by Kingsport Press, Kingsport,
Tennessee. Production is by
Gemini Smith, Inc.